WITHDRAWN
UTSA Libraries

Season of hope

Season of hope

Economic Reform under Mandela and Mbeki

ALAN HIRSCH

International Development Research Centre

Ottawa • Cairo • Dakar • Montevideo • Nairobi • New Delhi • Singapore

Co-published in 2005 by:
University of KwaZulu-Natal Press
Private Bag X01
Scottsville 3209
South Africa
E-mail: books@ukzn.ac.za
www.uknpress.co.za
ISBN 1-86914-041-9
and

International Development Research Centre (IDRC)
PO Box 8500
Ottawa, ON
Canada K1G 3H9
E-mail: pub@idrc.ca
www.idrc.ca
IDRC publishes an e-book edition of SEASON OF HOPE (ISBN 1-55260-215-5)

Edited by Sally Hines
Cover design by Flying Ant Designs
Cover photograph of Nelson Mandela by Graeme Williams
    (South Photographs/africanpictures.net)
Cover photograph of Thabo Mbeki by Alex Wong
    (Getty Images/Touchline Photo)
Typeset by Patricia Comrie

Printed and bound by Interpak Books, Pietermaritzburg

Contents

Acknowledgements   vii

List of abbreviations   ix

Introduction: 'A better life for all'   1

Chapter One: The economic legacy of apartheid   9

Chapter Two: From Kliptown to the RDP: 29
    The evolution of the ANC's economic policy

Chapter Three: Getting into GEAR   65

Chapter Four: Competing globally, restructuring locally   109

Chapter Five: Jobs and skills: 163
    Remaking the labour market

Chapter Six: Reaching for the economic kingdom: 193
    Black economic empowerment and small and
    medium business development

Chapter Seven: The two economies and the challenge   233
    of faster growth

Conclusion: Asking new questions   257

Select bibliography   267

Index   283

Acknowledgements

I prepared the first draft of this book as a visiting scholar at the Harvard Business School with access to the fabulous Baker Library and Harvard's other resources, supported by Canada's International Development Research Centre. Thanks to Marc van Ameringen and Rohinton Medhora of IDRC who arranged for the sponsorship and encouraged me to undertake and complete the project, and to Professor Richard Vietor at the HBS for accommodating me. Tom Karis, Dani Rodrik, and my wife Pippa Green read and commented on parts of the early draft of the manuscript, and Pippa on later versions too. Thanks also to Bill Freund who gave me valuable advice, both as a friend to whom I sent an early draft, and also as an anonymous reader for the publisher whose insights and prose style I could not mistake. Thanks to Eddie Webster for encouraging me to persist in trying to publish the manuscript. Thanks too to the other anonymous readers. The title of the book, *Season of hope*, was inspired by the use of the phrase by Trevor Manuel, Minister of Finance, in his budget speech in 2005, though the phrase can be traced back at least as far as Charles Dickens' *A Tale of Two Cities*.

I presented early versions of Chapters Two and Three respectively at the Walter Rodney Seminar at Boston University at the invitation of Dianna Wylie, and at the World Bank at an informal seminar convened by Jeffrey Lewis and Ataman Aksoy. Thanks to Alec Erwin, then Minister of Trade and Industry, and Zav Rustomjee, then Director-General of the Department of Trade and Industry, for allowing me to take extended leave to prepare the initial draft. Thank you too to my current employers at The

Presidency, especially Reverend Frank Chikane, Joel Netshitenzhe and Goolam Aboobaker for allowing me to update and publish what is not an authorised account, and is my sole responsibility. And thank you to my other colleagues in the DTI, The Presidency, TIPS (Trade and Industrial Policy Strategies) and elsewhere for their contributions to my knowledge and understanding.

This book is dedicated to Herbert and Shirley Hirsch who taught me to think critically about the way we live and the way we could live.

Abbreviations

ABET	Adult Basic Education and Training
ANC	African National Congress
AZAPO	Azanian People's Organisation
BEE	black economic empowerment
BEECom	Black Economic Empowerment Commission
BMF	Black Management Forum
BOT	built, operate and transfer (toll road)
BTI	Board of Trade and Industry
BUSA	Business Unity South Africa
CBM	Consultative Business Movement
CEAS	Central Economic Advisory Service
CEO	Chief Executive Officer
CMA	Common Monetary Area
COSATU	Congress of South African Trade Unions
CPI	consumer price index
CSIR	Council for Scientific and Industrial Research
DACST	Department of Arts, Culture, Science and Technology
DEP	Department of Economic Policy
DP	Democratic Party
DTI	Department of Trade and Industry
EAP	economically active population
ECD	early childhood development
EPWP	Expanded Public Works Programme
EROSA	Economic Research on Southern Africa
ET	Economic Trends group

EU	European Union
FRIDGE	Fund for Research into Growth, Development and Equity
GATT	General Agreement on Tariffs and Trade
GDFI	gross domestic fixed investment
GDP	gross domestic product
GDS	Growth and Development Summit
GEAR	Growth, Employment and Redistribution
GEIS	Generalised Export Incentive Scheme
GFCF	gross fixed capital formation
GNU	government of national unity
ICASA	Independent Communications Authority of South Africa
IDC	Industrial Development Corporation
IDRC	International Development Research Centre
ILO	International Labour Organisation
IMF	International Monetary Fund
ISP	Industrial Strategy Project
JSE	Johannesburg Stock Exchange (later Johannesburg Securities Exchange)
LFS	Labour Force Survey
MAWU	Metal and Allied Workers' Union
MERG	Macroeconomic Research Group
MIG	Municipal Infrastructure Grant
NAFTA	North American Free Trade Agreement
NAIL	New African Investments Limited
NAMAC	National Manufacturing Advisory Centre
Nedlac	National Economic Development and Labour Council
NEF	National Economic Forum (Chapters Three and Four)
NEF	National Empowerment Fund (Chapter Six)
NEM	Normative Economic Model
NGO	non-governmental organisation
NICs	newly industrialised countries
NIEP	National Institute for Economic Policy

NP	National Party
NUMSA	National Union of Metalworkers of South Africa
OHS	October Household Survey
PAC	Pan-Africanist Congress
PIC	Public Investment Commission (later Public Investment Corporation)
PIG	Provincial Infrastructure Grant
PWV	Pretoria-Witwatersrand-Vereeniging
RDP	Reconstruction and Development Programme
RIDP	Regional Industrial Development Programme
SACOB	South African Chamber of Business
SACP	South African Communist Party
SACTU	South African Congress of Trade Unions
SACTWU	South African Clothing and Textile Workers' Union
SACU	South African Customs Union
SADC	Southern African Development Community
SAMWU	South African Municipal Workers' Union
SANCO	South African National Civics Organisation
SARS	South African Revenue Service
SASO	South African Students' Organisation
SBDC	Small Business Development Corporation
SEDA	Small Enterprise Development Agency
SETAs	Sector Education and Training Authorities
SME	small and medium enterprise
SMMDP	Small and Medium Manufacturing Development Programme
SPF	Sectoral Partnership Fund
SPII	Support Programme for Industrial Innovation
SPV	special purpose vehicle
THRIP	Technology and Human Resources for Industry Programme
UBS	Union Bank of Switzerland
UDF	United Democratic Front
VAT	value-added tax
WTO	World Trade Organisation

'A better life for all'

When the African National Congress (ANC) came to power after South Africa's first democratic elections in April 1994, it faced daunting economic challenges: severe poverty and inequality, and economic stagnation. To fulfil its mandate to the electorate, nearly two-thirds of whom voted for the ANC, the new government had to redistribute wealth and incomes between privileged whites and deprived blacks (the latter group divided according to apartheid convention into 'coloureds', 'Indians' or 'Asians', and 'Africans'). But the economy was in decline, having virtually stagnated in real terms for a decade, with falling per capita incomes. Was there any point in redistributing a shrinking patrimony, with everyone getting poorer? And, yet, would not fuelling economic growth simply put more wealth in the hands of those who already had it? The big economic question faced by the ANC was: What would be the ideal relationship between growth and redistribution in South Africa? Or, more precisely, how could it set South Africa on the path of economic growth and at the same time ensure fair, just and politically necessary redistribution outcomes? Put yet another way: was there a way in which growth and redistribution in South Africa could complement each other?

This book describes how the new South African government addressed these challenges during the first decade of democracy, although its focus is more on economic policy and management than the distributional outcomes.

South Africa was one of the most unequal societies in the world – an almost unique 'outlier' in the unevenness of incomes as World

1

Bank economists put it in 1994. The average per capita income of whites was about 9.5 times higher than Africans. The distribution of wealth was even more unequal than income, as a result of land alienation and laws blocking Africans' access to private and commercial property. Access to government services was similarly skewed. When measured in 1989, 52.7% of Africans were living below the poverty line, compared with 1.6% of whites (Fallon and Perreira da Silva 1994: 39–42). In 1993 the poorest 10% of the South African population received 1.1% of the population's income, while the richest 10% received 45% (World Bank 2000: 239).

The spectre of a shrinking economy imposed a terrifying parameter on the new government. Between 1984–93, average per capita incomes fell in real terms (constant 2000 rands) from R23 006 to R19 996 (SARB 2004: S155). In other words, on average, South Africans were 15% poorer in 1993 than in 1984, and the recent years of the early 1990s showed the poorest economic performance.

Economic conservatives and representatives of business frequently warned the ANC that it should 'not kill the golden goose' in its efforts to rectify South Africa's inequalities, through higher taxes, for example. But the golden goose was already rather ill. Stated more appropriately, the task of the new government was to bring the golden goose to health, and simultaneously to meet the legitimate expectations of the newly enfranchised majority.

In the Reconstruction and Development Programme (RDP), which was the election manifesto of the ANC in the first democratic elections in 1994, the ANC addressed this conundrum by positing a virtuous circle: infrastructure development aimed largely at providing access for the poor would also contribute to economic growth through opening up the domestic market and increasing the efficiency of the economy. In turn, this would allow further improvements in the lives of the voters. A set of specific and fairly ambitious infrastructure targets was set out. The manifesto also recognised the need for specific economic reforms, including new trade, industrial and competition policies, and a commitment to avoiding macroeconomic imbalances such as unsustainable trade and budget deficits and high inflation (ANC 1994a).

Perhaps not surprisingly, the response of the establishment was not generally positive. *The Times* of London described a late draft of the manifesto as a failure and called for the policy to be abandoned (*Cape Times* 26 January 1994). Johannesburg's *Financial Mail* headed an editorial on the draft policy 'The Road to Hell' (21 January 1994). Nico Cypionka, a banking economist, said parts of the same draft were enough to make his 'hair stand on end' (*The Star* 3 February 1994). The centrist, largely white Democratic Party (DP) said that the ANC's plans were fiscally irresponsible (*The Argus* 12 April 1994).

In broad terms, the argument of this book is that the ANC government followed a consistent economic philosophy that had the following elements: at the centre is a social democratic approach to social reform – it is the state's job to underwrite the improvement in the quality of life of the poor and to reduce inequalities, but with a firmly entrenched fear of the risks of personal dependency on the state and of the emergence of entitlement attitudes. The state exists within a market economy that depends on private investment, and therefore a successful state creates an environment that supports high levels of private investment. This does not require the state simply to step aside for business, but rather that it should work with business and labour to develop growth-oriented strategies. The expectation was that because of the limitations of the domestic and regional markets, much of the growth would be driven by exports to major foreign markets. This required both measured trade liberalisation and effective industrial development strategies. Welfare initiatives were to consist mainly of the extension of infrastructure services such as transport, housing and communication, and on the expansion and improvement of social services such as health and education. All this would take place within a responsible macroeconomic policy, as the ANC did not wish to entrust international financial institutions or international banks with the country's future.

The ANC's approach is sometimes summarised as elements of a northern European approach to social development combined with elements of Asian approaches to economic growth, within conservative macroeconomic parameters. This remains the intellectual paradigm within which the ANC operates. Some of the outcomes may have been different from expectations – the stringency of the GEAR (Growth, Employment and Redistribution) policy from 1996–99, and the relatively slow growth of the economy and employment during that period surprised some, the rapid growth of the social security system after 1999 might have surprised others, but these can largely be explained as the consequence of conjunctural circumstances, or perceptions, possibly misperceptions of those circumstances.

In writing this book it has not been my intention to suggest an inexorable logic in the development and implementation of the economic policies of the democratic government. Choices were made in the past that might have been made differently, or delayed, or avoided in the light of present knowledge and circumstances. For example, the introduction and the character of the GEAR macroeconomic policy introduced in 1996 was the result of a number of vectors – unfounded rumours about President Mandela's health; unfounded concerns about the appointment of the first ANC Finance Minister, who happened also to be the country's first 'black'[1] Finance Minister; noisy criticisms of the ANC's economic leadership by labour and big business; international uncertainties leading to a teetering rand; the high interest rate policy of the South African Reserve Bank (SARB); and what the government belatedly realised was an excessively generous public sector wage settlement. Without one or several of these factors, the emphasis and orientation of the GEAR strategy might have been somewhat different. A similar argument could be made regarding a wide range of other policies and decisions. If in explaining the development and implementation of policy decisions it appears that I am arguing that the outcome was the only logical or possible one, it is simply because I am attempting to describe the factors contributing to a particular decision or policy.

South Africa's political transition cannot and should not be taken for granted. The stark backdrop to the South African transition in the early 1990s was the conflicts in Croatia/Bosnia-Herzegovina, Northern Ireland, Israel/Palestine and Rwanda/Burundi. Somehow, South African leaders were able to deflect their followers' attention away from fears and selfish interests.

As Mandela marched the path of reconciliation with determination and dignity, the 'political miracle' began to enter the realm of cliché. It was almost taken for granted in phrases such as 'now for the hard part', which is the name of the final chapter of Patti Waldmeir's insightful book on the South African transition, *Anatomy of a Miracle* (1997). The notion, 'now for the hard part', echoed independent Ghana's first leader Kwame Nkrumah's declaration that having entered the political kingdom, the goal was now to enter the economic kingdom.

Recognising that the political miracle was neither a miracle nor easy, but rather the result of extraordinary leadership, this book is about 'the hard part'. It would have been very difficult to deal even-handedly and extensively with all aspects of growth, redistribution, development and employment. I have chosen to focus on several key issues of economic policy and the response of the private sector to the policy framework, challenges and opportunities. The first key economic issue addressed in this book is the evolution of the economic policy of the major political and social force, the ANC. In this discussion, I aim to show how the economic thinking of the ANC has evolved, and to dispel some myths. The central myth is that the ANC suddenly switched course from old-fashioned socialism to orthodox neo-liberalism some time around 1993.

In Chapter Two I aim to show that the ANC's position (whether wrong or right, or somewhere in between) was based on an assessment of the conditions of the domestic and world economies, and a preoccupation with not giving up sovereignty to international financial capital, private or multilateral. It was not, as may accord with other interpretations, simply a victim of fashion, or of the browbeating of the International Monetary Fund (IMF) or foreign private bankers. This in turn explains the significant degree of stability and credibility built into the economic stance of the South African government since 1994.

Another area of focus, covered in Chapter Three, is an account and an evaluation of the democratic South African government's track record in the formulation and implementation of macro-economic policy – fiscal and monetary policy – looking at key moments such as the introduction of the GEAR strategy in 1996, its relationship with the RDP, and the course of its implementation. The way South Africa dealt with isolated currency shocks in 1996, 1998 and 2001 provides insights into choices that were made, and those that could have been made. Against the expectations of some bankers, *The Times* and the *Financial Mail* that the new government would spend recklessly, fiscal and especially monetary policies may have been excessively tight during the second half of the 1990s as a result of careful strategies driven by considerations of sustainability and sovereignty, and possibly due to a misreading of macroeconomic indicators by the central bank. Nevertheless, these tight policies eventually vanquished inflationary expectations and allowed for more expansionary policies in the second five years of the ANC government. Another insight to be gained from the ANC's macroeconomic policies is that because the ANC was confident of electoral success for at least 10 to 15 years, reaping the liberation political dividend, it did not feel forced to introduce risky, populist economic or fiscal policies to retain electoral support.

Chapter Four asks how the South African government decided to address the challenges of globalisation through trade and industrial policies and programmes. Many development economists will agree that this is where fundamental, though highly constrained, choices are made, and that macroeconomic strategies should be consistent with the development path that the country has chosen. A commitment towards an outward-oriented economy, modelled in some respects on the newly industrialising economies of the late 20th century was made with South Africa's offer to the Uruguay Round of GATT (General Agreement on Tariffs and Trade). Tariff

rationalisations and cuts were followed by the removal of other
demand-side interventions (subsidies) and the introduction of supply-
side programmes intended to boost investment, innovation, sales,
exports, and small business development, and hence employment.
In certain respects the programme has been unambiguously
successful; however, the pace of employment creation has been
disappointing. Is this the result of a time lag between restructuring
and real growth; is there a problem with the growth path chosen,
or a lack of policy co-ordination, or simply with the sequencing of
reforms?

Or was the problem in the labour market itself? Some economists, who believe that South Africa has made most of the right moves
with regards to macroeconomic and trade policy, explain the lagged
or slow response in investment and employment in terms of
deficiencies in the labour market. It is widely agreed that South
Africa is short of skilled and semi-skilled labour. The apartheid
system wreaked devastation in the field of human resource
development, as we shall read in Chapters One and Five. A debate
still rages around wages and labour market flexibility. Some analysts
believe that unskilled labour is too expensive in South Africa
relative to comparable markets, and that this is a result of labour
markets that are too inflexible due to labour union power and
legislation. Others believe that labour is more expensive than it
should be due to the costs built into the economy by apartheid, and
that costs can be reduced, but not necessarily through a frontal
attack on wages and union power. Some might not acknowledge
that there is a cost problem, and simply argue for improving the
capabilities of workers and managers through more and better
training.

Recently the temperature of the debate on black economic
empowerment (BEE) rose considerably. BEE is controversial, with
even members of the black economic elite complaining that it is
not broad-based enough and panders to a small emerging black
super-rich class. Part of this stems from a conflation of the issues of
empowerment on the one hand, and entrepreneur and enterprise

development on the other. For this reason the issue of small business development is addressed in Chapter Six, alongside a discussion of BEE. I argue that BEE, broadly defined, is as important to the sustained success of the South African political and economic revolution as any other single factor. The bottom line is that the new democracy will not be sustainable as a market-based system without really significant success in the field of BEE – the question is how to strike the right balance between a broad-based approach and the effective development of a black business class and a black middle class, and to select the appropriate tools for each task.

The final chapter reviews the key challenges of the future. Some of this is based on reflection of the experiences analysed in this book. But to base all future strategies on the results of historical strategies is (to paraphrase a Harvard business school professor) like driving with your eyes firmly glued to the rear-view mirror. Forward-looking debates about growth and employment should concern the anticipated future sources of growth, the key employment generators of the future. Forward-looking debates about distribution and delivery are necessarily more deeply rooted in the experiences of South Africa and other countries, but are also intimately connected to the debates on growth and employment.

A concluding note brings some key issues up to date, and reflects briefly on the government's achievement of its broader socio-economic objectives, and on the economic policies followed to achieve them.

Note

1. There are inverted commas around 'black' because I use the South African struggle terminology. All people who were not white were called 'black' in an inclusive sense, because they all suffered discrimination in South Africa. In fact, under apartheid's racial classification system, Trevor Manuel was officially classified as 'coloured', not 'African'.

CHAPTER ONE

The economic legacy of apartheid

The effect of pass laws and migrant labour

In 1955, in one of his most angry and passionate articles, young lawyer and activist Nelson Mandela wrote about a woman whose fate epitomised the economic oppression of apartheid:

> Rachel Musi is fifty-three years of age. She and her husband had lived in Krugersdorp [near Johannesburg] for thirty-two years. Throughout this period he had worked for the Krugersdorp municipality for £7 10s a month. They had seven children ranging from nineteen to two years of age. One was doing the final year of the junior certificate at the Krugersdorp Bantu High School, and three were in primary schools, also in Krugersdorp. She had several convictions for brewing kaffir[1] beer. Because of these convictions, she was arrested as an undesirable person in terms of the provisions of the Native Urban Areas Act and brought before the additional native commissioner of Krugersdorp. After the arrest but before the trial her husband collapsed suddenly and died. Thereafter, the commissioner judged her an undesirable person, and ordered her deportation to Lichtenburg [a distant rural town]. Bereaved and broken-hearted, and with the responsibility of maintaining seven children weighing heavily on her shoulders, an aged woman was exiled from her home and forcibly separated from her children to fend for herself among strangers in a strange environment (Mandela 1955: 46).

This was not an unusual story in South Africa between the 1950s and the 1980s. Sydney Mufamadi, now the ANC government's Minister of Provincial and Local Government, spent his early years oscillating between Venda in the far north of South Africa and Meadowlands in Soweto, near Johannesburg. As a youth he was known for his love of soccer. His mother brewed beer to supplement the family income. When she was raided by the police and her livelihood destroyed, Mufamadi found himself driven into student politics and black consciousness politics, and he became a founding member of the Azanian People's Organisation (AZAPO) in the late 1970s. Later he joined the ANC and the South African Communist Party (SACP) underground, and emerged as a dynamic and effective trade union leader (Harber and Ludman 1995: 111).

The position of African women in towns and cities was extremely tenuous – it was virtually illegal under the pass laws. Black men and children were almost as vulnerable, and many were also deported. Black people were prevented from making a living for themselves in the 'white areas', which included the towns and most of the rural areas. Even if Mrs Musi or Mrs Mufamadi had been caught making and selling bread, their activity could have been condemned as illegal, and they could have been deported.

Apartheid was a massively oppressive system that sought, amongst other things, to control the economic lives of all black people, and their residential location. Anyone without an approved job could be deported out of the urban areas. Most black workers in the urban areas, and all who worked on the mines, were annual migrants. These 'men of two worlds' were forced to reside with their families in distant rural areas, and to relocate themselves for 11 months of the year to work in the cities or on the mines.

Nelson Mandela was certain that the pass law (influx control) system had more to it than colonial racist sadism. All the major misdemeanours of apartheid, he said in 1955,

> are weapons resorted to by the mining and farming cliques
> to protect their interests and prevent the rise of an all-

powerful mass struggle. To them, the end justifies the means, and that end is the creation of a vast market of cheap labour for mine magnates and farmers. That is why homes are broken up and people are removed from the cities to ensure enough labour on the farms (Mandela 1955: 47).

The evidence strongly supports Mandela's hypothesis. Table 1.1 shows that African workers' wages on the gold mines actually declined in 'real' (accounting for inflation) terms between 1911 and 1971, from R225 (in 1970 rands, or US$300 in 1970 dollars) to an average of R209 per year in 1971. During the same period, especially during the phase of industrial development during and after the Second World War, and the phase of rapid growth in the 1960s, white mine workers' wages increased significantly. Not surprisingly, the relative number of white mine workers declined as the wage differential grew. For black mine workers, it was only after apartheid began to crumble with the recognition of black trade unions in the 1970s that black mine wages began to catch up.

Table 1.1: Average annual gold mine wages, 1911–82 (in rands).

Year	Whites		Africans		Ratio white to African wages (African = 1)
	Current prices	Real wage 1970 prices	Current prices	Real wage 1970 prices	
1911	660	2 632	57	225	11.7
1921	992	–	66	–	15.0
1931	753	2 214	66	186	11.3
1941	848	2 312	70	191	12.1
1951	1 609	2 745	110	188	14.6
1961	2 477	3 184	146	188	16.9
1971	4 633	4 379	221	209	20.9
1972	4 936	4 368	257	227	19.2
1975	7 929	5 035	948	602	8.4
1982	16 524	4 501	3 024	824	5.5

Source: Lipton (1986); Wilson (1972).

At the same moment key supplies of foreign migrant labour, which made up about 70% of black labour on the gold mines in the early 1970s, were threatened by the independence of the former Portuguese colony of Mozambique (Crush et al. 1991: table A.3). Till then, apartheid had been remarkably effective in keeping black mine workers' wages at very low levels.

Apartheid had also assisted in keeping wages low on South Africa's white/Afrikaner-owned farms. From the early years of the 20th century, black South Africans were restricted from entering the urban areas without permission: they had to have a valid 'pass'. At the same time, the rural 'reserves' where black South Africans were allowed to live (later also called 'homelands' and 'Bantustans') were restricted to a very small part of South Africa – 13% for three quarters of the population. The reserves, which were poorly located areas to start with, were deliberately held in poverty through the prohibition of private property and by a huge portfolio of restrictions on the economic development of black South Africans.

The pass laws were constantly resisted. Seventeen million black South Africans were prosecuted for pass offences between 1916 and 1986, when the pass laws were finally abolished (Ramphele and McDowell 1991: 5). During the Second World War the system had weakened as labour was in short supply in the cities, and the economy was expanding in response to the war. But in 1948, when the National Party (NP) came to power and created apartheid (Afrikaans meaning 'segregation'), the door was slammed in the face of black South Africans. The law was tightened, and pass law arrests doubled in the 1950s (Wilson and Ramphele 1989: table 11.01). As Verwoerd explained it at the time, 'emigration control must be established to prevent manpower leaving the *platteland* [white farming areas] to become loafers in the city' (Lipton 1986: 25). Many pass offenders were also put to work as prison labour on the farms.

The capitalist connection

The connection between apartheid and cheap labour is evident. In time, most historians have come to agree on this, though until the

1980s left-of-centre historians and social scientists were identified with this position. Mandela's statements on cheap labour in the 1950s were similar to the views expressed by contemporary communists and anti-apartheid unionists (see Bunting 1969; Mbeki 1984; Simons and Simons 1969). In the 1970s, the left intelligentsia revived and substantiated this analysis of apartheid in the context of resurgence of radical social analysis worldwide, and of the revival of the popular struggle in South Africa, now through worker and student movements.

Colin Bundy (1979) tells the story of how, in the second half of the 19th century, black South African cultivators were emerging as a competitive farming peasantry. However, the Prime Minister of the Cape Colony, mine-owner Cecil Rhodes, set out deliberately to eradicate what he saw as a threat to cheap labour on the mines. Harold Wolpe (1972) explains how the prohibition of private property and therefore land sales in the reserves inhibited the emergence of a large landless class, and helped prevent the full urbanisation of black migrant mine workers. He also shows how the workers' access to communal land-holdings subsidised the cost of labour for the mines. David Kaplan (1977) and Rob Davies (1979) show how the state balanced the interests of white labour, national capital and international capital against the black workers and peasants, and how power balances in the white elite shifted over time. Mike Morris (1976) shows how apartheid served the mine-owners and the white farmers by dividing the labour force into convenient exploitable segments. Wolpe, Martin Legassick (1974) and Duncan Innes (1984) stretch the argument further, claiming that other segments of capitalism, notably manufacturing, were also served by apartheid's cheap labour.

The logical conclusion, especially of the Legassick/Innes version of the argument, was that capitalism and apartheid were essentially intertwined in South Africa, and that the end of apartheid would require a socialist revolution led by the black workers. This conception helped inspire the new black trade unions that emerged in South Africa in the 1970s and 1980s, which made a huge contribution to the anti-apartheid struggle, though not through socialist revolution.

The best-known response from the liberal camp (using 'liberal' in the South African sense of socially liberal but economically conservative) was Michael O'Dowd's 'thesis', first articulated in 1964. O'Dowd argued that apartheid and capitalism were inherently incompatible and that economic growth would eventually lead to the disintegration of apartheid. Liberals tended to argue that apartheid was a sectional power play, catering to the sectional interests of Afrikaner labour and backward forms of capitalism. The essence of the liberal/radical debate in the 1970s was between these two caricatured positions: radical: apartheid and capitalism are two sides of the same coin – to fight apartheid you should fight capitalism; and liberal: capitalism and apartheid are inherently contradictory – support economic growth in a capitalist context in order to challege apartheid.

The debate about the connection between capitalism and apartheid became more nuanced in the 1980s with the contribution of work by Dan O'Meara (1983), Sam Nolutshungu (1983), David Yudelman (1983), Merle Lipton (1986) and Doug Hindson (1987), amongst others. The liberal position softened to acknowledge that the form of capitalism that predominated until the 1960s – mainly mining and agricultural – was deliberately and well served by the cheap labour system produced by segregation and apartheid. Equally, the left came to acknowledge that some more progressive capitalists had opposed apartheid, and that apartheid was beginning to curtail prospects for future capitalist growth.

Consequences for the 'beloved country'

In the meantime, apartheid had wrought havoc with South Africa, socially and economically. By critically injuring the black majority and by forcing the economy to conform to the increasingly contorted strictures of white rule, recovery from apartheid was made all the more difficult.

The great red hills stand desolate, and the earth had been torn away like flesh. The lightning flashes over them and the clouds pour down upon them, the dead streams come to life, full of the red blood of the earth. Down in the valleys women scratch the soil that is left, and the maize hardly reaches the height of a man. These are valleys of old men and old women, of mothers and children. The men are away, the young men and girls are away (Paton 1948: 13–14).

This is how Alan Paton described the ravaged hills of Natal in the late 1940s. Conditions continued to deteriorate in the reserves as the pass laws were tightened, as towns and cities were effectively policed, and as three million people were forcibly relocated to the reserves by the apartheid government between the early 1960s and the mid-1980s. By 1980, while 88% of the white population was urbanised, only 33% of the black South African population lived in the towns and cities. Population density in the black reserves was many times that in the white rural areas. The key reason was what South Africans called 'influx control'. As Colonel Stallard had put it in 1922, 'the black man' should only be in the urban areas 'to minister to the needs of the white man and should depart therefrom when he ceases to minister' (cited in Lipton 1986: 18).

The reserves, planned as labour reservoirs, and to deflect political conflict from the 'white areas', were filled beyond overflowing. Great tracts of land had become vast rural slums. The prohibition of private property meant that the land could seldom be rationally used, and human and physical degradation escalated. As Peter Fallon and Robert Lucas of the World Bank noted: 'In most developing countries, unemployment is lower in rural areas as agriculture tends to soak up excess labour supply, but this is not true in South Africa. Among Africans in particular, the probability of unemployment is much higher in rural than in urban and metropolitan areas' (Fallon and Lucas 1998: iii).

'The government [was], of course,' as Mandela saw it in 1959, 'fully aware of the fact [that] the people [in the reserves were] on the point of starvation.'

> They have no intention of creating African areas which are genuinely self-supporting (and which could therefore create a genuine possibility of self-government). If such areas were indeed self-supporting, where would the Chambers of Mines and the Nationalist farmers get their supplies of cheap labour (Mandela 1959: 64)?

Access to transport services, communications, water and power was extremely unfavourable for black rural dwellers. As late as the 1990s, 74% of black rural dwellers had to fetch their daily water, many over great distances, and almost none had access to electrical power. Less than 14% of the black South African population had access to telephones, while more than 85% of white households had access to telephones. Roads and rail lines favoured white rural producers and urban commuters. In the urban areas, blacks were often forced to live a great distance from industrial and commercial centres through a residential land law called the Group Areas Act. As a result, blacks were forced to spend 40% more of their income on transport than whites, coloureds, and Indians, though the latter two groups also bore some of the brunt of 'population resettlement' (May 1998: 139–163).

Perhaps the most powerful economic restriction on black people was that they could have no private ownership of immovable property. They were totally banned from ownership of any property or business in the 'white areas' that made up 87% of the country. They were not even allowed to own shares in public companies. In the remaining 13% of the country, communal property rights, under the management of traditional leaders – chiefs and headmen – prevailed through apartheid law. The restrictions on black business ownership even in 'black areas' were also prohibitive. Essentially, black South Africans were allowed to own a small number of small businesses of certain categories in scattered locations, and not at all beyond the black townships and reserves. The most successful black entrepreneurs were those who operated within the interstices of the law, some using white 'owners' for cover. But the restrictions on property ownership meant that the controls on black competition were overwhelming in practice, and few black businesses broke beyond the survivalist stage.

What about black advancement through salaried employment or the professions? This was blocked through the 'job colour bar'. First formally introduced on the mines in 1893, the job colour bar, which prevented black workers from advancing beyond semi-skilled occupational classes, was entrenched throughout the economy during the early decades of the 20th century, and extended during the 1950s. Outside of teaching black children, preaching to black congregations, and some professions where racial restrictions nevertheless applied, the opportunities for black economic mobility did not exist.

Education and social policies

Along with economic restrictions came a string of social restrictions on black people, which not only damaged their dignity, but also weakened the apartheid economy and made a successful democratic economy more difficult to attain. By far the most serious of these acts was in the field of education. Apartheid education policy set back human capital creation more than a generation, unconsciously forming the most serious of all economic constraints on the future expansion of the economy of a democratic South Africa.

Speaking in support of the 1953 Bantu Education Act, Dr H.F. Verwoerd, the Minister of Bantu Affairs, spelt out clearly the reason why blacks were to get a separate education:

There is no place for [the Bantu] in the European community above certain forms of labour . . . it is of no avail for him to receive a training which drew him away from his own community and misled him by showing him the green pastures of the Europeans, but still did not allow him to

graze there . . . [This led to] the much discussed frustration
of educated natives who can find no employment which is
acceptable to them . . . it must be replaced by planned Bantu
education . . . [with] its roots entirely in the Native areas,
and in the Native environment and community (cited in
Lipton 1986: 24).

The result was that the standards that applied to the education of
black children fell rapidly – education was not compulsory, school-
books were not free (unlike the arrangement for white children)
and subject policies in languages, maths and science limited career
options. In 1959, university segregation followed, with similar results.
The damage done by the Bantu Education system has been far
worse than South Africa's school attendance and literacy figures
suggest.[2] In fact many of those allegedly literate are functionally
illiterate for an industrial society, and many of those listed as
attending school make little real progress over many years due to
low attendance and pass rates.

Apartheid in public facilities and amenities was called 'petty
apartheid' by liberal whites, though it was not petty. It could be the
butt of humour of the absurd, though it was not funny. As apartheid
collapsed in the early 1990s, Ben McClennan, a political journalist,
compiled a collection of 'petty apartheid' incidents and reports that
he called *Apartheid: The Lighter Side*. Here is one example from a
1953 newspaper report:

If a Native [black] nurse carrying a European [white] baby
has to travel by South African railways, what section of the
train should she enter? The question arose at Grosvenor
Station on Tuesday evening. A Native nurse carrying a
European baby got into a non-European carriage in a
Johannesburg-bound train. She was immediately told to
alight by a conductor and, while she was stating her difficulty,
the train went off without her. A senior railway official
interviewed last night said: 'All I can say is that the mother

of the European baby should not have left it in the care of a Native in the first place' (McClennan 1990: 27).

In 1965 the *Cape Times* reported on the then unfolding beach apartheid programme:

> A witness asked the beach apartheid commission yesterday to declare about seven miles of Onrust River coastline White, and added that if White visitors took Coloured nursemaids to the beach, he would not like to see the nursemaids wear bathing suits. Mr PH Torlage, chairman of the commission, asked Mr H Whitely, secretary of the local Village Management Board how he would feel if a 'nanny was dressed in a bathing suit'? Mr Whitely replied: 'I would prefer to see them dressed as nannies' (McClennan 1990: 34).

The absurdity of petty apartheid did not stop the NP government from establishing a plethora of duplicated, inefficient and inferior institutions and facilities to satisfy the purity of the apartheid design and the racist selfishness of its constituents. The cost to society of building new townships, roads, railway stations, police stations, post offices, schools and management institutions was enormous. The cost to the new government of rebuilding unified institutions was very high – perhaps the most difficult was uniting nineteen separate racially and ethnically defined education departments into one national and nine provincial departments.

The apartheid economy

The economic effects of apartheid were not only the social consequences of its racial policies. Apartheid rule had long-lasting consequences on the broader characteristics and competitive capabilities of the South African economy too.

But first, the point must be made that the apartheid economy did not run into obvious problems until the 1970s. Racist capitalism seemed to work quite effectively during the period up to the end of the 1960s. By all normal indicators – rate of growth, rate of inflation, rate of job creation, rates of savings and investment – the South African economy was successful (Gelb 1991a). If one ignores the issues of the degree of equality and the standard of living of the majority, the one notable exception was the rate of profit in the manufacturing sector (Nattrass 1990a).

The success of the apartheid economy was based on a development model that ultimately proved fragile. One important element was the strength of gold as a foundation for the economy. Until 1971, the price of gold was fixed in US dollar terms under the Bretton Woods arrangement. This made gold different from other commodities; as the price was given, the only factor affecting the rate of profit was the cost of inputs. As we have seen in this chapter, the cost of the key factor – labour – was stable and low. Gold contributed more than a third of South Africa's exports, which, together with other mining, came close to half of South Africa's exports, and South Africa's share of 'western bloc' gold output remained as high as 75% with the development of a new group of mines in the 1950s and 1960s in the Free State gold fields.

The other major sector of the economy, manufacturing, had a totally different character. Built behind an increasingly complex protective barrier against imports, few South African manufactured goods, other than semi-processed primary products, were competitive enough to export. The manufacturing sector rested on an import substitution regime where consumer goods were highly protected, were consumed by the privileged white middle class and working class, and where capital and intermediate goods were imported at low or negative rates of effective protection, paid for by minerals exports. In sectors such as clothing, protectionism was so extreme, even in the 1990s, that while more than 90% of domestic consumption in clothing was locally manufactured, the local industry exported less than 10% of its output.

What caused the economic crisis that began in the early 1970s, and continued until 1994? In some respects it was no different from that of comparable developing countries at the time; the world was thrown into turmoil by the end of the 'golden age' of Keynesian capitalism, with falling growth and rising inflation (Moll 1990). However, there were factors that made South Africa different, and in some senses made it much more difficult to recover.

The fall in gold price

With the end of the gold standard in 1971, the ball game began to change for South Africa. The price of gold could fluctuate. With the onset of the oil price crisis in 1973, the price began to gyrate wildly. During the second oil crisis, which began in 1979, the gold price rocketed again, approaching US$900 per fine ounce. The Bretton Woods price had been US$35 per fine ounce. In spite of this, gold production in South Africa was declining from an annual peak of 1 000 metric tons of fine gold in 1970 to under 600 metric tons by the 1990s, due to rapidly falling ore yields. Instead of a foundation, gold had become a wild card.

Had the wild card been played well, South Africa could have protected its economy from excessive price shocks, possibly by creating special foreign exchange deposit arrangements for gold exporters. Instead, the fluctuating price was allowed to play havoc with the balance of payments and the value of the South African currency, which was floated during the late 1970s. Exchange control, and a dual rand which operated from 1960–95 with a brief break in the early 1980s, sometimes softened the fluctuations, but they were still severe.

Worse still, after the second oil crisis ended in the early 1980s, the role of gold in the global asset market changed. Under the Bretton Woods system from 1945–71, gold had been the standard of value, measured in US dollars. In the era immediately after the abandonment of the gold standard, gold remained a refuge during periods of uncertainty – and uncertainty there certainly was between 1971–84, with the oil crises, worldwide inflation, and the debt crisis that began in the late 1970s. In the mid-1980s everything changed. The liberalisation of international capital markets (alongside the liberalisation of trade barriers) meant that the role of gold as a store of value, as a refuge in uncertain times, greatly diminished. This was confirmed during the stock market crisis of 1987, and doubly confirmed during the Gulf War of 1992. The effects of these crises on the demand for gold were minimal. The gold price continued the downward drift that began in the early 1980s.

Not only had demand conditions changed, so had supply competition. New discoveries and new technologies meant that gold production elsewhere in the world, including the United States, Canada and Australia, grew during the 1980s and 1990s. Most of the new technologies could not be applied in South Africa's exceptionally deep mines. In addition, Russia, which is a major gold producer, rejoined the global market in the 1990s. South Africa's share of world gold sales fell rapidly. If this weren't enough, central banks and the International Monetary Fund (IMF) began selling gold off in the 1980s, and are continuing to do so – the creation of a European central bank sparked off yet another round of gold sales.

In short, gold had become a commodity, like wheat, coal or oil. Like most commodities in the modern industrial era, its relative price, or terms of trade, tended to drift downwards in the long run.

The manufacturing sector

Meanwhile, what had happened in the rest of the economy? The manufacturing sector grew rapidly during the post-Second World War era under an import substitution regime. Consumer industries thrived behind protective barriers on booming white incomes, and diversified into more complex durable products. Foreign investment, aimed at exploiting South Africa's protected domestic market, rose to nearly 30% of investment in manufacturing. At least as important was the investment by the government in parastatal corporations such as Eskom (electricity from coal), Iscor (iron and steel), Sasol (oil from coal) and several other producers of key inputs, such as fertiliser. The private sector also invested in input sectors, especially suppliers to the mines and energy sectors.[3] Manufacturing output grew at an annual rate of between 4.5 and 10% throughout the period 1946–75. With the exception of the late 1950s, employment grew at between 3.2 and 6.6% per annum (Black 1991; Nattrass 1990a).

The rate of growth of output and employment in the manufacturing sector fell steadily from the early 1960s. By the 1980s, both output and employment in manufacturing were declining on a broad front, the only exceptions being several plants making processed primary products, such as paper and bulk chemicals. Manufacturing remained protected behind tariff and non-tariff barriers, and remained essentially uncompetitive.

In the isolated conditions of the 1980s, compounded by growing disinvestments by foreign firms, a small number of South African conglomerates seized almost total control of the economy. By the end of the decade, five groups controlled companies worth close to 90% of the stock market value of all public companies based in South Africa. Just as government had indulged business in constantly acceding to pleas for higher protective barriers around local markets, government looked the other way as competition and rivalry melted away.

The beginning of the end

The imposition of sanctions on South Africa aimed at the apartheid regime further encouraged inward-looking policies. Government, the state-funded science councils, and the parastatal companies committed considerable resources – deploying the windfalls of high gold price revenues – towards domestic self-sufficiency in food (through roads and huge dam projects), power, weapons and telecommunications equipment. The commercial spin-offs of these projects were negligible; they were barely considered in the design. Not only were the windfalls largely poorly spent, they created financing commitments that lasted long after the gold price windfalls were distant memories.

The rising costs of maintaining the apartheid state, and the weakening economy and tax base meant that from 1984 to 1994 when the democratic government was installed, current government expenditure exceeded current revenue. The government's con-tribution to domestic savings was negative, while government consumption spending rose from 15% of GDP (gross domestic product) in 1983 to 21% of GDP in 1993 (McCarthy 1991). Some in the political opposition saw this as a deliberate debt trap set for the new government, but the simpler explanation of fiscal ir-responsibility and hubris seems more pertinent.

The private sector and parastatals had gone on an equally irresponsible foreign borrowing binge in the early 1980s, particularly in the period 1983–85 when foreign exchange controls were lifted. Foreign debt to GDP rose from 20% in 1980 to 50% in 1985. As a percentage of exports of goods and services, the debt rose from 56% to 149%, meaning that debt servicing through export revenues was under threat. Most problematic was the fact that US$14 billion out of the US$24 billion debt was short term. Heavily dependent on short-term foreign borrowings, the economy was vulnerable.

Several events precipitated a crisis. First the gold price fell from over US$500 to under US$300 per fine ounce between 1983–85 and fiscal and monetary policies failed to adjust. The rand fell fast, and borrowers who had not covered the currency risks adequately encountered payment difficulties. In 1985 President P.W. Botha made it clear in his widely publicised Rubicon speech that the government was not considering any significant political reforms. Within weeks foreign banks, led by Chase Manhattan, pulled the plug (Hirsch 1989; Ovenden and Cole 1989).

The result was a huge haemorrhaging of capital from South Africa, some of it through the withdrawal of credit lines and sales of South African assets, most of it done illegally by South African individuals and firms usually through various forms of transfer pricing. Some analysts of anomalies in the current account of the balance of payments estimate the illegal flows at more than R50 billion for the period 1985–92 (Rustomjee 1991). The bleeding only stopped in 1993 when the capital account of the balance of payments turned positive. Not surprisingly, gross fixed domestic investment shrunk every year bar two between 1983 and 1993, after which it turned positive.

A response from the South African Reserve Bank

For the late sanctions period when monetary policy recognised that the only way to counteract capital flight was by maintaining a high real interest rate policy that attacked inflation while preserving the value, or overvaluing the currency, monetary policy did not help improve the country's economic performance. Before 1989, when Dr Chris Stals became Governor of the South African Reserve Bank (SARB), the currency was allowed to drift to compensate for fluctuations in the gold price. In other words, as the US dollar price of gold declined, so did the rand in order to keep the rand profits of the gold mines healthy (Gerson and Kahn 1988).

One problem for the rest of the economy, especially potential exporters in the non-gold and platinum sectors, was that the fluctuations of the currency made the outcomes of export strategies unpredictable. The other was the overall trend for the terms of trade of non-gold products to deteriorate. As Brian Kahn pointed out, 'the effects of the gold price masked the underlying decline in the country's competitiveness'. He added that 'the terms of trade excluding gold declined consistently since the early 1970s, and by the end of 1986 they were approximately 43 per cent lower than their 1970 levels' (Kahn 1991: 62).

Governor Stals clearly indicated that his objective was to maintain the internal and external value of the rand. Stals faced a balance of payments crisis when a mini-boom in the late 1980s sucked in imports without the compensation of inward flows of capital. It was normal for South Africa to go into deficit on the current account during periods of growth, but the political and economic isolation of South Africa in the late 1980s inhibited any inflows of capital. Stals had to hike the interest rate, and add other emergency balance of payments measures. Though he usually justified high interest rates as an anti-inflationary measure, it clearly also helped slow imports by stalling domestic demand.

Until 1994, the assumption that seemed to underpin this approach – that because long-term capital would seldom enter South Africa policies had to protect short-term money – was justified. However, in the post-1994 period, long-term and direct foreign investment entered South Africa in significant volumes. It may be that Stals erred in maintaining these policies too long after 1994. These issues are explored in Chapters Three and Four. But we first need to review the apartheid legacy.

The economic inheritance from apartheid

Modern South Africa was built on one of the most vicious forms of labour exploitation in the history of capitalism. The evolution of segregation and the migrant labour system into an apartheid system, which sought to crush all black initiative and to protect all white interests, created a social system that soon fell behind world economic trends and was increasingly vulnerable to international economic shocks. The ending of the *de jure* gold standard and the oil crises in the early 1970s led to wildly fluctuating gold prices, foreign receipts and the exchange rate. Then the disappearance of a de facto gold standard – gold being seen as a refuge in times of international crisis – and, finally, the tightening of the sanctions noose in the early to mid-1980s, all helped to end apartheid, but left the South African economy battered and bleeding.

At great present and future cost, government social policy had turned the clock back to an era of racism and slavery when workers were seen as costs and as potentially dangerous enemies, not as human capital that rewards high levels of investment. Government economic policy helped further cripple the economy through protecting the increasingly monopolistic private sector at the expense of improvements in productivity and competitiveness, through investing in expensive political and strategic projects without reference to market considerations, and through irresponsible fiscal and monetary policies.

Not everything the apartheid government did was disastrous in all its effects. A review of South Africa's ranking in international

Table 1.2: South Africa's economic balance sheet on transition from apartheid (relative to other developing countries and countries in transition to capitalism).

South Africa's apartheid balance sheet	
Assets	**Liabilities**
Good transport infrastructure for business and white residential areas.	Inferior transport infrastructure for black homes and farms.
	Poor, inadequate, and unsafe public transport for workers.
Good communications infrastructure for business and white residential areas.	Very poor communications infrastructure in black urban and rural areas.
Good financial sector and regulation.	Minimal black private savings and no black ownership of banks.
	Declining savings performance of country.
	Government dissaving over 10 consecutive years.
Well-developed capital market.	Almost total absence of black ownership of land or economic assets.
Pockets of skilled labour and management.	Most labour very poorly educated and trained, and severe shortage of management skills.
Monetary discipline and declining inflation.	Growth inhibiting high real interest rates.
	Fiscal recklessness and huge government consumption expenditures.
Some good universities and science councils.	Poor quality of general education for black students.
	Most education facilities weak in mathematics, science and engineering.
Moderate levels of research and development spending and patent applications.	Very large proportion of research and development investment in defence industry.
Strong exports of primary products.	Uncompetitive protected manufacturing sector.

competitiveness ratings systems in the mid-1990s indicates that South Africa was poorly rated in labour-related indicators, but relatively strong in physical infrastructure, science and technology, and finance. In these three areas, the NP government had made major investments during apartheid, some of which remained economically valuable into the democratic era. But even in these strong sectors, the assets of the country were very poorly distributed – for example, white farmers in remote rural areas had access to tarred roads and highways of the very highest quality, while the majority of black rural and urban dwellers had to use rough-and-ready unpaved tracks to get to school or to work.

A balance sheet for South Africa at the end of the apartheid era, implicitly comparing it with other developing countries and countries in transition from socialism, would show that, at the time of transition in 1994, the assets were outweighed by the liabilities; but, with a little imagination and a great deal of determination, the assets could be used to lever up many of the significant liabilities into positive territory.

Notes

1. 'Kaffir' is a pejorative term used to demean black South Africans. At the time, white readers might not have understood the Xhosa word for corn (maize) beer, *uqombothi*.
2. The World Bank (1996) gave figures of 84% of the population in secondary school and 18% illiteracy in 1993, which fail to reflect the poor quality of education received in the Bantu education system.
3. Fine and Rustomjee (1996) argue that investments in support industries for minerals and energy sectors characterises post-Second World War South African manufacturing more accurately.

CHAPTER TWO

From Kliptown to the RDP

The evolution of the ANC's economic policy

A moment of truth

An icy midwinter meeting in Davos, Switzerland, was the setting
for the first formal statement of the economic policy of a democratic
South Africa. Here, at the World Economic Forum annual meeting
early in 1991, Nelson Mandela made the first really significant
statement of economic policy on behalf of the ANC since it had
been unbanned in February 1990 by President F.W. de Klerk. Davos,
the site of annual meetings of the world's economic elite, was also
the first venue where Mandela and De Klerk had shared a public
stage for more than a press conference. This, in itself, was a
statement, in the sense that De Klerk's decision to release Mandela
had been strongly influenced by a desire to make peace with South
Africa's potential investors and markets, while Mandela was
signalling that he recognised that the world's plutocrats wanted to
see him and De Klerk acknowledge their constituencies' mutual
dependence.

Mandela's speech at his first Davos meeting was shrouded with
controversy. The original draft of the speech had left space for a
section on the ANC's economic policies, which was to be prepared
by an ANC-allied economist in the United Kingdom. When the
insert arrived from London it was included in the draft speech.
However, when Mandela and his economic advisers read the section
they found that it was fashioned in a traditional socialist style,
virtually calling for the nationalisation of the commanding heights
of the economy. Tito Mboweni, 31 years old, one of Mandela's key

aides and an economist, had to redraft the economic section in great haste.

Mboweni was one of the bright young stars in the ANC. He trained in economics while in exile, first at the University of Lesotho, later at the University of East Anglia where he earned a Masters degree. He then took up a position in the ANC's department of economic planning in Lusaka, and was one of the first officials to move back to the ANC's new headquarters at Shell House in Johannesburg in 1990. Over the next few years, along with Max Sisulu, Trevor Manuel and their team, Mboweni helped to finalise and formalise the economic policy of the ANC for the real world of power.

Mboweni's rewrite of the speech tread a far more careful path, shying away from echoes of the old British Labour Party or eastern European socialism. The ANC had not held its important 1992 policy conference yet, so Mboweni had to say as little as possible while appearing to say more, without offending anyone. This he managed to do, and the version of Mandela's speech actually delivered at Davos in 1991 could best be described as carefully written, harmless and mildly reassuring for the collected band of plutocrats and international financial bureaucrats.

The difficulty of addressing potential foreign investors was summed up in an internal ANC document circulated during April 1991. The aim of the document was to advise ANC officials on how to conduct themselves in meetings with potential probing investors. 'Firstly,' instructed the briefing paper, 'we need to persuade foreign investors not to invest in South Africa until our conditions for the lifting of sanctions are met.' 'Yet,' noted the next point, 'we need to make an effort to sustain foreign investors' interest in investing in a Post-Apartheid South Africa. The South African economy desperately needs investment in new productive capacity' (ANC 1991d).

The story of Davos, 1991, might never have been known, were it not for the fact that Mandela's communications team released the first draft of the speech before Mboweni's rewrite. In South Africa the first version was published under alarmist headlines by the press, owned and controlled by whites, and close to big business. The second and final version was never as well known in South Africa as the speech that was never given.

A year later in Davos, Mandela was unambiguous and clear. Though the policy conference was still to be held in May, the position of the ANC had evolved to the point where Mandela felt he could make some definitive statements. He talked about a 'mixed economy', using a term that had been introduced into the lexicon of the ANC by economists seeking to hold on to more interventionist socialist policies, but turned the term into a synonym for social democratic capitalism. In Mandela's mixed economy, 'the private sector would play a central and critical role to ensure the creation of wealth and jobs'. The public sector would be strong, but would be modelled on western European social democracies such as France and Germany (Mandela 1992a).

Moreover, the ANC had decided to address, directly, the concerns of potential foreign investors. Without being too specific, Mandela recognised that, in order to meet its objectives of job creation and poverty alleviation, the ANC would have to 'address such questions as security of investments and the right to repatriate earnings, realistic exchange rates, the rate of inflation, and the fiscus' (Mandela 1992a).

In addition, Mandela made it clear that there was to be no rash assault on the assets of white-owned South African firms. He realised that this would also be an important signal to foreign investors. The South African economy, he predicted, 'will offer very good prospects for the investors present in this room, both South African and international' (Mandela 1992a). Considering the fact that the ANC still supported economic sanctions against South Africa, and would continue to do so until there was a constitutional settlement, this was as far as Mandela could go.

The people's charter

But where did the economic policy of the ANC come from, and was it true, as some analysts have suggested, that the ANC changed its tune some time in the early 1990s in order to placate foreign investors and the multilateral banks in Washington?

It might be more accurate to say that ANC policy had come full circle. In 1955 the ANC and its Congress Alliance partners met in a huge popular gathering, a 'Congress of the People', at Kliptown near Johannesburg. Three thousand people gathered for two days in wintry late June to endorse the first policy document designed to enlist a broad alliance in a struggle for a non-racial, democratic South Africa.

The Freedom Charter remained the ANC's only broad statement of social and economic policy until May 1992 when a huge, representative ANC conference in Johannesburg endorsed the 'Ready to Govern' policy. In the life of the Freedom Charter it came to have many guises and interpretations. The first declaration in the Charter is perhaps the definitive one. It reads:

> We, the people of South Africa, declare for all our country and the world to know that South Africa belongs to all who live in it, black and white, and that no government can claim authority unless it is based on the will of the people (ANC 1955: 81).

These sentiments, redolent of the phraseology of late 18th century anti-aristocratic and anti-colonial revolution, perfectly capture the spirit of non-racial, national, democratic revolution. This 'non-racial' dimension of the struggle against apartheid was essentially new; previously the ANC, though steeped in democratic liberalism, understood that it represented the majority of South Africans of indigenous African origin. As the ANC's programme of action had stated only seven years previously, in 1949: 'Like all other people, the African people claim the right to self-determination' (ANC 1949: 80).

In the vicious face of apartheid, the struggle intensified, and democrats of different hues and social classes were pushed together. Some 'Africanist' black South Africans left the Congress Alliance

a few years later to form the Pan-Africanist Congress (PAC), but the
ANC with its Congress Alliance, which included organisations for
non-Africans (until they were accepted directly into the ANC in
1969) and the trade-union federation SACTU (South African
Congress of Trade Unions), remained the central opposition.

The chief economic clause of the Freedom Charter went a bit
further than Tom Paine, the printer and pamphleteer of the
American and French revolutions, would have. But things looked
a lot bleaker for the black South African middle classes than they
had for the tradesmen in America or the sans-culottes in Paris. The
declaration 'The People shall share in the Country's Wealth' was
elaborated as:

> The national wealth of our country, the heritage of all South
> Africans, shall be restored to the people;
> The mineral wealth beneath the soil, the banks, and
> monopoly industry shall be transferred to the ownership of
> the people as a whole;
> All other industries and trade shall be controlled to assist
> the well-being of the people;
> All people shall have equal rights to trade where they choose,
> to manufacture, and to enter all crafts and professions (ANC
> 1955: 82).

Other than the second sub-clause, on nationalisation, the economic
clause would have it appear as if the Congress Alliance represented
a bourgeois struggle against feudalism. Even the second clause, on
public ownership of banking and mining monopolies, fitted into
the social democratic mainstream in the 1940s and 1950s when
United Kingdom and West European labour and socialist parties
sought to expand the economic role of government. For example,
between 1945 and 1951, the Labour government in the United
Kingdom nationalised the Bank of England, civil aviation,
telecommunications, coal, the railways, long-distance road haulage,
electricity, gas, iron and steel. They also built a welfare state that

offered social insurance and a national health system. In doing this they followed the Labour Party's social democratic manifesto, *Let Us Face the Future*. With regards to the welfare state, they were also following proposals developed by the Liberal Party supporters, William Beveridge and John Maynard Keynes (Sassoon 1996: chapter 6).

Mandela felt, at the time, that the nationalisation clause could be explained in context. It was true that the demand for nationalisation would strike a fatal blow against the 'financial and gold-mining and farming interests that have for centuries plundered the country and condemned its people to servitude'. However, Mandela continued, 'the breaking up and democratisation of these monopolies would open up fresh fields for the development of a prosperous, non-European bourgeois class. For the first time in the history of this country, the non-European bourgeoisie will have the opportunity to own in their own name and right mills and factories, and trade and private enterprise will boom as never before' (Mandela 1956: 49).[1]

Thirty-six years later – in 1992 – Mandela referred to this passage in his 1956 article and acknowledged: 'Immediately after the adoption of the Freedom Charter, and even up to the present, there has been extensive debate about the intention of the clause which reads: "The people shall share in the country's wealth"' (Mandela 1992b).

There can be no doubt that the ambiguities of this part of the Freedom Charter were intentional. The Congress Alliance was a broad church, stretching from rural traditional leaders through peasants and workers to professionals, intellectuals and business people. The ANC itself was almost as broad. The Freedom Charter was intended to be inclusive; attempting to represent so many diffuse, though related, interests with a crystal clear document would have been futile.

The radical 1960s and 1970s
During the 1960s and 1970s, ANC economic policy leaned towards the left. One reason was the radicalising influence of anti-colonial

African socialist movements. First Abdel Gamal Nasser in Egypt, then Kwame Nkrumah in Ghana, then Julius Nyerere in Tanzania and Kenneth Kaunda in Zambia, frustrated by the lack of economic progress of their popular constituencies, moved decisively towards state interventionist policies. These policies were, rightly or wrongly, collectively known as 'African Socialism', and spread to other African states. The main characteristics of African Socialism were nationalisation of large companies, usually with compensation, a variety of land reform strategies, the expansion of the state, and an increasing reliance on the use of state-owned companies and the state apparatus itself for the economic advancement of individuals. The weakness of the African middle class in the post-colonial era, due largely to the destructive effects of colonialism and the lack of preparation for decolonisation, was the main driving force behind African Socialism. By the mid-1970s, left-wing critics had begun to describe African Socialism as 'state capitalism', or, in relation to its most degenerate forms, 'kleptocracy'.

A second influence on the economic thinking of the ANC in the 1960s–80s period was the fact that the organisation had been driven underground. After being banned in 1960, massively harassed with arrests, detention, torture and long-term imprisonment, the ANC made the decision to resort to armed opposition to the South African government. The ANC went underground without the support of most liberals, the business community, or the international community other than independent African countries, Scandinavia, and the socialist countries of Eastern Europe and Asia. This had the effect of 'pigeon-holing' the ANC in a 'socialist box' to an even greater extent than it was before.

And, in the early days of exile at least, beyond Sweden, the socialist states were the only non-African countries prepared to offer moral and material support to the armed struggle. Combined with the apparent fact that Soviet socialism seemed more successful than the west allowed, the South African Communist Party (SACP) element in the Alliance was able to gain greater credibility and influence than before the armed struggle.

Not long after the ANC went underground, the intellectual tide in those parts of the western world affected by the student and worker revolts of 1968 was shifting towards the left – the new left. The economic crises of the 1970s characterised by the new phenomenon of rising unemployment *and* inflation suggested to some that the failure of Keynesian capitalism meant that capitalism was unsustainable. Undoubtedly these currents influenced the thinking of the younger ANC intellectuals in exile, as well as young opposition intellectuals who were not forced to or had not chosen to leave South Africa.

The shift to the left is reflected, however superficially, in the ANC's first important policy document of the 'exile era'. This was a document called 'Strategy and Tactics', adopted at an ANC conference in Morogoro in Tanzania in 1969. The description of economic oppression linked to national (racial) oppression is familiar. What is less so is the statement:

> But one thing is certain – in our land this problem [poverty and inequality] cannot be effectively tackled unless the basic wealth and the basic resources are at the disposal of the people as a whole and are not manipulated by sections or individuals, whether they be White or Black (ANC 1969: 392).

In the next paragraph there is a specific reference to a capitalised Socialism, and the role the revolutionary working class would play in the construction of 'a real people's South Africa'. There is also a reference to the military struggle for political and economic emancipation as a 'first phase', though the subsequent phase(s) are not described (ANC 1969: 392). While the terms are still vague and general, the language is less 18th-century petit bourgeois liberalism and far more Cold War-era anti-imperialism.

By the end of the 1970s, ANC leaders were asking themselves whether they should make explicit the organisation's commitment to the ideology of Marxism-Leninism. The 1979 drafters of the strategic 'Green Book' argued that while 'no members of the commission had any doubts about the ultimate need to continue our revolution towards a socialist order', it was not thought appropriate for the ANC to say quite as much 'in the light of the need to attract the broadest range of social forces among the oppressed'. Instead, the report referred to 'phases of the struggle' without actually using the term socialism. The most explicit statement was the following:

> The aims of our national democratic revolution will only be fully realised with the construction of a social order in which all the consequences of national oppression and its foundation, economic exploitation, will be liquidated, ensuring the achievement of real national liberation and real social emancipation. An uninterrupted advance towards this ultimate goal will only be achieved if . . . the dominant role is played by the oppressed working people (ANC 1979: 724-726).

This view was consistent with the position adopted by the black and white organisers of many of the new black trade unions, which during the 1970s and early 1980s became a dominant internal force struggling for freedom. Three years before the Green Book, the leader of SASO (South African Students' Organisation), Diliza Mji, had made an analysis of the pro- and anti-revolutionary forces and concluded: 'It is against this background in a capitalistic set-up like it is in South Africa, we have to align ourselves with the majority of working people and be with them.' Mji pointed to yet another factor pushing the anti-apartheid struggle in this direction: the fact that the United States had chosen to support the apartheid regime, quite explicitly under Kissinger and Nixon, showed that South Africa was being defended as the last bastion of capitalism in Africa. It was evident that if apartheid was being defended in order to defend capitalism, the two were indivisible and had to be attacked together (Mji 1976: 740). Several of Mji's contemporaries in the black student

movement ended up as prominent union leaders in the late 1970s
and early 1980s. Some of them, such as Jay Naidoo, Sydney
Mufamadi and Cyril Ramaphosa, are now cabinet ministers or top
business leaders.

Exploiting apartheid's fissures

By the late 1980s, as politics shifted towards the possibility of a
negotiated resolution to the South African conflict, the shape of
the ANC's economic policy returned to a more conventional form
– gradually diluting the revolutionary socialist spice with which the
policy was flavoured between the late 1960s and the mid-1980s.
There were several contributing factors.

One was the emergence of an economically vital East and South-
East Asia following economic paths that were market-oriented, but
with high degrees of government intervention. The conventional
view for the success of Japan, South Korea, Taiwan and countries
in South-East Asia was that they had followed orthodox laissez faire
free-market policies. By the end of the 1980s, work by prominent
western economists such as Alice Amsden and Robert Wade had
shown that, although the macroeconomic policies, other than the
exchange rate and exchange control, were orthodox and conservative, the governments of the newly industrialised countries in
Asia played a huge role in supporting human resource and technology development, and in directing public and private investment
flows (Amsden 1989; Wade 1990). This challenge of non-western/
non-white nations to the economic hegemony of the west *within
the capitalist system* began to impact on the thinking of some ANC
leaders and intellectuals (for example, see Erwin 1989: 93).

Another factor influencing economic thinking of the ANC was
the failure of Soviet socialism and its rejection by the ordinary people
of Eastern Europe. For some, the experience of Poland in the early
1980s was enough evidence; for others Gorbachev and the fall of
the Berlin wall eventually influenced their thinking. Some of those
who spent part of their lives in Eastern Europe or in African socialist
countries made the most radical shifts.

The ANC and the SACP always remained separate organisations. In a sense, the SACP was a political club within the ANC. Its analysis had become very influential in the 1950s, as we saw in Chapter One in Mandela's economic analysis of apartheid. In the conditions of underground struggle, where the support of the Soviet Union and the German Democratic Republic, and later, Cuba, were absolutely crucial, the influence of the SACP in the Alliance had grown. Some have argued, overenthusiastically, that the SACP de facto 'took over' the ANC between the late 1960s and 1990, when it was legalised (Ellis and Sechaba 1992).

The line adopted by the SACP up to and including the report 'The Path to Power' in 1989 remained orthodox Soviet socialism, in spite of Gorbachev. Early in 1990 Joe Slovo, the Secretary-General of the party, published the paradigm-shifting 'Has Socialism Failed?'. Nobody had more authority in the traditional South African left than Joe Slovo. He was a pillar of the armed struggle as one-time Chief-of-Staff of the ANC's military wing Umkhonto we Sizwe, he was Secretary-General of the SACP, and later was elected its chair. Slovo had joined the Young Communist League in the early 1940s in Yeoville, a lower middle class and mainly Jewish suburb of Johannesburg. He remained an energetic and influential leader of the anti-apartheid struggle, and was a senior member of President Mandela's first Cabinet until his death from cancer in 1995.

Slovo's analysis was simple: socialism had failed not because the underlying economic philosophy was wrong, but because it was undemocratic in implementation in the USSR and elsewhere, allowing the formation of a parasitic and repressive state. Said Slovo: 'In short, the way forward [for the SACP] is through thorough-going democratic socialism . . .' (Slovo 1990: 25).[2] While the article supported multi-party, pluralistic democracy, it had no clear economic prescriptions. By 1990 this hardly mattered – all the key players in the ANC and the internal opposition in South Africa were converging around the idea of a modernised form of social democracy. For social policies the intellectual leaders now looked to Scandinavia and northern Europe, even Canada, rather than the USSR. For economic policies they were studying East Asia.

Indeed, ANC leaders were careful to avoid revolutionary socialist terminology in the Constitutional Guidelines published by the ANC in 1988 as a public gesture towards a negotiated settlement. The guidelines refer to a mixed economy, 'with a public sector, a private sector, a cooperative sector, and a small-scale family sector'. There would be corrective action to address past inequalities, and the 'private sector shall be obliged to co-operate with the state in realising the objectives of the Freedom Charter in promoting social well-being' (ANC 1988: 12). Not the 'liquidation of economic exploitation' terminology of the Green Book.

The language of the Harare Declaration of 1989 was similarly moderate. The Harare Declaration was a statement of the Organisation of African Unity (OAU) setting out terms for a negotiated settlement for South Africa, and setting out some key parameters for negotiations. Included amongst the parameters was a statement of principles that was, in a sense, a prototype bill of rights for the new South Africa. The ANC played the principal role in drafting this document, including the statement of principles. In general, the principles establish a liberal, pluralistic democratic order with an implicit separation of powers. In particular they refer to an entrenched bill of rights that would protect civil liberties, and 'an economic order that shall promote and advance the well-being of all South Africans' (ANC 1989: 15). It would be hard not to interpret these aspects of the Harare Declaration as a self-conscious projection of the ANC into the political mainstream, far from the currents of radical revolution.

But, for the broader layers of ANC and SACP leadership, Slovo's paper was like the intellectual equivalent of a sudden supply of pure oxygen to a person who had been slowly asphyxiating. It took a little while to adjust to the sudden change in the atmosphere. Released, as it was, in the same month as the unbanning of the ANC and the SACP, the paper had a powerful impact on the next round of policy debates; the first debates conducted with the prospect of imminent state power.

Between the mid-1980s and the early 1990s, the ANC returned

to the philosophical world of the Freedom Charter, a world combining middle-class nationalism and working-class egalitarianism. It took a little while, though, to work out what this meant in practical economic terms.

Preparing for power

When the ANC and the SACP were unbanned, and Nelson Mandela was released, Mandela's early statements on economic policy were confrontational and opaque. In his initial speeches he referred to nationalisation as an option, explaining this in terms of the desire to redress deep historical economic inequalities. It was also a reaction, and a counter-measure to the NP government's attempt to hastily privatise existing publicly owned companies to prevent them from falling into the hands of a future ANC government. Mandela was not concerned about creating economic uncertainty at that time; seizing a power advantage for the ANC was more urgent. Some commentators also claim that more radical internal leaders of the liberation movement heavily influenced the initial speeches – had exiled ANC policy leaders written the speeches they might have been more moderate (for example, see Waldmeir 1997: chapter 8).

The use of nationalisation as a bargaining tool, and as a means of inhibiting decisive action by the NP government (which remained in power, at least *de jure*, for more than four years after Mandela's release), was evident in Mandela's speech to an assembly of 300 white business executives in May 1990. He opposed the process of privatisation outright. 'It would only seem reasonable', he argued, 'that so important a question as the disposal of public property be held over until a truly representative government is in place.' And he was, for the business community, infuriatingly vague on the question of nationalisation. As he put it:

> We believe that there must be further discussion on the issue of nationalisation of assets that might not at the moment be publicly owned. The ANC has no blueprint that

these or other assets will be nationalised, or that nationalisation will take this or the other form. But we do say that
this option should also be part of the ongoing debate, subject
to critical analysis as any other, and viewed in the context of
the realities of South African society. It should not be ruled
out of the court of discussion simply because of previously
bad experience or because of a theological commitment to
the principle of private property (Mandela 1990).

This seemingly rather ominous vagueness represented a tactic by
the ANC to undermine the power of the existing government, and
to begin to assert the ANC's power in relation to the established,
essentially white, South African business community. It is true that
the ANC's position was not entirely clear on all aspects of economic
policy – its powerful ally, the SACP, was still committed to Soviet-
style socialism as late as 1989.

Tito Mboweni wrote about the complexities of the ANC engaging
with business in an internal memo. 'The private sector is', he
explained, 'very sceptical about the policies of the liberation
movement and would like to change them in its favour. The ANC,
on the other hand, wants to engage the private sector mainly for
political reasons . . . to win the support of the broadest section of
South Africa's civil society.' He noted, 'the interest for this dialogue
is mutual, albeit for different reasons, sometimes diametrically
opposed to each other' (ANC c.1991c).

Another reason for the complexities of the ANC's economic
Gordian knot was the role that increasingly powerful trade unions
played in the internal liberation struggle. The internal struggle
against apartheid depended on the organisational weight of the
trade unions as a major source of its strength. The unions had no
doubt that workers should have a great deal more power in the
South African economy, though they did not necessarily agree on
how this should be achieved. Some preferred traditional socialist
strategies, others looked to a unique new hybrid of worker power
and economic planning.[3]

However, the apparent uncertainty of ANC policy shortly after its unbanning should not hide the fact that its economic thinkers had already given a good deal of thought to the desired nature of the post-apartheid economy. During the second half of the 1980s, before the unbanning of the ANC, there were at least seven international conferences on the 'post-apartheid economy' in venues as far apart as Boston and Beijing. These conferences provided the opportunity for sympathetic social scientists from within and outside of South Africa to get together with ANC intellectuals and leaders to begin to address post-apartheid economic challenges (Padayachee 1998: 434).

Beyond the professional policy conferences, there was a series of meetings between ANC-in-exile leaders, and mainly white business and non-governmental leaders from within South Africa (to the anger and condemnation of the NP government). As early as 1986, these discussions began to address economic questions. Gavin Relly, then chief executive of the Anglo American Corporation, told the ANC in 1986 that 'we accept the likelihood of some form of mixed economy with a measure of state planning and intervention', because 'there is a quite justifiable emphasis on the part of Black South Africans on a more equitable distribution of wealth to compensate for the errors of omission and commission of the apartheid era' (*Sunday Times* 1 June 1986). This statement was made after one of a series of meetings between white non-government leaders and the ANC that began in 1985 in Lusaka, and continued, in different forms and places, until the ANC was unbanned.

One very large version of such a meeting was organised in Lusaka, Zambia, in the middle of 1989. The South African delegation of 115 included 23 academics, 20 business people, and 6 newspaper editors. The 123 ANC representatives included 20 members of its National Executive Committee, and were led by the ANC President, Oliver Tambo. In the economic commission, the ANC repeated the formulation as enunciated in the Constitutional Guidelines, anticipating the Harare Declaration. While the ANC statement referred to direct control over the mines, banks and monopoly industries (echoing the Freedom Charter), it noted:

> The exact forms and mechanisms of state control are left open in our programmatic perspectives. The element of private participation in state enterprises is occurring more and more in socialist countries . . . and has not been addressed.
>
> Nationalisation, which involves a mere change in legal ownership, does not advance social control . . . In some conditions of premature nationalisation it can actually result in impeding social control by the destruction or downgrading of industry. This occurred in Mozambique [after 1974] (Louw 1989: 81).[4]

Meanwhile, behind the policy conferences and political seminars, groups of researchers were beginning to develop a broad body of work to inform post-apartheid policy leaders. The ANC set up a Department of Economics and Planning in the mid-1980s (later the Department of Economic Policy), but its initial function revolved around project management and fund-raising. It did, however, participate in the establishment of a research group based in the United Kingdom, called EROSA, or Economic Research on Southern Africa. Leading researchers were drawn from universities and the private sector in London. EROSA prepared a series of sectoral reports for the ANC, and some broader analyses of policy options. While EROSA was linked to the ANC through some highly placed intellectual leaders, the influence of the group on the ANC's thinking was patchy. However, when the ANC was asked early in 1990 to contribute to a newspaper supplement on proposed economic policy for the next government, the author was Vella Pillay, a banker and ANC member, who was close to EROSA (Padayachee 1998).[5]

At about the same time, in 1986, a South African research group was constituted to serve the policy needs of the recently formed Congress of South African Trade Unions. COSATU was then officially politically independent, though it was not a great surprise when, after the unbanning of the ANC, the ANC and COSATU constituted a formal alliance, along with the SACP. The new research group, called the Economic Trends group (ET), was a loose collective of university-based, oppositional economic researchers from around South Africa, most of whom were white.[6] The co-ordinator until the end of the decade was Stephen Gelb, a Canadian-trained South African economist who had co-authored a very influential analysis of the South African economic crisis (Saul and Gelb 1981).

The key point of contact for researchers in COSATU was Alec Erwin, then Education Secretary of the National Union of Metalworkers of South Africa (NUMSA), but an influential thinker in COSATU beyond his formal status. Erwin had lectured in economics at the University of Natal in Durban until he resigned in the late 1970s to become a full-time trade union organiser. He was later to become Deputy Minister of Finance in Mandela's first Cabinet, and early in 1996 joined the Cabinet as Minister of Trade and Industry.

Initially, the Economic Trends group was required to conduct research to advise COSATU on policy in relation to economic sanctions, but as the end of apartheid began to appear on the horizon, ET shifted to an analysis of the causes of the South African economic crisis (the focus of the last section of Chapter One of this book). It was important to understand the economic crisis in order to develop suitable policies for a post-apartheid government, or so that COSATU could influence such a government. The analytical findings of the ET group were contained in a series of working papers and in a book edited by Gelb (1991b).

The ANC starts writing
We have identified a series of parallel, sometimes conflicting, and sometimes interlinked processes contributing to the formulation of an economic policy by the ANC in the early 1990s: formal pre-1990 documents stemming from the ANC's headquarters in Lusaka, Zambia; meetings of academics and political and business leaders;

and at least two significant policy groups. During the course of 1990, the formal position of the unbanned ANC began to take shape in a series of key documents that would lead to the ANC's national policy conference in 1992.

The first significant formal ANC-linked document drawn up after the legalisation of the ANC arose out of a conference in Harare, which concluded on 2 May 1990. Harare, Zimbabwe, was an appropriate setting for the meeting, which was the first time that economic researchers from inside South Africa, mostly associated with COSATU, and ANC-linked economists from outside South Africa met with the purpose of hammering out a common policy framework. Harare is located between Lusaka, the ANC's headquarters in exile, and Johannesburg, South Africa's major city. In addition to ANC officials and South Africa-based researchers, mainly linked to ET, some EROSA researchers attended too. At the end of the conference, a paper was issued entitled 'ANC and COSATU Recommendations on Post-Apartheid Economic Policy' (ANC and COSATU 1990).

Though the paper had no formal status, it was considered to be a relevant policy statement by ANC officials, to the extent that Tito Mboweni presented the paper at a conference in Lesotho a month later. In any case, the paper was publicly released and reported widely in South Africa's financial press.

Several significant formulations were contained in this document. There was recognition of the importance of international competition in products, and the need to make South African production more competitive. While the responsibilities of the state were defined broadly, its economic role was defined more narrowly, in terms of 'some form of macro-economic planning and coordination'. There was a very strong statement of the importance of fiscal conservatism, concluding: 'A future non-racial democratic government would not replicate the recent practice of using borrowings to finance current state expenditure' (ANC and COSATU 1990). Balance of payments problems and inflation were also to be avoided. All these formulations picked up on themes that were being debated in South Africa in ET forums and beyond. Some of the strongest language refers to the importance of re-regulating capital markets to encourage appropriate investments. This represented, in part, the stamp of the EROSA delegates' more interventionist approach to investment and planning.

While the problem of monopolistic conglomerates was highlighted, dismemberment of these clumsy business giants was the main proposed remedy. Nationalisation was noted as a possible strategy, though the document emphasised the need for a 'viable' state sector. One of the objectives of the document, like Mandela's speech to white business in the same month mentioned earlier, was to prevent privatisation by the then current government. The document explicitly threatened the possibility of renationalising companies that were privatised by the current government. The threats worked, and privatisation ceased between 1990–94. In the late 1980s, the state-owned steel company, Iscor, and the state's oil company, Sasol, had been sold, except for a small share of each retained by the state-owned Industrial Development Corporation (IDC).

The rest of the document referred to sector specific issues regarding manufacturing, mining and agriculture; labour rights; human resource and gender equality issues; and aspects of re-distribution through welfare and housing programmes. In all, with the exception of threats designed to hamstring the strategies of the then current government, and some comments on the capital market, it was a conventional, modern social democratic economic policy document. The growth model relied on macroeconomic stability, competitiveness and exports, while the state was responsible for equity and the redistribution of wealth and income in order to right past wrongs.

The other notable economic policy document of 1990 was that put together by ANC economists in their own right and on their own, again in Harare, and again including exiles as well as some who had remained in South Africa. This time there was no official COSATU presence, and no non-South African advisers. The meeting ran over four days and produced a document published by the ANC's Department of Economic Policy (DEP), under the title 'Forward to a Democratic Economy'.

By and large, the ANC document echoed the ANC/COSATU recommendations prepared five months earlier. There were similar references to the redistribution of wealth and income and the restructuring of manufacturing, agriculture and mining. One additional element was the explicit statement that '[p]rivate business has a major role to play in the economy of a democratic, non-racial South Africa' and 'a future democratic government should strive to build confidence with the private sector and encourage maximum cooperation in pursuit of democratically defined development objectives'. The failings of the private sector in regard to the woeful under-representation of black managers and businesses, and its extreme concentration of ownership were noted, now increasingly in the language of reform. However, if co-operation was not forthcoming from the private sector, 'a future democratic government could not shirk its clear duty in this regard' (ANC [DEP] 1990).

'Ready to Govern'

It was decided to relocate the offices of the DEP to the new ANC headquarters in Johannesburg. The ANC had bought a 26-storey building from Shell, which did not like its location in downtown Johannesburg near the commuter train station and informal taxi ranks. It did not take the ANC long to begin wondering whether the R25 million it paid for the building showed the ANC's capacity to exploit Shell's opportunistic generosity, or Shell's business acumen relative to the ANC. Even during the 1994 election campaign, the ANC did not need the whole building for officials, but it was never able to rent out much of the rest of the building. Since then the ANC has moved its headquarters to the more modest Luthuli House in a quieter part of downtown Johannesburg.

From 1990, Shell House bustled with enthusiastic, young and old activists and intellectuals. The 19th floor, where the DEP was located, was well blessed. The DEP manager was Max Sisulu, until he left for a course at Harvard University. Max was the second oldest son of Walter Sisulu who had been Secretary-General of the ANC for many years until he was locked up on Robben Island with Nelson Mandela. Max Sisulu is an intelligent, quietly confident man, who managed to win the confidence of the range of mostly younger economists who looked to him for leadership and direction. He later left his post as Chief Whip in Parliament for senior positions in the defence parastatal Denel, and later in the privatised oil company Sasol.

One of Sisulu's two lieutenants in the DEP was Trevor Manuel, a highly regarded leader in the Western Cape of the United Democratic Front (UDF), an ANC-oriented internal movement. Manuel, born in 1956, had no background in economics; he had trained in civil engineering at a technikon in Cape Town. Since then his career had largely been professional activist in community, then regional, and then national politics. By 1990 he was a manager of the Mobil Foundation – Mobil overlooked the fact that most of his time was spent on ANC politics. Manuel is highly focused and a quick study, with strong political skills. He made macroeconomics his area of focus, and learned fast, without making serious mistakes. When Sisulu left for Harvard in 1992, Manuel took his place, and kept it, even after Sisulu's return a year later. Trevor Manuel was appointed Minister of Trade and Industry in Mandela's first Cabinet, and proved such a success that he was appointed the first 'black' and the first ANC Minister of Finance early in 1996.

The other young leader was Tito Mboweni, born in 1959, who was Nelson Mandela's economic adviser at Davos. Mboweni covered the trade and industrial sectors of the economy, with a special interest in competition policy. Mboweni took the labour portfolio in Mandela's first Cabinet. Other staffers included Ketso Gordhan (born 1961), a Sussex University development studies graduate who ran the ANC's election campaign in 1994, took a seat in Parliament, and soon left to take the job of Director-General of Transport, and recent graduate Vivienne McMenamin who later moved on to run the economic development office of the city of Durban. Zavareh

Rustomjee (born 1957), a chemical and industrial engineer and economist who was later appointed Director-General of Trade and Industry, joined after receiving his Ph.D. in economics from the University of London. Paul Jourdan, who had spent 16 years doing development and policy work in Mozambique and Zimbabwe, had accumulated degrees in geology and mining economics, before returning to South Africa as the ANC's mining policy co-ordinator. After returning Jourdan received a Ph.D. from Leeds, and then went on to take another (part-time) Masters degree at the University of the Witwatersrand. He was appointed special adviser to Trevor Manuel when Manuel became Minister of Trade and Industry. Derek Hanekom, DEP agricultural policy co-ordinator, had used his farm as an underground ANC base until he went to jail for it. He was made Minister of Land Affairs in the first Cabinet, and later also took over the agriculture portfolio. Along with some junior officials, these ANC employees worked with ANC-aligned economists around the country, developing policies and trying to ensure that they were communicated to and canvassed with the grassroots membership of the ANC.

A key task for the DEP was attempting to manage the almost impossible demands of foreign business and government requests for meetings to discuss economic policy, and fulfilling obligations to liaise with the local business communities. The DEP office also drove an active policy development programme – what it thought was its primary task, at that stage. The intention was that the initial work programme of the DEP (and similar departments in health, education, etc.) should culminate in a national policy conference, which would finalise and endorse a comprehensive social and economic policy for the ANC. This could act as the foundation for an election platform. There was an underlying desire to prove to the world that the ANC had the technical competence and the political coherence to produce a workable policy.

Through a structure of regional economic representatives, initially nominated by ANC structures in the regions, and through the work of officials employed in the DEP, workshops were held round the country to discuss economic policy issues. The DEP circulated a rewritten version of the 'Forward to a Democratic Economy Document', and later distributed a workshop package on economic policy (ANC 1991a, 1991b).

The issue most extensively debated in the regional workshops, in my experience, was the section on nationalisation. The DEP documents explained that although nationalisation might be an option, it could drain the financial and managerial resources of the new government, and therefore might not be manageable. Moreover, they explained that redistributing wealth from the rich to the poor would not solve the problems of the poor, because there was not enough wealth, and the economy had to grow to create more wealth to be redistributed.

Perhaps more interesting in both documents was the section on the 'growth path' where the meaning of 'growth through redistribution', the current slogan, was described. The DEP explained that income streams would be redirected towards the poor (who had a higher propensity to consume), and at the same time the productive sector would be restructured to meet the new demand. In the longer term, the new strength of the productive sector would be directed towards export markets.

This formulation was naïve compared with other ANC economic formulations at the time. It masked a choice that the ANC was as yet unwilling to make: between stimulating demand through the redistribution of income, or through increasing productivity to compete in export markets. Both paths could be accommodated by the slogan 'growth through redistribution'. In the case of the export-oriented path, redistribution would have been through the social wage in the form of education, health and other social services that could improve the capacity of existing and new industrial workers. This approach, later embodied in the Industrial Strategy Project's (ISP's) vision, was less Keynesian and more Asian in its approach, and its proponents failed at this stage to make its parameters very clear.

After several delays, the ANC's grand policy conference was held

in May 1992 at the national agricultural show grounds – NASREC –
a collection of outdoor arenas and aeroplane hangar-type halls
located near Soweto. Hundreds of elected ANC delegates from
around the country stayed in shabby downtown hotels in then run-
down Johannesburg. The fleet of buses that whisked the delegates
to the conference was escorted by noisy swarms of traffic police on
motorcycles. Up until that time, most delegates still saw the traffic
police as part of the repressive apparatus that had fought against
democracy. Now, it seemed, the tables were really turning.

The conference lasted three days, a day longer than the Kliptown
conference 37 years earlier. This time it was for real – the policies
adopted would begin to bind the ANC to an election platform and
would help guide the first democratic Cabinet.

In the economic commission there were two key debates: one
over the clause on the role of the state in the economy with respect
to nationalisation; the other was the clause on relations with the
multilateral financial institutions: the World Bank and the
International Monetary Fund (IMF). There were other clauses, not
the focus of attention at this meeting, that probably were more
significant in setting the agenda of the future ANC government.

The nationalisation debate ended only after the ANC's
president, Nelson Mandela, was asked to participate. The result
recorded in *Ready to Govern* was a victory for the moderate social
democratic formulation. '[T]he state', it was argued, 'should respond
to the needs of the national economy in a flexible way . . . the
balance of evidence will guide the decision for or against various
economic policy measures.' In this context, the democratic state
would consider either or both '[i]ncreasing the public sector in
strategic areas' or 'reducing the public sector in certain areas that
will enhance efficiency, advance affirmative action, and empower
the historically disadvantaged . . .' (ANC 1992: clauses D1.6–D1.7.2).
Not only was nationalisation moved out of the ideological sphere
into the realm of pragmatism, so was privatisation.

The clause on the IMF and the World Bank ended with wording
that satisfied all, though again weighted towards the moderate view.

Relations with the World Bank and the IMF would be conducted in such a way as to 'protect the integrity of domestic policy formulation and promote the interests of the South African population and the economy'. The ANC would also strive to 'reduce dependence on international financial institutions' (ANC 1992: clause D4.4). What this meant in practice was that the government would avoid excessive public or private borrowing from abroad.

The trade policy section began with a commitment that 'trade policy will aim at raising the level of productivity and improving the competitiveness of domestic and Southern African producers'. Any economist, especially in highly protected South Africa, would interpret this as a commitment to a trade policy reform programme. This was backed up by a commitment to 'participate in international institutions governing multilateral trading arrangements', in other words, the General Agreement on Tariffs and Trade (GATT). These commitments were elaborated in other clauses that referred to avoiding job loss and support for 'new branches of production', but the significance of the clause was clearly in the basic commitment to trade liberalisation (ANC 1992: clauses D8.1; D8.2).

The clause on foreign investment also broke new ground. It committed an ANC government to adopting the principle of 'national treatment' towards foreign investors, which meant equal treatment with South African companies before South African law. Again, there were some qualifications appended, but the commitment eventually worked its way through to be enshrined in the democratic regime's new constitution (ANC 1992: clauses D8.3–D8.7).

These two steps indicated that the ANC was embracing the strategy of global integration more enthusiastically than before; 'growth through redistribution' understood in a Keynesian sense of managing domestic demand had begun to disappear. Instead, the two principal components of the ANC's national economic strategy – redistribution and growth – were now separated into complementary programmes, rather than being dealt with in an integrated way (ANC 1992: clause D1.2). Afraid of the dated

Keynesian connotations, the slogan 'growth through redistribution' was dropped altogether. Perhaps the old-fashioned Keynesian slogan of 'growth through redistribution' should have been systematically replaced with a more modern, Asian-inspired version, emphasising redistribution in the form of cheaper wage goods due to lower tariffs, and better government services for the poor, especially in health and education, leading to higher productivity and exports, and therefore growth. Perhaps the drafters thought, consciously or otherwise, that this was too subtle a shift to manage in a huge, mass-based policy conference, or that it would confuse external observers.

Filling in the details
At the DEP's Harare meeting in September 1990 it had been agreed to set up a national economic policy institute that would fund economic research projects to aid the ANC in its policy development process. The ANC called for and participated in a study supported by the International Development Research Centre (IDRC) of Canada, an independent state-supported body. Canadian trade economist, Gerry Helleiner, led the mission, which included Benno Ndulu, a Tanzanian and one of Africa's top macroeconomists. The commission recommended that the policy institute should support macroeconomic policy research as a priority. Monetary and fiscal policy were key responsibilities of government that the IDRC team felt were the most in deficit in the ANC policy community. This recommendation was influenced by the fact that the IDRC was already committed to a major 'microeconomic' policy research project linked to the ANC through COSATU – the Industrial Strategy Project (ISP). So, the ANC-linked institute started out in an interim form as the Macroeconomic Research Group (MERG), located in the economics department at the University of the Witwatersrand in Johannesburg.

MERG was intended to focus on options for the ANC in fiscal and monetary policy, but it soon became clear that the project's mandate would be wider. In his address launching the project, ANC president Nelson Mandela emphasised fiscal policy issues, especially on the expenditure side of the account. The ANC had more or less accepted that taxation systems were not the key to redistribution, although it strongly endorsed progressive systems of taxation. While monetary policy issues were not mentioned, items referred to beyond fiscal policy included housing, land, transport, education, health, social security, mining and energy.

While the substance of the policies would be important, the image of the ANC in the media was important too. 'The ANC is portrayed in the media', complained Mandela, 'at best as being incapable of formulating economic policy, and at worst as preparing for a massive nationalisation programme' (Mandela 1991). The ANC had to correct this image in the view of the general public and its supporters.

There was confusion amongst some MERG researchers about the status of their output – so much so that this still influences the way people see the MERG process. Some researchers apparently thought their work would be endorsed as ANC policy; others understood that their work would be considered by the ANC along with the work of other sympathetic projects, such as the ISP. After all, the researchers were simply researchers, and had no direct mandate or licence from the ANC.

This would not have mattered had an attempt at a MERG synthesis report not ended in some chaos. MERG funded a range of discreet projects (including the Trade Policy Monitoring Project at the University of Cape Town which I set up and ran). It also aimed to produce a unified report on macroeconomic policy. The report was managed by a steering committee that included several British economists who had been involved in the EROSA programme. The report was to be constructed as a synthesis; however, the authors of various parts of the synthesis did not all agree on a range of general and specific issues. The various groups of researchers were never effectively brought into a discussion to attempt to resolve these issues, and the steering committee failed to do so.

When the report was presented to the ANC's DEP, and even when it was later published, it contained contradictions and unresolved conflicts (MERG 1993). The chapter I contributed to, on trade, industrial and competition policy, contained contradictory policies based on differing philosophies. One researcher withdrew from the process at a rather late stage as he felt members of the steering committee were usurping his policy formulation responsibilities. One of the South African members of the steering committee was not included in the final editing process. Of the final editorial committee, only one of the four editors was a South African – the rest were British academics.

The muddled nature of the final report was probably one of the reasons the report was received lukewarmly by the ANC; another was that the conflicts between the researchers had become something of a public controversy; a third might have been that some of the policies might be seen to be contradicting the positions adopted in *Ready to Govern*.

Nevertheless, the MERG report has been resurrected as an icon for the left. The MERG report is now commonly portrayed as a coherent left-wing alternative to the ANC mainstream. According to this view, by 1993, when the report came out, the ANC had already 'surrendered' to the established business community. In another version, MERG was soon betrayed by the ANC.[7] However, the report was less revolutionary than muddled. The distinctive aspects of the report required the government to play a stronger role in the private and public investment decisions of society, and called for certain targeted interventions. Most of these ideas were not ideologically controversial in the ANC; their 'back-burner' status was more an outcome of a realistic (or pessimistic) assessment of the likely capacity of government administration after the first democratic elections. Policies that had worked well in East Asia might not be able to be implemented immediately in South Africa because of the incompetence and potential treachery of the old state apparatchiks and the expected inexperience of new civil servants.

Perhaps one point of real debate, which only crystallised on the publication of the ANC government's GEAR report in 1996, was over the size of an acceptable fiscal deficit. The MERG report, like an early World Bank report (Fallon and Perreira da Silva 1994), had bold macroeconomic prescriptions, contrasting with the ANC's preoccupation to get the deficit down to 3% of GDP. Another debate concerned the independence of the SARB, where the ANC took the conservative view to maintain and entrench the independence of the central bank. It feared that the statement of contrary policies would unnecessarily unsettle international capital markets' views of policy stability in South Africa. The MERG report saw a more developmental role for the SARB, again after the Asian model.

In spite of the partisan crust that has since coagulated around the MERG report, in general the MERG project supervised useful policy research outputs. Another useful though far narrower policy research initiative was the ISP. This descended from the COSATU-linked Economic Trends group, and went through several phases. Its goal was to determine how to revive the manufacturing sector in South Africa in order to preserve and create jobs, and to create wealth. The outcome was an interesting synthesis drawing on the East Asian experience, which emphasised the role of government in improving competitiveness, meshed with an appreciation of recent work on modern production methods, the new growth theory which emphasised the role of technology in productivity and competitiveness, and a view of the world economy that was alive to its opportunities, but wary of its potential pitfalls. It was supply-side oriented, not in a Reaganomics sense of tax-cutting for the rich, but in an operations management sense of reorganising and re-engineering the workplace. This subversion of the concept of 'supply-side' was one of the distinctive and influential features of the ISP.

The project produced a set of monographs on industrial sectors, and several studies on cross-cutting issues such as small business development, innovation, trade policy, and competition policy. Many of the reports came to inform future policy, not surprisingly as many of the authors took senior economic policy positions in government within a year or two of the democratic elections.

The project also produced a synthesis report published as a book (Joffe et al. 1995). The key policy proposals focused on reorganising the work process and hence industrial relations, elevating training, increasing competition in the domestic market (through trade and competition policy) while simultaneously encouraging co-operative relations between certain types of firms, and developing instruments to support small business development and innovation. The expectation was that future growth was more likely to come from exports than from the expansion of the domestic market, which was over-borrowed and under-saved – except where there were significant effects from the redistribution of income and wealth and through the erection of new houses: building materials and semi- and durable consumer goods. No matter how effective such redistribution, the ISP felt that more growth would have to come from export markets. Perhaps one reason for this, contrasting South Africa with the original Asian tigers of Japan, South Korea and Taiwan, was that the land reform in South Africa seemed unlikely to be as efficient and effective as it had been in those countries – nor did it have as much potential, with the supply of arable land in South Africa being very limited.

The subversion of the concept 'supply-side measures' showed that the ISP found many of South Africa's economic problems and potential solutions (with the key exception of the exchange rate) to be in the sphere of microeconomics. The issue of the precision to which interventions should be targeted that would be appropriate for South Africa was never quite resolved. While most of the ISP researchers favoured targeted interventions in theory, some doubted that the South African government would have the capacity to manage such interventions without being captured by special interests or simply wasting resources.

The compromise answer was to design general incentives that would allow firms or sectors to self-select themselves, and to design them in such a way as to make them suitable only for firms with a high potential to grow and make good profits. In Chapter Four we will look at how the government attempted to put these ideas into practice.

Economic policy as election manifesto

While the largest, black-dominated trade union federation in South Africa – COSATU – had a relationship with the ISP, the latter was ultimately responsible for its own output, and that output did not necessarily represent the views of COSATU, although by and large, at the time, it did. COSATU was emerging as a key electoral ally of the ANC, but could not go into an election pact without indicating to its members what an ANC government would deliver for the working class. Moreover, some COSATU leaders felt that the ANC leadership did not take economic transformation seriously enough, and that it was their task to help the ANC set its economic transformation agenda. From these concerns emerged the Reconstruction and Development Programme. The RDP was published as the ANC manifesto before the elections, and, in a modified form, as a government white paper later in 1994. The manifesto is now commonly known as the 'base document'.

When the RDP manifesto was published, weeks before the general election of 1994, it represented the participation, not only of formal members of the ANC's alliance – the ANC, COSATU and the SACP, but also the civic federation, SANCO (South African National Civics Organisation), whose main cause was housing. A range of other non-governmental organisations was also consulted. The document was a blueprint for a productive social democratic haven. Aside from a few mildly dogmatic statements, for example about the need for a public housing bank, or the need to retain all infrastructure services in public hands, the RDP proposed a series of practical solutions and targets. Though the programmes were roughly costed by MERG, it was not certain that all these targets could be reached in the time given – generally the five-year term of office of the new government.

There were two key constraints that were not adequately

quantified. One was how government revenue flows would be improved. The RDP explicitly committed itself to fiscal prudence, and hence the reallocation of existing revenues rather than the gathering of new taxes.[8] The second constraint, not seriously thought about at the time, was one provided by the lack of sufficient skilled managers in the new government, and the lack of proven techniques of policy co-ordination and implementation.

The establishment of an RDP office, in the Office of the President, run by a Minister without Portfolio, former COSATU leader, Jay Naidoo, and managed by one of COSATU's top or-ganisers and strategists, Bernie Fanaroff, was an attempt to finesse both the problem of mobilising financial resources, and the problem of the co-ordination of policy and implementation of programmes. But the RDP office was never able to deal with the problem that its functions were in part a subset of those of the Department of Finance, and that its initiatives were, in part, seen as impositions on the line departments of government. This led to the disap-pointing performance of the RDP office as an institution, and to its dissolution early in 1996. The dissolution of the RDP office weeks after the appointment of the first ANC Minister of Finance (the first two Ministers of Finance were drawn from the business community) was not a coincidence.

One notable shift from the ANC's *Ready to Govern* position was a return, in the RDP, to the notion of an inextricable link between redistribution and development, the latter term being seen as more than, but dependent on, growth. Redistribution and development were linked in the same modified Keynesian way that was present in the 1990 documents of the ANC. Redistribution of wealth and income would lead to rising domestic demand, and these goods should be supplied by local manufacturers, leading to a virtuous circle:

This programme will both meet basic needs and open up previously suppressed economic and human potential in urban and rural areas. In turn this will lead to an increased

output in all sectors of the economy, and by modernising
our infrastructure and human resource development we will
also enhance export capacity (ANC 1994a: 6).

So, in certain minor respects, the RDP diverged from the policies
embodied in *Ready to Govern*. There was less hesitancy about the
role of the public sector, and more optimism about the direct
complementary relationship between growth and development. But
with regard to key macroeconomic positions, the RDP was orthodox.

'The largest portion of RDP projects', it indicated, 'will be
financed by the better use of existing resources.' This implied, in
essence, milking the defence budget, which was considered
excessively large, even though it had declined under De Klerk's
government. 'In the long run', argued the base document, 'the
RDP will redirect government spending rather than increasing it
as a proportion of GDP' (ANC 1994a: 142–143).

The document also referred explicitly to concerns about
government dissaving, that is: borrowing more than it spent on
public investment. 'A severe imbalance exists at present between
insufficient capital expenditure and excessive consumption
expenditure.' It drew attention to the 'existing ratios of the [fiscal]
deficit, borrowing and taxation to GDP'. 'Particular attention would
be paid to these ratios', it added, in order to maintain 'macro-
stability' during the implementation of the RDP (ANC 1994a: 143).

The RDP was clearly an attempt to set out an Asian-type
heterodox policy that combined investment driven hard by the
public sector with institutional reform and orthodox macroeconomic stability.

COSATU gave the RDP policy a stamp of approval. Ebrahim
Patel, one of the drafters of the RDP and one of the leading left-
wing thinkers in COSATU, was happy with the RDP document. 'It
makes public COSATU debates, is a confirmation of policy positions
and has its origin in earlier documents.' Patel might have preferred
a more radical document, but 'the RDP accepts and acknowledges
the limits of power', he noted (*Weekly Mail* 21 January 1994).

Taking the RDP into government

The ANC entered government with a history of policy development and policy debate, which had continued throughout the early 1990s, largely in the public arena. It also had a set of economic policies that had been hammered out over time. It is quite justified to ask, at this stage, so what? Many policies are developed in political parties and alliances, especially when they are out of power, only to be forgotten when the party takes power. Sometimes this is deliberate fraud; other times it is a result of political factors entering into Cabinet appointments that shift the direction of policy for the relevant portfolio.

Indeed, in South Africa, there were examples of extensive and sophisticated policy development processes by the ANC that were ignored by the new Cabinet Minister and his or her Director-General, partly because those individuals had not been involved in the policy process and had other ideas.

In the case of the economic portfolios, however, there was remarkable continuity. Key ministers and deputy ministers were, with a few exceptions, the same people who had led the ANC's policy processes – particularly Tito Mboweni, Alec Erwin, Trevor Manuel and Derek Hanekom. New senior parliamentarians had also helped lead the economic policy processes – people such as Rob Davies, Max Sisulu, Chris Dhlamini and Ben Turok. Many of the key provincial economic leaders were soon leading ex-COSATU officials, who had a grasp of the issues and close relationships with the relevant ministers and parliamentarians. Moreover, many of the senior officials in key government economic departments were soon drawn from the ANC policy community, though this happened much faster in some economic departments than others. In the case of economic policy, therefore, the history of the policy development process is relevant. The leaders of the policy processes became the governmental leaders – cabinet ministers and bureaucrats – assigned with the responsibility of implementing policy. In the next four chapters we review their performance.

Notes

1. Interestingly, the passage on the 'non-European bourgeoisie' was excluded from the version of the article included in the Ruth First collection of Mandela's writings (1965).
2. Ironically, though Slovo called on the Party to win its support 'through democratic persuasion', the SACP has not yet tested the electoral waters on its own, beyond the umbrella of the ANC.
3. Alec Erwin (1989), then of NUMSA, thought, for example, that the power of the working class could be used to impose rational planning processes on the South African economy. See Baskin (1991) for the best general analysis of South African unions in the run-up to political liberation.
4. For some of the ANC thinking leading to this formulation, see Davies (1987).
5. Padayachee has summarised and periodised economic policy inputs into the ANC, though his article contains opinions I do not share, and is unevenly reliable.
6. My own involvement has been extensive – I do not write as a dispassionate observer. I joined the Economic Trends group in 1988; participated in ANC economic policy work (including speech drafting) from 1990, wrote a report for the Industrial Strategy Project, established the Trade Policy Monitoring Project, and later the Trade and Industrial Policy Secretariat, participated in the Macroeconomic Research Group book project as co-author of a report and contributor to a chapter, joined government in 1995 and currently work in the South African Presidency.
7. Most strongly stated by Marais (1998: 158–160); also suggested in Padayachee (1998: 437–439); and in an otherwise useful article, 'How the ANC bowed to the market', by John Matisonn (*Mail & Guardian* 11 November 1998).
8. 'In the long run, the RDP will redirect government spending rather than increasing it as a proportion of GDP' (ANC 1994: 142–143).

CHAPTER THREE

Getting into GEAR

Buying insurance

An apocryphal story about Fidel Castro and Che Guevara was popular in South African opposition circles in the 1970s and resurfaced in the early 1990s. According to legend, when Castro and the Cuban revolutionaries took power, Castro asked at an early planning meeting: 'Who is an economist here?' Thinking that Castro had asked, 'Who is a communist here?' Che put up his hand. 'OK,' said Fidel. 'You run the central bank.'

Unlike the Cuba of the legend, South Africa had a number of leaders of the newly dominant political party, the ANC, who were skilled in economics, though obviously not experienced in managing government. Some had post-graduate degrees in economics; some had post-graduate training in economic policy management; some had been given the opportunity to be special interns in investment banks such as Goldman Sachs. The second rank in the ANC was often more schooled formally, though less experienced managerially.

That is why many in the ANC were surprised when the two key economic positions in the new government were retained by the incumbents who had been appointed by the apartheid government. One was Chris Stals, the Governor of the South African Reserve Bank (SARB); the other was the Minister of Finance, Derek Keys.

President P.W. Botha appointed Stals in the midst of South Africa's politically leveraged debt crisis. Before his appointment, Stals had run the Treasury.

65

Stals was widely known as the key architect of South Africa's debt standstill agreement, reached with international bankers early in 1986. Chase Manhattan led a flight of banks and credit lines from South Africa in mid-1985 after President P.W. Botha made a defiant speech against reform. With a plunging oil price that led to a plunging gold price and then a plunging rand, a dispro-portionately large proportion of short-term international bank-to-bank loans precipitated a debt crisis. Stals negotiated a well-structured deal after Botha, under the threat of sanctions, made an announcement about reforming the influx control laws. When the ailing M.H. de Kock retired as SARB Governor in 1988 with a mediocre record as central bank manager, South Africa was lucky to get Stals.

Keys was appointed Minister of Economic Affairs (including Trade and Industry) by the reforming President F.W. de Klerk in 1992. Shortly afterwards, Keys also took over as Minister of Finance from Barend du Plessis, a former schoolteacher and a political ally of P.W. Botha. Keys was one of several National Party (NP) nominees in the post-1994 Cabinet which, although it was dominated by the ANC, was constituted as a government of national unity (GNU) according to an agreement embodied in the interim constitution. (There were also Inkatha Freedom Party members of the GNU Cabinet.) Keys had previously been CEO of the large, Afrikaner-based mining conglomerate Gencor, which he helped to transform into a world-class player.

While still under De Klerk's government, Keys had begun to bail out a very leaky ship. On the trade and industry side, he helped forge a new partnership between business, labour and government in the National Economic Forum (NEF). In finance he began to stem the growing budget deficit – the gap between government revenue and its expenditure, which his predecessor had managed to double in a few short years.

After presenting a sensible first budget for the new government (his second budget), Keys resigned late in September 1994, for personal reasons. It later transpired that he had been offered a top position in Gencor's operation in the United Kingdom. Instead of replacing Keys with an ANC politician, President Mandela appointed Chris Liebenberg as Finance Minister. Liebenberg, a professional banker, had been chief executive of the Nedcor group, one of South Africa's big four banking houses. He had distinguished himself in the apartheid era, during the transition towards democracy, by giving early and visible support to the Consultative Business Movement (CBM). The CBM was a pressure group set up by some relatively liberal business leaders who sought a meaningful interaction with the ANC, when many members of the business community were still afraid to be seen talking to the ANC, who had been demonised as terrorists for decades.

While he was somewhat liberal politically, Liebenberg was known as a steady, predictable banker. Mandela announced Liebenberg's appointment at a hastily convened press conference early in July after rumours of Keys' resignation started to affect financial markets. He made the announcement, as he put it, because 'the boys from the stock exchange and elsewhere seem to be very jittery'. He also felt compelled to assure journalists that there had been 'no change whatsoever in government policy' (*Cape Times* 6 July 1994).

The haste with which Mandela was forced to respond to the rumours of Keys' resignation indicates the kind of pressure and suspicion that the new South African government laboured under. This was a new, untried government, said the markets. This is a black African government, they added. It will have to prove itself over and over again, realised Mandela and the ANC Cabinet. Until proof was on the table, Mandela was forced to make gestures such as retaining Stals and appointing Liebenberg, though there were several ministers, deputy ministers and frontbenchers that could have stepped into Keys' shoes had competence been the only criterion.

When President Mandela appointed the respectable Liebenberg, he not only had to engineer a change in the constitution to allow for a person who was not an elected member of Parliament to serve in the Cabinet, he also had to adjust the Cabinet to compensate the NP for losing a seat in the GNU. Liebenberg did not represent any political party.

The overwhelming condition for macroeconomic policy for the first ANC government was that whatever the evidence they received to the contrary, the markets expected the Cabinet to make mistakes. If mistakes were made or even suspected, they were fed to the rumour mill that buttered the bread of currency and securities dealers. Once Mandela was recognised as a responsible and careful leader, his future, as if everything rested on it, became the main object of speculation. Periodically, throughout his term of office, rumours about Mandela's health, for example, fed currency speculation. Frustration with these tendencies led Trevor Manuel, after being appointed Minister of Finance in 1996, to once angrily refer to the market as 'amorphous'. Though this was essentially true, the media and the market punished him for his tactlessness.

Though many in the financial world may have hoped for the best for South Africa, they expected the worst. Stories about South Africa continued to take on the dark shades of the apartheid era. The South African story had long been associated with drama and tumult. Few outsiders dared to tell the South African story in any other terms. Mandela's government was not wholly successful in its struggles to counter a racially tinged pessimism about Africa, and to encourage the world to accept the South African 'miracle' as a carefully constructed compromise. This, at least partly, explains the preoccupation of Mandela's successor, Thabo Mbeki, with the theme of 'African Renewal', but this is a story we will come back to later.

Because the ANC operated, at least from 1992, under the assumption that financial markets would second-guess them whenever given an opening, it was forced to be more conservative than it would have been had it been the government in a well-established democracy. This was the main reason that the ANC, before and after the elections, publicly committed itself to economic policies that would not antagonise influential world economic players. The three most obvious policies falling into this category were the intention to reduce the government deficit, the general commitment to remove restrictions on exchange control, and the agreement to include a strong form of central bank independence in the constitution.

Another motivation for fiscal and monetary conservatism was the ANC's fear of giving up South Africa's limited economic sovereignty to the International Monetary Fund (IMF) and/or the World Bank as the result of a financial crisis. As ANC parliamentarian Ben Turok put it: 'A new democratic South Africa will need to defend its interests against the predatory actions of international capital and institutions like the International Monetary Fund [and] the World Bank . . .' (*Sunday Times: Business Times* 13 March 1994).

The irony was that in order to stave off the power of international finance, the ANC committed itself to policies approved by the same financiers. In order not to get too indebted to those who could turn their debt against them, they had to be conservative and pander to some of their prejudices.

And yet, the electoral platform of the ANC was the Reconstruction and Development Programme (RDP). The legitimacy of the ANC rested on its ability to deliver an improved life for its constituents – poorer South Africans excluded from power and privilege under apartheid. Moreover, it had to do this inheriting an economy in severe decline, with huge, growing government debt and interest burdens, low or negative growth, declining per capita income, capital outflows, and poor competitiveness in most of the economy. In short, the ANC government had to undertake a general restructuring of the economy *and* a reorientation of the economy towards the historically excluded masses at the same time.

Is it easier to confront growth and distribution issues at the same time, or is it easier to attend to one first then the other? South Africa's experience suggests that it is easier and more sensible to address the two challenges simultaneously. Restructuring for growth is politically difficult – it encounters the problem that those who lose from restructuring usually have more powerful voices than those who will gain in the future but for now have no voice. Therefore, to engage in restructuring with a powerful constituency with a great deal to gain through redistribution should make it easier to do the two reforms together. Moreover, some key aspects of restructuring for growth entail a good measure of redistribution of resources, certainly in the South African case – human resource development and small business development are two obvious examples.

This view is supported by comparative examinations of political and economic reform. When Joan Nelson and her colleagues compared transitions in several Latin American and eastern European societies, they found that it was easier to carry out effective economic reform in some of the countries of Eastern Europe, where the political change was more radical. As Nelson put it, 'where democratic reforms marginalize old political elites and actors, and where public opinion is prepared for fundamental economic changes . . . the launching of [economic] reforms is facilitated' (Nelson 1994: 13). This statement covers much of the South African case.

Mending a leaky tank

In the run-up to the transition, the government's budget was haemorrhaging. The budget deficit had reached a record high of 8.5% of GDP (gross domestic product) in 1992–93 (SARB 1998b).[1] But to compare the country's finances in the apartheid era, when it was split into several allegedly independent countries, the fiscal accounts of the central government and the 'independent home-lands' should be combined. If this is done, the consolidated deficit reached 9.5% in 1992–93, easing off to just under 8% in 1993–94 (estimated figures) in Keys' first budget (Fallon and Perreira da Silva 1994: table 2.6). From 1978–91 the fiscal deficit had averaged between 4 and 5%, but in 1991–92 fiscal restraint disintegrated. This led some ANC supporters to speculate that the old regime had deliberately set a debt trap to constrain the actions of the ANC government. The new government, which came into power in April 1994, had no spare cash and was locked into debt obligations for years to come. Whether or not there was a deliberate debt trap strategy, the new government certainly was weighed down by its obligations.

Part of the story was the rising cost of paying people to defend apartheid. The percentage of government expenditure that went to the payment of its employees, rose from 26.5% of government spending in 1978-82 to 35.5% of spending in 1992-93. From 1981-92 the number of employees in the central government and the provinces grew by more than a third, while the number of employees of the 'independent homelands' more than doubled (Fallon and Perreira da Silva 1994: 109).[2] The apartheid regime was shoring up its defences by selling patronage, but at the long-term expense of the health of its finances.

Change in the composition of government expenditure itself contributed to lower growth. As Table 3.1 shows, the amount spent on recurrent expenses – that is, not invested for the future – rose very rapidly during the 1980s. From 70.3% of spending in the late 1970s, recurrent expenses rose to nearly 86% of government expenditure in 1993. The main reason was the rising government

Table 3.1: Patterns in government spending, 1978–93.

	1978–82	1983–87	1988–93	1991	1992	1993
1. Capital expenditure %	20.1	18.0	12.6	12.7	9.3	13.4
2. Recurrent expenditure %	70.3	80.4	86.4	85.1	89.8	85.8
2a. Remuneration of employees %	26.5	31.4	34.9	36.7	38.4	35.5
2b. Interest payments %	8.3	10.6	13.3	13.1	13.4	14.0
3. Total expenditure/GDP %	31.3	32.8	36.2	36.5	36.8	40.6
4. Fiscal deficit/GDP %	-4.2	-4.1	-5.0	-4.5	-5.6	-9.5

Note 1:   Each fiscal year ends 31 March.
Note 2:   Rows 1 and 2 plus net lending make up 100% of government expenditure.
          2a and 2b are *some* of the components of 2.
Source: Fallon and Perreira da Silva (1994: table 2.6).

wage bill. Another reason was the mounting government debt which, combined with rising interest rates, meant that the interest paid by government to finance its debt nearly doubled as a proportion of government expenditure between 1978–93. Rudolf Gouws, a respected banking economist, told the new Parliament's finance committee that the government had inherited a 'fiscal mess' (*Cape Times* 17 August 1994).

Steering a careful course

This was not a promising moment for the new government to attempt to implement new policies and programmes. The state apparatus was under-funded and over-borrowed, the apparatus for revenue collection was in a dire state, and the economy was limping along, having only recently entered positive growth territory for the first time in four years. Facing this, the government seemed to have a number of options: it could raise tax levels, either/or both income tax and a 14% value-added sales tax; it could increase government borrowing; or it could borrow heavily from abroad, as new sources of funds were available to the new government. At least some of these actions seemed necessary if the ANC government was to deliver on its election promises or, more importantly, shore up the fledgling democracy with real benefits for the mass of the people.

But it did not do any of those things. Instead, the ANC committed itself to reducing the budget deficit as a percentage of GDP, and to bringing down the overall government debt burden eventually. It was thought that the debt burden was crowding out private sector borrowing – what was certain was that the debt to GDP ratio raised fears of macroeconomic instability that could drive away private investment capital. So, the government came down heavily on over-expenditure. Alec Erwin, then Deputy Minister of Finance, reported to Parliament that a 'crash-team' was taking drastic steps to correct all cases of over-expenditure (*Business Day* 14 September 1994). In addition, the government planned to improve revenue collection, and reallocate funds from low-priority areas to high-priority areas. Before and after the elections, ANC leaders were quoted on several occasions saying that they would fund new social programmes through funds reallocated from downgraded or redundant functions (see, for example, *Cape Times* 16 March 1994).

What did budget reallocation mean in practice? If we compare 1990/91 expenditures with those of 1995/96 we will see that the major losers were defence, economic services and general government services. Defence was cut from 16% of the budget to 9%; general government services were cut from 8 to 7%; while subsidies that encouraged manufacturers to locate in remote homelands were cut from 2.5 to 1.3% of the budget. Most of the reallocated funds went to social services, including: education up 1.6 percentage points to 26.2%; health up half a percentage point to 12.3%; housing up half a percentage point to 2.3%; and social security and welfare, up 3.5 percentage points to 11.9% (South Africa Foundation 1996: 54). Also, a RDP fund was set up for special projects, starting with R2.5 billion – about 2% of the budget.

All of these increases were intended to contribute to the equalisation of services provided to the historically disadvantaged black population, though in some cases the overall standard could not be as high as it had been for privileged whites in the past. Up to 1994, social services for whites were hugely more generous than those provided to other 'race groups', especially black South Africans. For example, the ratio of government spending per school pupil, black to white, was one to seven in the mid-1980s (Wilson and Ramphele 1989: 141) and these figures had been even worse in the 1960s and 1970s.

All in all, not an extremely dramatic shifting of funds. The huge backlog in the provision of public facilities such as roads and water, and services such as health and education might take longer than the RDP originally envisaged.

By late 1994 the government realised that reallocation could not address the fiscal challenges confronting it, and it announced a 'six-pack' belt-tightening strategy. The key new elements were: a voluntary cut in salary for parliamentarians, ministers, and the President; the redeployment of and cutting back on civil servants (initially through voluntary retrenchment packages); a commitment to the full or partial privatisation of state assets and enterprises to reduce debt or supplement the RDP; and the reorganisation of fiscal relations between the central government and the provinces (*Cape Times* 31 October 1994).

The government was not keen to raise tax levels. South Africa was already, at least on paper, a heavily taxed society. Company and personal marginal income tax rates were over 40% of income. Though the basic company tax was 35%, there was a secondary tax on distributed profits that could raise the rate to 42.5%. Derek Keys had cut company taxes, but they remained high by international standards, as did personal income taxes. The ANC felt raising income taxes could scare off potential investors, and held off. There was a once-off levy in the 1994 budget to help pay the costs of the transition, particularly the elections, but this made it more difficult to justify any other additional tax. The major indirect tax, the value-added tax (VAT) of 14% on all purchases of goods and services, was seen by the ANC and its supporters as a regressive tax. It penalised the poor, who spent almost all their income on VAT-taxable goods and services. Raising it would damage the credibility of the ANC in its own backyard. Instead, the new government decided to focus on improving the performance of the revenue collection machinery under the existing tax dispensation.

The ANC was equally reluctant to borrow heavily from abroad. A World Bank report published almost simultaneously with the 1994 election suggested that higher levels of government investment expenditure was one of five key strategies for faster growth and redistribution in South Africa (Fallon and Perreira da Silva 1994: chapters 5 and 6). Implicit in the report is the notion that a growth promoting budget deficit could be financed through foreign borrowing at low enough levels not to worry the new government. More precisely, the World Bank economists felt that the government should urgently underpin growth with substantial investments in South Africa's social and physical infrastructure that aimed to redistribute facilities, resources and opportunities (Fallon 1993).

Tony O'Reilly, the Irish-born Heinz chair, president, CEO, and the major shareholder in the Independent newspaper group, which bought control of South Africa's biggest newspaper group in 1994, strongly urged the government to borrow heavily to get the economy going. O'Reilly, whose purchase of the Argus newspaper group was supported by Mandela and the ANC, said in July 1994, 'We have got to kick-start this economy, and it will not be kick-started by world business' (*Cape Times* 6 July 1994). Months later, after South Africa made progress in its credit ratings, he reiterated his message. He warned of the perils of under-borrowing, and urged the government to 'take appropriate risks to jump-start this economy, and jump start it tomorrow' (*Cape Times* 10 November 1994). This in an economy where the growth rate had doubled from 1.3% to 2.7% from 1993–94. Brian Kantor, a senior macroeconomist at the University of Cape Town, also called for a more ambitious borrowing programme (*Cape Times* 25 August 1994).

Nevertheless, the South African government refused to bite. Though some foreign bonds were issued, their main purposes were to refinance existing credit, to restructure the debt portfolio and its maturity profile, and to set benchmarks for other South African borrowers (CREFSA 1997).

Why did the government not take greater advantage of loan offers from private and public international lenders? One reason was undoubtedly the fear, noted earlier, that badly timed and badly managed borrowing could leave the government in the hands of the IMF. A second reason was that the government lacked confidence in its ability to invest the money effectively. The fiscal machinery was in a mess, and the capacity of most of the government departments to spend money effectively was far from proven. In retrospect, this concern was fully justified in 1994. A third and related reason was that the fiscal squeeze was a good rationale for a radical shake-up of the public service, something urgently needed in almost all South African government departments and organisations in the early phase of the transition to democracy.

The new government preferred to err on the side of caution. The new government leaders had little experience of managing a country's finances and suspected that the civil service managers they inherited were not necessarily competent or trustworthy. Their own handpicked staff was only beginning to enter government, particularly in the Department of Finance, which did not have an ANC minister or director-general until 1996, and even more slowly in the SARB. They feared that the long-term costs of making a mistake were potentially greater than the costs of missing an opportunity. This new government was able to think in longer terms than most democratic governments, partly because of the extraordinary vision of the new leadership, and partly because it had good reason to be confident of being returned to government in the second democratic elections in 1999.

In any case, the Minister of Finance was preoccupied with critical issues that had to be addressed before he could turn his attention to expansionist strategies. Simply constructing the 1995/96 budget was a 'nightmare' according to new Minister of Finance, Chris Liebenberg, because of the complexity of incorporating former homeland finances into a single national account (*Business Day* 11 November 1994). Even then, many homeland offices were still running semi-autonomously. The Department of Finance was reluctant to transfer homeland finances to the relevant province – nine provinces had been created in the constitutional settlement. South Africa had to transform four existing provinces and nine homelands, of which several were 'self-governing' or 'independent', into nine provinces in one nation. It was at the homeland level that the nation's finances were most problematic, and some problems evident in 1994, such as redundant and untraceable civil servants (the term 'ghost workers' was invented to describe this problem), took a decade to resolve in some provinces.

A key fiscal target set by the government in November 1994 was to reduce the budget deficit from the 6.8 to 4.5% of GDP over a five-year period, with an expected GDP growth rate of 3% per annum on average. As Table 3.2 shows, the deficit target was easily accomplished, growth on average was close to 3%, but the government could not immediately reverse the trend towards higher consumption expenditure.

Table 3.2: Macroeconomic trends, 1991–2003 (at two-yearly intervals).

	1991	1993	1995	1997	1999	2001	2003
Government consumption/GDP %	19.8	20.1	18.3	19.8	18.3	18.3	19.1
Public sector investment/GDP %	5.9	4.3	4.3	4.6	4.7	3.9	4.9
Government annual deficit/GDP %	-2.7	-7.3	-4.6	-5.0	-2.8	-1.9	-2.3
Government total debt/GDP %	37.2	40.4	49.0	49.2	50.2	45.6	40.2
GDP growth at 2000 prices	-1.0	1.2	3.1	2.6	2.4	2.7	2.8

Source: SARB *Quarterly Bulletin*, various.

Hands on the brake

Article 224 of South Africa's Constitution is headed 'Primary Object' of the central bank, though it goes further than that. It reads:

(1) The primary object of the South African Reserve Bank is to protect the value of the currency in the interest of balanced and sustainable economic growth in the Republic.

(2) The South African Reserve Bank, in pursuit of its primary object, must perform its functions independently and without fear, favour or prejudice, but there must be regular consultation between the Bank and the

Cabinet member responsible for national financial matters (Constitution of the Republic of South Africa 1996).

In 1994, Stanley Fischer, soon to become number two in the IMF, suggested a terminology for describing central bank independence. Fischer used the term 'goal independence' to describe the extent to which the central bank could set its own goals (low inflation, high growth, low unemployment or whatever), and the term 'instrument independence' could cover the extent to which central banks were free to deploy whatever instruments they chose – trading government stocks, trading foreign exchange, manipulating the interest rate, or whatever (Fischer 1994). It has been widely believed that central bank independence, especially instrument independence, is 'a good thing' because it insulates the currency from short-term-oriented politicians. However, in a democratic society, goal independence would insulate the central bank from the values of the sovereign state, which is not desirable. The results of sufficient independence are expected to be low inflation and a sound foundation for growth.

Recent surveys show that central bank independence is not an absolute virtue. The evidence increasingly suggests a trade-off between high independence and low inflation, and moderate independence and higher growth (see Eijffinger and De Haan 1996; Blinder 1998; Forder 1998). Of course, no independence and uncontrolled inflation would still be disastrous.

Applying Fischer's terminology, the South African Constitution clearly enshrines 'instrument independence' (the choice of policy instruments through which the Bank achieves its objectives) in the phrase: 'must perform its functions independently and without fear, favour or prejudice'. And the Constitution does not allow 'goal independence'. The Constitution sets the goal of the SARB in the clause which reads: 'The primary object of the South African Reserve Bank is to protect the value of the currency in the interest of balanced and sustainable economic growth in the Republic'

(Constitution of the Republic of South Africa 1996). This is the interpretation of a South African Chamber of Business (SACOB) report, which noted that 'instrument independence' and 'goal dependence' are consistent with international practice and 'probably also supportive of international investor perceptions and business confidence' (SACOB c.1993: 27). On the left, the wording of the constitutional clauses on the SARB has been characterised as a victory for 'capital' or 'international finance capital' (Marais 1998).

But was SACOB right to think that the SARB does not have 'goal independence'? The constitutional clauses define the goal vaguely, and then insulate the SARB from outside interference. The SARB has some room to interpret the goals of monetary policy, giving weight to what Alan Blinder, former vice-chairman of the United States Federal Reserve Bank, called the central bank's 'interpretive role' (Blinder 1998: 54). What do 'balanced' and 'sustainable' actually mean in clause 224(1)? The Minister of Finance is given access to the Governor's ear for 'regular consultations', and since 2001 has established an inflation-targeting regime, but the autonomy of the bank remains considerable.

Stals often referred to the goal of preserving the 'internal and external value of the rand' (Stals 1994b: 27). (The rand was floated in the late 1970s.) He would have approved of the fact that there was no obligation on the SARB to consider economic growth in broad terms, nor was there any mention of an obligation to create jobs, such as the 'maximum employment' objective in the legal foundation of the Federal Reserve Bank of the United States. Stals' vision was always explicitly closer to the 'purist' approach of the Deutsche Bundesbank, which is directed by law simply to 'safeguard the currency' (Blinder 1998: 54).[3]

His job as central banker under the new government, felt Stals, was just the same as it had been before. 'We have spent the past five years establishing relative domestic financial stability. We must spend the next five years ensuring we maintain that stability,' he said shortly after President Mandela's new government was installed. 'Our contribution to the RDP', he added, 'is to ensure monetary stability.' He emphasised that the major problem he still had to deal with was the pressure on the balance of payments (*The Star* 27 May 1994).

What Stals failed to recognise was that the circumstances of the post-apartheid government were very different from those before 1994. International capital was now potentially available, in all shapes and forms. Also, the prospects for greater political stability and certainty under a credible, democratic government meant that capital could flow in relatively quickly.

Stals had two preoccupations: the first being inflation, and the second being the balance of payments. In a country such as South Africa, where imports are high at 20 to 30% of GDP, and where the inclination for imports to grow during periods of GDP growth is very high,[4] one anti-inflation strategy is to prevent the price of imports rising by maintaining the external value of the currency. The two targets were closely linked. A high interest rate had the combined effects of strengthening the currency and slowing the economy. In the South African case, the effect on imports of the currency appreciation resulting from the higher interest rate was normally more than offset by the contraction of the domestic economy. So, while sucking in short-term capital, imports were constrained, tackling inflation and the balance of payments simultaneously.

Stals was not afraid to use the interest rate to protect the value of the currency and the balance of payments. As Table 3.3 shows, the real bank rate (the difference between the SARB rate and the consumer price index) varied between 1 and 5% in the early 1990s, and rocketed up to over 13% in the late 1990s. The real prime interest rate rose as high as 17.5%. As Paul Krugman reminds us, in the era beyond the fixed currencies of the Bretton Woods agreement, the 'iron law of international finance' is that it is impossible for countries to maintain stable exchange rates and currency convertibility, and still have the freedom to use interest rates to support economic expansion (Krugman 1991: 60–61).

The way that Stals tackled monetary stability was old-fashioned monetarism. In March 1994 he confirmed that the SARB felt that 'money supply targeting remains . . . the most sensible anchor for monetary policy . . .' For 1994, he announced, the acceptable range for the rate of increase in M3 was 6 to 9% (Stals 1994a: 25–26). M3 is the quantity of broadly defined money, including deposits and credit. As Table 3.3 shows, the results for M3 growth in 1994 (15.7%) were not even close to the SARB's acceptable range, and yet the rate of inflation continued to fall.

Table 3.3: Percentage change of key monetary indicators, 1992–2002 (selected years).

	1992	1994	1995	1996	1997	1998	2000	2002
M3 supply	8	15.7	15.2	13.6	17.2	14.6	7.5	12.8
Private sector credit growth	8.7	17	17.8	16	14.4	16.7	10.8	4.4
Inflation CPI	13.9	9	8.7	7.4	8.6	6.9	5.4	9.2
Inflation: core (i)	16.8	8.9	7.9	7.5	8.6	7.5	7.8	9.3
Bank rate level (ii)	15	12	15	16	17	20.6	11.75	12.5
Real rate of interest Proxy (iii)	1.1	3	6.3	8.6	8.4	13.7	3.95	3.2
Nominal effective exchange rate	-4.8	-9.3	-5.7	-13	-5.4	-15.7	-5.9	-21.7
Real effective exchange rate	1.8	-3	0.2	-8.3	0.8	-11.8	-1.3	9.9
Current account/ GDP %	1.5	0.1	-1.5	-1.3	-1.5	-1.7	-0.4	0.3

(i) Consumer price index (CPI) excluding food and non-alcoholic beverages, mortgages, and VAT. From 2000 this is CPIX, i.e. CPI minus mortgages for metropolitan and other urban areas.
(ii) As of 30 June each year, or thereabouts. (Up to 1993, rediscount rate on Treasury bills; from 30 April 1993 to March 1998, accommodation rate against overnight loans; from 8 March 1998, repurchase-based auction system, Repo rate.)
(iii) Bank rate minus inflation CPI. This is between 3 and 4% below the predominant prime interest rate over the period.
Source: SARB *Quarterly Bulletin*, various.

In 1995, with an upswing well under way, Stals had two choices. On the expectation that continued positive economic trends would encourage more and more long-term investment that would compensate for rising imports, he could have continued with a moderately tough monetary policy and allowed for a gradual depreciation in the currency with modest single digit inflation targets. Instead he embarked on a much tighter monetary policy: he raised the Bank rate to 15% (3% above the mid-1994 level), increased the reserve requirements for commercial banks, and issued guidelines that indicated maximum desired credit extension levels to the banks.

He explained his action by referring to the rapid rate of M3 growth, driven by an even greater rate of growth of credit extension to government and private borrowers – credit grew by 21% in all during 1994. Stals feared the credit expansion would overheat the economy and lead to inflation (Stals 1995). In fact, as Table 3.3 shows, while M3 continued to grow rapidly in 1995, 1996 and 1997, inflation continued to decline, except in 1997 when the 20% depreciation of the rand in 1996 had an adverse effect.

The tight money policy meant the real interest rate more than doubled from 3% in 1994 to more than 6% in 1995 and more than doubled again to 13.7% in 1998. This had two effects: firstly it started to choke off what was a private sector, investment-driven expansion; secondly it attracted excessive volumes of short-term capital inflows undermining the prospects of a stable currency.

Volatile short-term capital, particularly in the South African case, largely takes the forms of bank-to-bank loans, short-term loans to public corporations and authorities, liabilities related to reserves and, most volatile, private sector, short-term, non-direct investment. Intermediate-term capital would include long-term loans and portfolio investment, while the most stable form of investment is direct investment (for more detail, see Khatri et al. 1997; Kaskende et al. 1998).

Developing countries, particularly a country such as South Africa where the propensity to save has fallen very low,[5] and where the early period of the growth cycle is characterised by higher rates of import growth than export growth (Kahn 1987), need significant injections of foreign capital to underwrite growth.

Table 3.4: Capital movements 1992–2002.

Year	Capital inflows			Capital outflows			Balance
	Direct	Portfolio	Other	Direct	Portfolio	Other	
1993	33	2 427	-6 332	-974	-10	-813	-5 679
1994	1 348	10 298	-1 554	-4 388	-290	-1 055	4 359
1995	4 502	10 651	17 217	-9 059	-1 631	-1 899	19 784
1996	3 515	17 983	7 492	-4 485	-8 407	-2 704	13 394
1997	17 587	51 563	-1 330	-10 831	-20 983	-8 957	27 049
1998	3 104	50 452	6 534	-9 841	-30 077	-2 872	17 296
1999	9 184	83 883	-9 322	-9 659	-31 537	-10 034	32 515
2000	6 158	11 793	10 828	-1 878	-25 628	947	5 976
2001*	58 404	-24 000	-10 226	27 359	-43 626	-12 324	-4 413
2002	7 929	5 348	-1 162	4 216	-9 619	12 016	18 728

* The high figures in the direct investment columns for 2001 result from a transaction between
Anglo American and De Beers, which resulted in Anglo American moving its domicile to London.
Source: SARB *Quarterly Bulletin*, various.

There are two ways for foreign capital inflows to underwrite growth in South Africa. The first is for high real interest rates and a relatively strong currency to attract mainly short-term capital. However, sooner or later the high interest rates will cause the currency to appreciate, reducing competitiveness, or it will cut off domestic expansion, or both. In any case, it leads to a repeated boom-and-bust cycle. The second alternative is for longer-term capital to be attracted by steady longer-term growth, at the expense of the gentle depreciation of the currency because of the lag between the deficit on the current account and the inflow on the capital account. A strategic government-borrowing programme aimed at investments to improve productivity could help to prevent the lag being a very long one.

The latter course, when accompanied by general fiscal and monetary discipline, is potentially more beneficial than the former course. An analytical study published in one of the SARB's *Quarterly*

Bulletins supports this argument (Smal 1996). Why take the former course, then, as Stals did? There are several possible explanations.

One is confidence. Stals had long worked in a country where confidence in the future was very low, leading to few long-term private investment projects, and expedient, short-term relations with the outside world. He may have felt that the lagged long-term direct investment and project-related loans would never materialise on a scale to allow the economy to move towards balanced external accounts, let alone growing reserves. There was no government-borrowing plan.

In addition, South Africa had just embarked on a programme of exchange control reform. Exchange control had started during a political crisis in 1960, was briefly lifted between 1983 and 1985, and then reimposed during the 1985 debt crisis. Both the ANC and Stals had talked about the need for liberalisation, though it was never quite clear what the end-point of that liberalisation should be – complete as in fully developed countries such as the United States and the United Kingdom, or partial. What Stals and the ANC agreed was that liberalisation should be gradual. The first step was to abandon the separation of the financial rand – a closed international capital market where every sale had to be matched by a purchase – and the commercial rand used for current trans-actions. The passage of exchange control reform is summarised in Box 3.1. Though a key motive for exchange liberalisation was to increase confidence in the South African economy, after the disastrous experience of 1983–85 it was an act of faith. Stals must have been worried about the unknown outcome of liberalisation.

Box 3.1: Exchange control liberalisation in South Africa, 1995-2003

21 February 1995
Stals announces that the financial rand will soon be scrapped.

10 March 1995
Liebenberg scraps the financial rand, significantly freeing inward foreign investment market.

13 July 1995
Stals announces permission for investments abroad by institutional investors, by approval, in the form of asset swaps with the foreign purchasers of South African assets.

Stals announces the partial withdrawal of the SARB from the forward cover market where it had subsidised borrowings by local public and private companies.

14 June 1996
Manuel announces:
1. Relaxation on limitation on domestic borrowing by foreign investors from a level of 50% of their shareholders equity to 100%;
2. The ceiling on institutional investors foreign investments through asset swaps, limited to 5% of total assets in 1995, raised to 10% of total assets;
3. Institutional investors would also be allowed foreign transfers of currency for 1996 of up to 3% of net inflow of funds during 1995, subject to 2. above;
4. Exporters were freed to offset the cost of imports against the proceeds of exports, within limits;
5. Personal and commercial travel allowances were also freed up significantly.

During 1996
Capital exports as investment in southern Africa given preferential treatment by SARB.

12 March 1997
Manuel announces (most for July implementation):
1. Almost all controls on current account transactions removed;
2. Travel allowances increased again (to R80 000 for individuals);
3. Individuals allowed to hold approved foreign currency deposits, to invest in Southern African Development Community (SADC), and to use foreign earned income other than proceeds from exports;
4. Corporates allowed to invest R30 million abroad and R50 million in SADC beyond the Common Monetary Area (CMA), to invest a percentage of assets in portfolio investments abroad under approval, and to retain foreign currency earnings for up to 30 days (previously 7 days);
5. Institutional investors again allowed to invest offshore, up to 3% of net inflow during 1996, allowed a further 2% to invest in non-CMA SADC countries, and to broaden the definition of institutions qualifying for asset swaps to include regulated fund managers;
6. Companies defined as foreign and hence limited as regards local borrowing broadened from 25% foreign ownership to 50% foreign ownership;
7. US dollar/rand futures to be allowed on local futures exchange.

11 March 1998
1. Limit on offshore investments by South African corporations raised to R50 million, and to R250 million for SADC countries;

2. Individuals in good tax standing allowed to invest R400 000 abroad, previously R200 000.

1999–2001
Three major South African firms allowed to shift their domiciles to London for funding reasons, and loosening of remaining controls on South African citizens and corporations.

26 February 2003
Minister of Finance announces that citizens will be allowed, within a designated time period to legalise or repatriate illegally held foreign assets, on payment of a penalty.

In pushing up the bank rate, Stals might also have been overly influenced by the M3 and credit extension figures. Stals seemed convinced that credit and broad money supply expansion would lead to overheating and inflation, though there was no evidence from the economy that this was indeed the consequence. What Stals may have missed here was the rapid restructuring going on in South African society and the economy, with a more secure black working class and a fast-growing black middle class opening bank accounts and adopting new financial facilities, as well as the expansion of micro-credit after an amendment to the Usury Act in 1992.

He was clearly worried about the low levels of domestic saving. It is possible that he felt that bank savings would continue to shrink as long as the inflation beast was not yet dead and buried. South Africa had experienced negative interest rates for a very long period between the mid-1970s and 1988, during which it was rational to be a debtor, not a saver.

Another concern was his view of the South African economy's ability to respond to the new opportunities offered by the more competitive currency. He thought labour markets were not flexible enough to allow depreciation to have long-term positive effects on competitiveness. Workers would bid their real wages back up to where they were before the depreciation.

A fourth possible reason was the way that the SARB tended to stabilise the currency when it got wobbly – in addition to intervening in the spot market, it got involved with the forward market for foreign exchange. This began through the provision of forward cover because of the absence of a commercial forward cover market in South Africa. When South Africa ran short of foreign capital, as during South Africa's debt crisis from 1985–93, the SARB offered preferential long-term rates to encourage South African borrowers to seek funds abroad (Khatri et al. 1997: 33–38). For most of the 1990s the main form of SARB intervention in the forward market was through foreign exchange swaps. When it used swaps to intervene in the spot market, it usually resulted in the SARB being 'oversold' in foreign currency to prop up the domestic currency.

Frequently, the net oversold position was as much as six or seven times as high as the gross foreign reserves position (foreign reserves being the central bank's holdings of foreign currencies and gold). The gross foreign reserves position tended to oscillate between the very low levels of about two and three billion US dollars, often less than the value of two months of imports (Khatri et al. 1997: 35). So the reserves were insufficient for the SARB to use them effectively as a bulwark against currency fluctuations. Currency swaps were far more heavily used.

Because the SARB had to settle its accounts in foreign exchange, it may have had an interest in further propping up the domestic currency so that the final settlement was not too expensive – in other words, so that the difference between the price of the rand at time p and at time p+1 was not too large. Some commentators suggested that the use of the forward market to stabilise a falling rand might have led to a vicious circle, where the SARB was forced to expend more and more resources protecting the rand and its position. Jonathan Leape's team at the London School of Economics argued: '. . . the size of the oversold position at particular points in time has raised suspicions that the need to reduce the oversold position became an independent factor guiding exchange rate and even interest rate policy' (Khatri et al. 1997: 44).

Whatever its intentions, the strategy of the SARB regarding the exchange rate and interest rates influenced the composition of capital inflows. A tight money policy with high real interest rates and an exchange rate strategy that tends towards overvaluation encourages short-term capital inflows because of the interest to be earned and the expectation that depreciation will not eat these short-term gains away. However, by discouraging investment and consumption in South Africa's real economy through high interest rates, and by decreasing competitiveness through a relatively overvalued currency, this policy did not encourage private, long-term, direct investment. Moreover, short-term capital inflow bubbles can burst, as happened in 1996 and 1998 when South Africa experienced two rather brutal 'mornings after', during which the currency corrected itself downwards by around 20%. The currency shock in 2001, though similar in effect, had different causes.

Was there a smoother path?

Was another path open to the SARB? Analysis of Latin American experiences with capital flows and exchange rates implicitly suggests that the South African experience in the 1990s was hardly atypical. When developing countries begin serious market-oriented reform processes, the pre-existing external credit constraint will relax. It should result in a long-run sustainable volume of capital inflows, but it will also 'generate a short run overshooting in the *inflow* of capital into the country'. Short-run capital inflows will exceed their long-run equilibrium value until the market completes its adjustment. In some cases the adjustment process takes a few years (Edwards 1998: 16).

The capital inflow during the adjustment period will lead to an overly appreciated real exchange rate, which when the inflow adjustment tails off, will require a 'massive adjustment'. 'The dynamics of capital inflows and current account adjustment will require, then, that the equilibrium real exchange rate first appreciates and then depreciates', argued Sebastian Edwards (1998: 16).

Anticipating such events would seem to be no more than good common sense. In several Latin American countries and in Israel, as Edwards notes, such shocks have been anticipated and counter-measures have been adopted. Indeed, South African economists began writing about the potential negative effects of post-democratic capital inflows into South Africa well before the 1994 elections (Kahn 1992; Hirsch 1993). The obvious question is: why did the SARB not anticipate this major shock, and why did it not attempt to counteract its effects? Indeed, its interest rate policies almost seemed to be designed to exacerbate the effects of the adjustment to the removal of the external credit constraint, rather than ameliorate them – perhaps because of a conflict between the inflation target and the exchange rate target in the context of capital inflows. There are no indications that Stals anticipated negative effects from the should-have-been-expected capital inflow. In fact in 1995 he admitted that the volume of capital inflows surprised him. Was this simply a case of an old general fighting the last war (capital flight) instead of the current one (unemployment)?

If Stals had anticipated the adjustment shock, and if he was concerned about currency fluctuations and the loss of competitiveness, what could he have done differently? Can developing countries design their exchange control regimes to insulate themselves from some of the negative effects of volatile short-term capital flows? Can they influence the composition of capital inflows to encourage a higher proportion of the more stable form of inflows, particularly long-term loans and direct foreign investment?

Had Stals recognised that he was winning the fight against inflation, that the relationship between M3 expansion and inflation had weakened in a more open competitive economy, and that some of the M3 data was a result of structural rather than behavioural change, he could have softened interest rate policy, encouraging domestic growth and long-term capital inflows.

Secondly, he, or the Minister of Finance, might have intervened directly in South Africa's international capital movements. Though Edwards is sceptical about the long-term effects of capital controls on the external value of the currency and interest rates, he does accept that such controls do slow down exchange rate appreciation, and give the monetary authorities greater autonomy temporarily in interest rate policy. More importantly, Edwards accepts that a country that has imposed such controls, such as Chile, has effectively skewed its capital inflows towards long-term serious money, and away from volatile hot money (Edwards 1998: 28, 30, 36). Even the IMF's managing director, Michel Camdessus, urged that, while capital flow liberalisation was necessary, 'the last thing you must liberalise is very short-term capital movements' (Edwards 1998: 13).

In the absence of an international agreement to inhibit volatile capital flows, some international economists see no reason why individual countries should not take such a step themselves (Helleiner 1998a). The risk countries take is opening themselves to scorn and misinterpretation (like Malaysia in 1998). The usual method is some form of explicit tax inhibiting short-term capital flows to and from developing countries. Chile has used several forms, including non-remunerated deposits in local banks and taxes. Rudiger Dornbusch took a lead from John Maynard Keynes and James Tobin in suggesting a transactions tax (Dornbusch 1998).

Moving onto new terrain

In the months before the 1994 elections, while some whites were amassing stores of canned foods and candles, many white stockholders were inclined to dump their equities. The market was not excessively weak, but some local investors thought that institutional and foreign buyers had not realised that the ANC would win the April election, and that there would be a major fall in share prices in reaction.

As it turned out, selling stocks in 1994 was a bad strategy. When the elections were won without too much fuss, the threat of a white-right reaction dissolved. After nervousness during the first half of

1994, markets settled down quickly, reassured by the reappointment of Derek Keys as Mandela's first Finance Minister, and Chris Stals' agreement to a five-year contract as Governor of the SARB. Conservative whites moved their candles and canned foods back from hideouts to kitchens. Foreign capital flowed in fast, and certain sectors of the Johannesburg Stock Exchange (JSE), such as construction and information technology, surged upwards.

Capital was attracted by high interest rates, the resumption of growth in the South African economy, bank borrowing, and public sector gilt issues. In October 1995, Chris Stals admitted that capital inflows 'exceeded the most optimistic expectations of the pre-election period'. Over the 18-month period ending in June 1995, there was net capital inflow of R18.6 billion, or over US$5 billion. By contrast, the previous 10-year period had seen net annual outflows of at least R5 billion (*The Star* 16 October 1995). Net foreign purchases of equities mounted to US$1.3 billion in 1995. With the JSE bottled up because South Africans still had very little freedom to invest abroad, the rise in demand for equities soon translated into rising share prices.

Days before Stals' statement, the IMF had mentioned South Africa in a list of developing countries (which also included Indonesia and Brazil) that had to pay more attention to the way they were managing the inflow of foreign capital. In the *World Economic Outlook*, the IMF noted that in general there was no need to reconsider liberalising financial markets because of the potential for market turmoil. But an IMF spokesman did say that South Africa should take special note of the recommendation to proceed cautiously along the road to free international capital markets (*The Argus* 5 October 1995). A clear implication of the statement was that the IMF was concerned about the composition of South Africa's capital inflows, which were heavily skewed towards short-term, potentially volatile capital.

Later in October, the Union Bank of Switzerland (UBS) issued a report praising the government's policies. But, noting that the foreign direct investment component was only US$700 million (less than 10%) of the capital inflow, the UBS indicated concern that the rand was vulnerable to shifts in short-term funds. 'Foreign perceptions are such that any negative developments in South Africa could easily trigger an outflow of short-term capital . . .' (*Cape Times: Business Report* 23 October 1995).

For a few months markets held firm. Then, early in 1996, the UBS issued another report indicating that the rand was overvalued by 7-10%. This was persuasive in the context of the surge in capital inflows and a still-rising real interest rate. Days later, rumours about President Mandela's health sent the rand tumbling. The excess 10% was shaved off the rand's value in less than two weeks, before the end of February 1996.

Again the markets seemed to settle. Then, in late March, shortly after Chris Liebenberg presented his second budget, Trevor Manuel, who had been Trade and Industry Minister, replaced Liebenberg as Minister of Finance. Liebenberg resigned, probably in terms of an agreement he had with Mandela when he accepted the position in 1994. Alec Erwin, who had been Deputy Minister of Finance, took over as Trade and Industry Minister, and the RDP was dissolved as a separate government entity. Its functions were relocated: financial management to the Department of Finance; and planning and co-ordination, in a low-key form, to the office of the Executive Deputy President, Thabo Mbeki.

The RDP Office had failed to spend much of the funds committed to the programme, and the government decided that it was duplicating the functions of individual departments. A special economic growth Cabinet committee under President Mandela had been wrestling with the need to improve economic policy co-ordination for months. It was preferable that the departments themselves were empowered to meet the challenges of reconstruction and development. Now with an ANC Minister, the Department of Finance was ready to co-ordinate this drive. Liebenberg stepped gracefully aside and returned to the private sector, having helped ease the transition to the first ANC Finance Minister.

If ever there was a baptism of fire, it was Trevor Manuel's, on his appointment as the first ANC and the first 'black' Minister of

Finance in South Africa. Manuel had shown in his 22 months as Minister of Trade and Industry that he was a good manager and leader, and was as tough as teak. He showed this in pushing through an initially unpopular trade liberalisation programme, and he showed it in Cabinet, where he was not afraid of confrontation when he stood on firm ground.

Toughness was the quality Manuel needed most in his first half-year as Minister of Finance. The rand, which had stopped its descent during mid-March, began to plunge again after the Cabinet reshuffle was announced. One reason was Manuel's appointment. 'The markets' seemed concerned that there was an ANC Minister of Finance, that he was 'black', and that he was not a financier. Perhaps they suspected that he would buckle under the demands of his Cabinet colleagues; perhaps they thought he would make other mistakes – his bull-headed approach to trade liberalisation left some commentators concerned that he might try to liberalise exchange controls too fast (*The Star* 30 March 1996). Perhaps some traders were merely exploiting uncertainty and selling short.

Another reason for the weak rand was the blossoming of an intense debate about economic policy. During 1995, SACOB had said several times that it felt that economic policy needed stronger co-ordination. It felt that the RDP document and white paper really did not provide clear enough guidance. The comment was first made in response to a Cabinet decision to set up a special committee to focus on growth, led by the President (*Sowetan* 10 August 1995). Later SACOB's comment was echoed in the ANC, which stressed the need for the co-ordination of macroeconomic policy (*Business Day* 16 October 1995).

In 1996, four weeks before Manuel's appointment, the South Africa Foundation, a pressure group for the largest South African companies, brought out an economic report called *Growth for All*, which set out the economic options, as they saw it, with brutal frankness (*Business Day* 1 March 1996). One key argument was that South Africa's high unemployment was in large measure due to inflexible labour markets. The proposed solution: if jobs were to be created, the trade unions had to be circumvented through a dual labour market. One labour market would be for skilled and unionised workers, another for unskilled and non-unionised workers. Other remedies included anti-crime strategies, leaner government, brisker privatisation and export promotion. In some respects – monetary policy for example – *Growth for All* might have been a useful contribution to the economic debate in South Africa, but the report was clumsily composed and non-strategically dumped into the public arena.

The ANC shot back immediately through Tito Mboweni, the Minister of Labour, in his capacity as chair of the ANC's economic policy committee. Mboweni lambasted proposals to cut the budget deficit and hoist VAT, and rejected the suggestion that privatisation could fund poverty relief, as naïve. But he reserved his most withering comments for the 'most ridiculous of all' proposals – the two-tier labour market – which he described as an 'affront to democracy' (*Sunday Times* 10 March 1996). Mboweni had spent exhausting months finding a compromise between labour and business for the new Labour Relations Act, and big business seemed to be trying to undo the agreement.

Before long, the ANC found itself attacked again, this time from the left. Vella Pillay, who had worked for the Bank of China in London, and was a long-time adviser to the ANC who had led MERG (the Macroeconomic Research Group project – see Chapter Two), was now the director of MERG's descendent – the National Institute for Economic Policy (NIEP). NIEP had been set up with foreign financial assistance to aid the ANC in policy formulation. Having failed to find a way to do this effectively, it found itself developing strategies and critiques from a step to the left of the ANC mainstream. Pillay ridiculed the debate between the ANC, the unions, and the South Africa Foundation, calling it a 'debate for simpletons'. He criticised the ANC's fiscal policy, suggesting that instead of cutting the budget deficit the government should be expanding the deficit to 7 or 8% of GDP (*Cape Times: Business Report* 12 March 1996).

Days after Manuel's appointment, the labour movement dipped its own oar in the water with a policy document called 'Social equity and job creation' (COSATU et al. 1996). The document was issued on behalf of the three major union federations. Like the business document, the labour document made many sound points, in this case from a left-Keynesian position. Had the two documents been the basis for an academic debate rather than a struggle for influence, it would not have been too hard to find common ground. But, following the publication of *Growth for All*, the tone of the debate was too strident, as if some participants saw it as a struggle for the soul of the ANC.

The South African Communist Party (SACP), a member of the ANC alliance, along with the Congress of South African Trade Unions (COSATU), also hit out at big business's now exposed underbelly. Jeremy Cronin, imprisoned for underground ANC work in the 1970s, a political philosopher and a talented poet, was Deputy Secretary-General of the SACP. In an op-ed piece in a national business daily, Cronin struck out at the underlying assumptions he saw reflected in *Growth for All*. He focused more on the subtext than the details. *Growth for All*, he felt, assumed that the market would solve South Africa's problems and that government was extraneous. He isolated unguarded comments that indicated insensitivity towards the long-oppressed sections of South African society and arrogance about the role of the business community. *Growth for All*, he implied, was out of place in the new South Africa (*Business Day* 24 April 1996). Gwede Mantashe, Assistant Secretary-General of the National Union of Metalworkers of South Africa (NUMSA), contrasted the approach of business in the *Growth for All* document with that of members of the business community then working in a Presidential labour market commission, trying to meet minds with government and labour (*Business Day* 22 April 1996).

In the midst of this rancorous debate, the currency plunged again, losing another 10% in value between late March and early May. Since the middle of February the rand had lost marginally over 20% (CREFSA 1996: figure 7). The government had to respond. It had to nail its economic colours to the mast as there was now a politician, not a banker at the helm of the fiscus; it also had to show onlookers that it was prepared to take charge – that it would not allow itself to be buffeted from side to side by the country's most powerful social forces: organised business and labour.

Hands on the wheel

The government had been working on an economic policy document. Government earlier asked the Central Economic Advisory Service (CEAS), an apartheid-era government agency that fell under the RDP office, to prepare a macroeconomic policy statement. The resulting statement was based on the Normative Economic Model (NEM) prepared for the De Klerk government in the early 1990s. The NEM was based on a conservative and static set of assumptions, particularly regarding the balance of payments. Like Stals, it failed to recognise the potential for capital inflows. The new document was irrelevant in a rapidly changing society. It was never published, and the CEAS was dissolved within a year of this failure.

The next effort was a project of the RDP office itself. This was undertaken as an interdepartmental project, to be co-ordinated and drafted by the RDP. One problem with this effort was that it grew almost unstoppably as each agency of central government ensured that its interests were represented. Once the decentralised drafts were collected, the RDP office rewrote them to no one's satisfaction. A summary paper – the 'draft National Growth and Development Strategy' was released in February 1996, but was downplayed by government.

A group of officials, clustered around the Department of Finance and the Development Bank, and including senior officials from the Departments of Trade and Industry and Labour, started working late in 1995 on a more focused macroeconomic policy document. Several academics were enlisted to test macroeconomic models, and World Bank economists who had worked on the South African model used in the 1994 World Bank paper were also drawn into the project. After Trevor Manuel was appointed, he adopted the project and instructed the co-ordinators to speed it up so that he could present it before the end of the debate on the 1996/97 budget. He intended that it should answer the questions that were being asked of him, offer a clear and coherent set of economic policies and strategies, and show that government was prepared to take charge rather than bob around like a cork in the ocean. This, he and the Cabinet hoped, would restore stability to the currency and related markets, amongst others the short-term capital traders who had been getting out of South African gilts from the middle of February.

The result was the GEAR strategy – its full name being 'Growth, Employment and Redistribution: A Macro-Economic Strategy'. The GEAR approach linked greater fiscal prudence to the ability to ease off a still-tight monetary policy and encourage private local and foreign investment. Government dissaving was a key target. The policy group believed that as long as the government debt grew rapidly it would put pressure on interest rates; conversely, escaping the debt trap and reducing the debt burden would allow interest rates to soften, leading to higher investment levels. As Trevor Manuel put it in his speech introducing GEAR to Parliament on 14 June 1996, '. . . in the recent past, the shortcomings of policy coordination has placed an excessive burden on monetary policy as the major instrument to maintain macro balances. This has led to higher real interest rates' (Manuel 1996: 7). Manuel and his team expected interest rates to fall with inflation under control and the government-borrowing requirement decreasing.

To this end, Manuel made the deficit reduction target more stringent than that announced by Chris Liebenberg in 1994. Liebenberg had set the target for bringing the fiscal deficit down from 6.8% of GDP in 1994–95 to 4.5% of GDP in 1999–2000. The expected deficit for 1996–97 was about 5.4% of GDP. Manuel, realising that this would not reverse government dissaving, certainly at current interest rates, set the new targets at 4% in 1997–98, 3.5% in 1998–99, and 3% of GDP in 1999–2000. Other fiscal reforms would include 'public service restructuring', which implicitly included revisiting an overly generous deal struck with the public service unions in 1995, revamping the budgeting process into a three-year rolling budget, some tax restructuring, and a major drive to improve revenue collection.

Box 3.2: Main proposals of the GEAR strategy

The elements of the proposed package are:
- a faster fiscal deficit reduction programme to contain debt service obligations, counter inflation and free resources for investment;
- a renewed focus on budget reform to strengthen the re-distributive thrust of expenditure;
- a reduction in tariffs to contain input prices and facilitate industrial restructuring, compensating partly for the exchange rate depreciation;
- a commitment to moderate wage demands, supported by an appropriately structured flexibility within the collective bargaining system;
- an exchange rate policy to keep the real effective rate stable at a competitive level;
- a consistent monetary policy to prevent a resurgence of inflation;
- a further step in the gradual relaxation of exchange controls;
- speeding up the restructuring of state assets [including privatisation];
- tax incentives to stimulate new investment in competitive and labour absorbing projects;
- an expansionary infrastructure programme to address deficiencies and backlogs;
- a strengthened levy system to fund [industrial] training on a scale commensurate with needs.

Source: Department of Finance (Summary document) (1996: 1-2).

Manuel expected inflation to rise in 1997 as a result of the effects of the 1996 currency depreciation on the cost of imports, and he expected the real bank rate to fall from 7% in 1996 to 5% in 1997, and eventually to 3% in 1999 and 2000. In wording agreed to by the SARB, GEAR aimed to 'maintain the current competitive advantage created by the depreciation of the rand . . . [through keeping] the real effective exchange rate of the rand at a competitive level' (Department of Finance 1996: 10). This would be underpinned by further import tariff and exchange control liberalisation.

There were other elements in the GEAR strategy: new trade and industry programmes aimed at encouraging new investment through tax breaks and credit facilities; industrial innovation; small business development and export growth through a range of programmes; and to give teeth to the competition authorities. In the labour market, the government indicated its intention to improve productivity through better industrial training, to improve competitiveness through 'more flexible' labour markets, and to seek a national agreement to link wage growth to productivity growth. The government also indicated its intention to speed up privatisation, and to support more government investment, especially in municipal infrastructure, when spending on public servants' salaries and wages came under control.

The final element of the GEAR strategy was perhaps the most important – co-ordination of economic policy and implementation within government, and between government and its 'social partners' (business and labour). In words that foreshadowed an inevitable audit, the GEAR authors wrote:

> Within government, especially in the fields of monetary, fiscal, trade, industrial and labour policies, there is also a critical need for coordination. Inconsistent approaches in any of these areas have the potential to destabilise the credibility of the overall macroeconomic framework (Department of Finance 1996: 21).

GEAR was a serious attempt at a co-ordinated strategy. All the key government departments implicated in the strategy, as well as the SARB, participated in the analytical process that preceded the strategy, and endorsed its outcome. The Deputy President, Thabo Mbeki, made an introductory speech underlining its importance. 'This policy', he said, 'is the central compass which will guide all other growth and development programmes of the government.' He also indicated that the macroeconomic strategy would be situated within the broader 'National Growth and Development Strategy' (Mbeki 1996: 137–140). The intention to locate GEAR within a broader growth and development strategy receded into the background until 2003, and debates on GEAR tended to assume that it was the alpha and omega of the government's economic policy.

Grinding gears

GEAR was generally well received by local and international business and, when it became clear that Manuel was serious about implementing GEAR, markets began to settle. Before the end of 1996 capital flow signals were strongly positive again (no doubt helped by the escalating real interest rate).

The left was less sanguine. Labour leaders were very concerned about the conservative fiscal stance of the strategy, and also interpreted the monetary policy proposals as too conservative. COSATU complained that the document made too many concessions to foreign investors without any guarantee that they would respond by delivering their capital. Mbazima Shilowa, General Secretary of COSATU, commented that COSATU and the SACP were finding it very difficult to deal with the ANC. Implying that they had not been properly consulted, he said, at a SACP seminar: 'It means something has gone terribly wrong that such a document is able to emerge and be on the table' (*Sunday Times* 7 July 1996).

Manuel may have provoked criticism from the left in his speech introducing GEAR when he said: 'The parameters are not up for negotiation at this stage.' Though he did add that the implementation of the programme rested on close co-operation with social partners (business and labour) and that 'there is undoubtedly so much of the detail which we will have to work through together' (Manuel 1996: 14), what remained with the ANC's allies was the perception of a closed door on substantive negotiations.

With the rand still unstable, Manuel probably felt that to show weakness of resolve was to reopen the currency speculation season. Government needed to show its willingness to take on the responsibilities of government.

Manuel's twin departments of Finance and State Expenditure moved fast and with remarkable success considering their limited resources. Though the 1996–97 budget deficit was a little higher than expected at 5.6% of GDP, in 1997–98 it fell to 4.4%. This exceeded the GEAR target of 4.0%, but slower-than-expected GDP growth had reduced government revenues, while rising interest rates were adding to the debt-servicing burden. Other finance reforms were set in motion too – particularly the reconstruction of the government's budgeting process.

The Department of Trade and Industry (DTI) also moved quickly, with several of its new programmes in place before the end of 1996, and others following the next year. But, in light of the fact that the rand was beginning to appreciate again and interest rates were rising, the DTI had second thoughts about accelerating an already dramatic tariff liberalisation programme. The Labour Department moved steadily towards an improved national skills framework, but more slowly on labour market flexibility and a national wage/price agreement. Privatisation moved forward, though government was often held up by the trade unions that were concerned about job losses and the delivery of services to the poor. A national framework agreement three years later improved the climate for privatisation.

A more serious case of uncoordinated policy, which punctured the GEAR strategy, came from the SARB. By late 1996, with the real bank rate at 9.5% (nominal: 17%), the currency had stabilised and international capital flows were positive. Inflation, at 7.5% for the year, was more than 2% better than the GEAR target and the fiscal deficit was coming down. It was time for the SARB to play its role in getting GEAR going through gently relaxing the real interest rate. As Maria Ramos argued, shortly before being appointed Director-General of Finance, while monetary policy should remain firm, after GEAR it no longer had to take the strain of keeping a grip on the economy alone (*The Star* 15 June 1996).

But interest rates continued to rise. Early in 1997, Stals explained his refusal to cut interest rates: 'the growing deficit in the current account had to be reversed'; there was an imminent 'danger of escalating inflation'; and the 'escalating growth rates in the domestic monetary aggregates . . . had to be reversed' (Stals 1997: 32). Though the SARB had participated in preparing GEAR, it was not comfortable operating within the GEAR targets, based on the GEAR model.

Taking it further, in March 1998 Stals referred to an expected annual inflation rate of 0–5% for the world as an indicator of South Africa's objectives, although he qualified this by saying that the range could not for now 'be accepted as a formal commitment or firm inflation target for the Reserve Bank' (Stals 1998: 38).

One result of the SARB's excessively tight monetary policy, which saw an increase in the real bank rate from 3% in 1994 to 13.7% in 1998, was that it choked off South Africa's expansion. Domestic investment and consumption tailed off, and even the growth of exports slowed due to the appreciation of the currency during 1997. Homebuyers had to repay mortgages with real interest rates of at least 11% during 1997 and up to 18% in 1998, for example. GEAR had planned for a slight depreciation of the exchange rate in 1997; instead the currency appreciated by at least 0.8%. Most of this preceded the interest rate hikes provoked by the Asian, Russian and Brazilian crises in 1998.

The other result of the high interest rate was that, as in 1995, it skewed the composition of the new inflow of foreign capital towards short-term money. Foreign investors could expect good returns for a limited period of time, as long as they got their exit strategy right to beat the next wave of depreciation. But the kind of foreign investors that would come for the long ride, who would look for steady growth and political and economic stability, might be put off by Stals' rather short-term approach to monetary policy. So, the boom-and-bust cycle of 1994–96 seemed likely to repeat itself again, except that the boom was smaller.

Stals' preoccupation with low inflation and a strong currency seemed to override the commitment of the SARB to co-operate with the GEAR strategy. His fixation was never more evident than in the middle of 1998 when the panic emanating from the Russian crisis hit South Africa. Stals intervened massively to try to retain the value of the currency at close to five rand to the US dollar. He did this largely through swaps in the forward currency market. As soon as traders became aware of this, they bet heavily against the rand. Stals lost, the rand fell by 20% to R6.70 to the dollar, and the real bank rate was forced up to 14%.

Why did Stals behave in this way? By the end of 1998 there was speculation in the South African media that one of Stals' main concerns was to prevent losses or even gain a profit on the SARB's forward book (*Financial Mail* 11 December 1998). Jonathan Leape also expressed concern that the size of the oversold book could influence the exchange rate strategy (Khatri et al. 1997: 33–38). But it is hard to imagine that a seasoned central banker such as Stals could sacrifice so much in the economy at large only to avoid excessive losses in the forward market by the SARB.

Another reasonable explanation is that Stals failed to grasp the effects of structural change on money market aggregates and on prices in South Africa. The redistribution of wealth and power since the early 1990s had a huge impact on South Africa, which will be dealt with in more detail in Chapter Six. This has meant a significant extension of credit facilities and opening up of a range of banking accounts that may well not have had an equivalent effect on consumer expenditure. The integration of the South African economy, new payments technologies, and the introduction of new forms of credit have also influenced the credit extension figures (see IDC 1998: 9). Even if credit expansion boosted demand, it had become far more difficult for manufacturers, wholesalers and retailers to exploit constricted markets or to pass on price increases to consumers. The most important structural change in this respect was the very significant decline in import tariffs on consumer products since 1995, which was preceded by the reduction of import surcharges in the early 1990s. South Africa was behaving far more like an open competitive market today than it did in the early 1990s. Had these structural changes been better understood by the SARB, monetary policy might have contributed more effectively to GEAR.

The performance of GEAR

What were the results of GEAR? The strategy included a set of projections indicating desired macroeconomic policy indicators, such as the fiscal deficit and average tariff rates, and indicators of outcomes, such as job growth and real export growth. In some areas performance exceeded the expectations of GEAR, which was measured as a five-year programme, ending at the end of 2000. The GEAR model aimed for a fiscal deficit down to 3% of GDP, government consumption down to 18.1% of GDP, and inflation (CPI) down to 6% per annum. All of these targets were beaten, with figures of 2.2%, 18% and 5.4% respectively. Some of the economic targets were more or less met, such as a real manufacturing export growth rate of around 10%.

The two significant disappointments were job growth and investment. The target for job growth was 2.9% growth in formal non-agricultural employment per year. Jobs grew at about 2.5% per year in the period 1995–2003, but more than half of these new jobs were in the informal sector (Statistics South Africa Labour Force Survey March 2003; Bhorat 2003; private correspondence with Ingrid Woolard, senior researcher at the Human Sciences Research Council in 2003). Investment performance was even more disappointing, especially in the later GEAR period: in 1999 and

2000 investment by private, parastatal and public sectors all shrank, instead of growing at around 10% per annum. Growth, not surprisingly, was also disappointing, averaging 2.6% over the GEAR period, instead of the projected 4.2%.

The tight monetary policy of the late 1990s, which was partially in response to the Asian, Russian, and Brazilian crises, and a 20% depreciation of the rand, certainly contributed to low investment and growth. Fiscal policy was probably also an important factor. It may well be that the positive effect of government reducing its borrowing (which had been crowding out private investment by raising the cost of capital) was more than outweighed by the effect of reduced government investment with its potential to crowd in private investment (Davies and Van Seventer 2004).

Or it may simply have been a matter of timing. The reduction in government borrowing may have been slower to take effect than the reduction in government investment. In fact, overall government debt only began to fall significantly as a percentage of GDP after 1999. One reason for the significant improvement of public finances at the end of the 1990s was the tightfistedness of the Minister of Finance, Trevor Manuel. The other was the effectiveness of the South African Revenue Services (SARS) under Pravin Gordhan, a pharmacist and leading anti-apartheid activist in South Africa in the 1980s, who took over SARS in 1999. Public revenue collection improved to such an extent that Manuel could for several years, especially the period 2000–03, increase real government spending, reduce the budget deficit and reduce government debt levels as a percentage of GDP, while significantly cutting income tax rates. In this sense, the fruits of GEAR were only reaped from 2000. It was also in the early 2000s that private companies began to raise capital in the form of bonds, signalling that government crowding out had ended.

It was at this point, in 2000 that the fiscal stance began to move into a more expansionary phase. Before 2000, the most significant developmental interventions through the fiscus were noteworthy increases in expenditure on social services, largely health, education and social welfare. Expenditure on social grants rose from R10 billion in 1994 to R38.4 billion in 2003, and the number of beneficiaries grew from 2.6 million to 6.8 million. Targeted grants, such as the child support grant, were introduced. The education budget rose to make up a quarter of all government expenditure, with significant increases in enrolment in early childhood development and in secondary schools, where enrolment increased from 70% in 1992 to 85% in 2001, while the pupil-teacher ratio declined from 43:1 to 38:1. In health, the focus was on primary health care and related programmes (Policy Co-ordination and Advisory Services 2003: 16–21).

The extension of infrastructure services was a significant intervention too, though some of these were financed by public corporations, rather than the fiscus itself. The result was that, for example, the proportion of households with access to clean water grew from 60% in 1996 to 85% in 2001, while the number of homes with access to electricity increased from 32% to 70% over the same period (Policy Co-ordination and Advisory Services 2003: 24).

Infrastructure expenditure began to grow more rapidly after 2000. Between 1998 and 2001 government fixed capital formation fell for four consecutive years, but this began to turn around in the early 2000s. Since 2001, government and public corporation infrastructure spending has increased at a rate of about 6% per year, and this is expected to continue at least until 2006. The strongest growth is in infrastructure development by the provinces, which grew from R11 billion in 2001 to R18 billion in 2003 and is expected to grow to R24 billion by 2006. This indicates another significant fiscal trend – a steadily growing proportion of funds flowing to the provinces and to municipalities, for the provision of social services and infrastructure investment.

The GEAR period, 1996–2000, was supposed to see a simultaneous improvement in the management of public finances and investment response that would raise growth levels. Only the former happened. There are probably four main reasons why the growth performance of the GEAR era disappointed. The first was excessively tight monetary policy, especially in the 1996–98 period. The second was the macroeconomic crises in Asia, Brazil and Russia in 1998, which pushed South Africa to an even more conservative monetary policy. The third factor was that the very tight fiscal policy, partly a consequence of the need to reorganise government at national, provincial and local levels, reduced government investment expenditure. Lower level and microeconomic reforms proved considerably more difficult than the reform of the Treasury and trade policy. Finally, the private sector, both nationally and internationally, remained cautious about South Africa's future.

The GEAR strategy was not implemented in an entirely consistent and co-ordinated way, especially regarding monetary policy. It was also unrealistic, perhaps, about the timing of positive investment responses, and about the ability of the new government to develop effective institutions, plans and investment modalities. But criticism about the fundamental design remains debatable. GEAR certainly set the stage for a stronger performance in the new millennium.

Notes
1. The South African fiscal year runs from 1 April to 31 March.
2. Many people were recruited and promoted in the 1980s in a vain attempt to shore up the apartheid system with a black bureaucratic middle class.
3. Blinder thinks that even the United States law is too vague.
4. 'The income elasticity of the demand for non-oil merchandise imports is 1.47 . . . When domestic income increases, the percentage change in imports is considerably larger than the change in domestic income' (Smal 1996: 30).
5. Gross domestic savings as a percentage of GDP fell from 25.3% in 1983 to a low of 14.3% in 2001 (SARB 1998b: column 6286J).

CHAPTER FOUR

Competing globally, restructuring locally

Manuel stands his ground

Presenting his 1999 budget to Parliament, Trevor Manuel, Minister of Finance, looked back. 'Integrating South Africa into the world economy has been a major challenge,' he recalled. 'We inherited an uncompetitive, inward looking, protectionist economy. Since 1994,' he added, 'we have sought to open up the economy in a measured and sustainable way' (Manuel 1999: 1).

As Minister of Trade and Industry between May 1994 and March 1996, Manuel had to implement South Africa's trade reform programme. The reform schedule was written into the 1994 Marrakesh agreement of the General Agreement on Tariffs and Trade (GATT), which followed the Uruguay Round of negotiations.

South Africa was a founder member of GATT in 1948 when there was no 'special and differential status' for developing countries. When, during the 1960s, GATT allowed differentiation between developed and developing countries to permit the latter to receive more gentle treatment, South Africa did not consider changing its status. Its white rulers believed they lived like wealthy western European or American societies, and would have seen developing country status as an insult.

During 1993, before the new government was elected, the ANC and the Congress of South African Trade Unions (COSATU) suggested that the South African government should enquire about changing the country's status to 'developing country'. Stef Naudé, then Director-General of Trade and Industry, was told that the United States would ensure that this would never happen. Neither did Japan nor Western Europe offer any assistance; apart from anything else, they were far too preoccupied finalising the Uruguay Round of negotiations to think about how they might assist South Africa. Nevertheless, South Africa was assured that, in some respects, it would be allowed greater flexibility – similar to the 'economies in transition' of Eastern Europe.

By and large, though, the trade policy community in South Africa could accept the retention of 'developed country' status as far as the Uruguay Round was concerned. Developed country status meant the biggest cuts in protection, implemented at the quickest pace. The South African economic policy community, from the union federation COSATU through the ANC, big business and the De Klerk government, agreed that the economy had become overprotected, that building a new platform for growth would require restructuring the real economy, and that substantial trade policy reform was a necessary, if insufficient, element of such restructuring.

It was one thing to agree in principle, but another thing to carry the project through. Manuel soon learned the costs. Even before the 1994 elections, the South African Clothing and Textile Workers' Union (SACTWU) persuaded the ANC to improve the terms of the GATT agreement. This required the ANC leader, Nelson Mandela, to call United States President, Bill Clinton, to ask for a special dispensation for the clothing and textile industries in South Africa. Though he had not yet been elected as President, Mandela carried more weight internationally than President de Klerk. The union and the industry wanted to extend the down phasing of tariffs to a 12-year period, rather than the mandatory 5 years. South Africa was not party to the separate Multi-Fibre Agreement that covered many fabric and garment importers and exporters.

The South African textile and garment industries employed over 200 000 people living in poor communities. Behind tariffs higher than 100% for clothing and not far below 100% for textiles, the industries had fallen out of step with world production and marketing trends. Many workers in the clothing industry lived in the Western Cape province, which was a tight electoral race for the ANC. For these reasons, Mandela agreed. At little or no cost, Clinton agreed too. Nevertheless, the ANC lost the Western Cape to De Klerk's National Party (NP).

A year later Trevor Manuel found himself facing the clothing workers again. At a huge public conference organised by his adviser on small business, Alistair Ruiters, Manuel was participating in the finalisation of a new policy for small business. But the clothing workers used this occasion to protest against the implementation of the tariff phase-down programme. They blamed it for what they saw as ongoing job losses in the garment and textile industries. This may have been the first vocal public protest against the ANC in government by a member of the ANC's constituency – the union concerned, SACTWU, is a member of COSATU, which is one leg of the ANC's tripartite alliance. The third leg is the shrunken South African Communist Party (SACP).

As a young activist in Cape Town in the late 1970s, Manuel had been a voluntary literacy teacher amongst the poor. Some of his students were garment and textile workers, or members of their families. Now Manuel was faced with representatives of the same communities telling him that his policies were causing garment and textile workers to lose their jobs. Though he may have wished he could explain his policies to the workers in small groups like the literacy classes he once taught, he could not.

But he never wavered in his policy position. Manuel left no one in any doubt that he was firmly committed to the trade reform process, even though it might appear to hurt some of the communities he knew and loved, and depended on politically. And his colleagues in the ANC leadership backed him.

Contours/prospects of the economy

Why was the ANC so sure that trade policy reform was necessary, though they knew that the strategy might be politically costly in the short to medium term? Had it been brainwashed by the World

Bank and the International Monetary Fund (IMF) or seduced by international bankers, as some of its critics believed?

To any economic observer in South Africa in the early 1990s, it was clear that the country had entered an economic cul-de-sac. The economy was shrinking. Its assets were being run down – gross fixed investment was negative for four consecutive years to 1994, and capital was in full flight. National income was stagnating, and per capita income had declined every year since 1982, except 1988. Government debt was rising to dangerous levels, with the general government fiscal deficit over 9% of gross domestic product (GDP) in 1993.

What were the potential sources of growth? What sectors could the country rely on to get the economy going again so that problems of poverty and unemployment could be addressed?

The traditional strength of the economy had been gold mining. But the physical volume of gold extracted from South Africa's deep-level mines began to fall, inexorably, after reaching peak production at 1 000 tons in 1970. Even the very high price paid for gold during the two oil crises of 1973–75 and 1979–81 failed to boost gold output. The quality of accessible ore was deteriorating – whereas a ton of ore produced 13.3 grams of gold in 1970, it only produced 5.3 grams of gold in 1987 (Freund 1991). Though the tonnage of ore processed rose, the output of gold fell. By 1998 gold production had fallen to 473 tons, which was the lowest gold yield since 1956. Meanwhile, in the United States, Canada, Australia, and elsewhere, gold production grew cheaper and more efficient in geological formations more amenable to modern mining methods.

South Africa's deep-level, low-yield mines depended more on cheap labour than innovative extraction methods to maintain a sufficient margin between the cost of mining gold and the world price. Wages for black mine workers began to rise in the 1970s when the mine-owners turned away from cheap migrant labour from Mozambique. South Africa's eastern neighbour had suddenly won independence from Portugal after a democratising military cabal overthrew the Portuguese dictatorship in 1974. The mine-owners feared the volatility of the new state of Mozambique, and may have feared that the Mozambican miners were infected with a new blend of socialism that FRELIMO developed for the country.

When black workers on South Africa's mines began to organise themselves successfully, their justifiable demands for improved wages and working conditions added to the difficulties of the mine-owners. The owners compounded their own difficulties by being extremely slow to innovate production methods, to improve training, and to develop more sophisticated labour relations. When gold lost its starring role as an international store of value in the wake of the liberalisation of international financial markets in the 1980s, South Africa's gold mining industry was slow to acknowledge the changed circumstances, and even slower to react.

Other metal and mineral products, such as platinum group metals, coal and basic chemicals, experienced some growth in output and exports during the 1980s. A major new export in the early 1980s was pulp and paper produced by new mills in eastern higher-rainfall regions. Some sugar cane lands were converted to wattle production to feed the mills, but the new plants had a small net effect on the economy as a whole. They did boost the profits of Sanlam and Anglo American, two of the large financial corporations that were becoming increasingly gargantuan in the context of a stunted economy.

Export growth in semi-manufactures such as dimensional metal products (rods, bars, plates and coils), basic chemicals, pulp and paper, as well as more fabricated metal products positively correlated with productivity growth and overall economic growth in the 1970s and 1980s, whereas before 1970 manufactured exports made no contribution to growth at all (Holden 1990). But the contribution of these sectors was far less than would have sufficiently compensated for the effects of declining gold output and the low gold price.

What about agriculture? Could it provide jobs and exports on which to base a new round of growth? One limitation on the use of agriculture as a source of growth is the small supply of arable land. Only 10% of South Africa receives more that 750 millimetres of rain per year. Much of the country is desert or semi-desert, and variations of rainfall are severe enough to result in frequent drought cycles. Indeed, variations in agricultural output can push the GDP growth rate up or down by as much as 1.5%. Agriculture's contribution to GDP varies, averaging around 4%. The combined contribution of agriculture, fish and timber to total South African exports declined from 19% in 1957 to 5% in 1985 (Cassim et al. 2003; Holden 1990).

A second limitation is the fact that much agricultural land is owned by large landowners who are white and undercapitalised and do not have incentives to increase employment or output. Productivity and yield growth in the agricultural sector ran aground after the early 1970s, after years of lavish government support for farm investments. The land reform programme, intended to return a significant proportion of land to black people, started slowly in the agricultural sector. Though it has accelerated since 1999, the link between land reform and agricultural development remains fairly weak.

There are undoubtedly opportunities for agricultural expansion in high-value products such as wine, berries, fruits, nuts, and processed agricultural products, but South Africa's distance from major markets has been a drawback. Many of South Africa's competitors have a close relationship with their major customers, such as that between Europe and North Africa, or between the United States, the Caribbean and Latin America. Before the conclusion of a 'free trade agreement' with the European Union (EU) in 1999, some South African fruits attracted tariffs of over 20% in the EU, whereas products from favoured rival producers outside of the EU attracted barely any tariffs at all. EU tariffs on South African canned pears added 23.2% to the price in 1997, while in the United States they added 16.6%, and in Japan, 14.4%. EU import tariffs on South African canned apricots, as another example, were 25.1%, with the United States at 32.4%, and Japan at 16% (Kaplan and Kaplinsky 1998: 7). Since the conclusion of the EU-South Africa free trade agreement, the situation has improved a little, but remains difficult. As the conflict that wracked the World Trade Organisation (WTO) trade negotiations since Cancun in 2003 show, the inclination of the EU, Japan and the United States to subsidise domestic agricultural production and exports, in addition to protecting against imports through tariff and non-tariff barriers, has barely diminished, and even 'free trade agreements' have extensive qualifications and limitations.

In short, while South Africa has several competitive agricultural products, some of which will contribute to growth and employment creation in the future, domestic climatic constraints and world market conditions mean that agriculture can never be a complete answer to South Africa's growth and employment challenges. This was evident to policy makers in the early 1990s.

There were possibilities of employment and export growth in the services sector. Indeed, exports of services grew at 5.7% per year between 1988 and 1996, whereas the value of manufactured exports grew by only 3.2% per year (in US$). However, exports of services amounted to one quarter the value of exported manufactures in 1996 (Cassim et al. 2002: table 3). Services were not generally highly protected, and seemed to require less of a major policy reform than promotion. It was assumed that the services sector would benefit from the removal of protection on other sectors. The key service sector to promote would be tourism, a point we will return to later. On reflection, South African policy circles

Table 4.1:   Components of GDP, 1971–2001 (1995 constant prices).

Broad production sectors	Ave. share % 1971–80	Ave. share % 1981–90	Ave. share % 1991–2001
Mining and agriculture	16.1	13.3	11.4
Manufacturing	29.5	29.6	27.6
Services	54.3	57.0	61.0
Total	100.0	100.0	100.0

Note: GDP is measured at factor cost.
Source: Cassim et al. (2003).

certainly underestimated the potential of the services sector for growth, exports and particularly employment while policy was being formed in the 1990s, and certainly failed to consider carefully the key drivers for the sector.

Debating industrial policy

For these reasons, the focus of economic development fell on the manufacturing sector. Actually there were other reasons too. One institutional reason for focusing on manufacturing was the influence of the trade unions in the policy process. The most sophisticated unions, as far as economic policy was concerned, included the very broad National Union of Metalworkers of South Africa (NUMSA), and the clothing and textile workers' union, SACTWU.

ANC economists themselves tended to have a soft spot for the manufacturing sector. Whether in the Marxist tradition or the structuralist school of development economics, or even in the mainstream of economic history, the dynamism of the industrial sector was the mythic life source.[1] This view was reinforced by the Japanese success after 1945, for which the dominant explanation heavily emphasised the importance of a strong and outward-oriented manufacturing sector. Even the World Bank report, *South Africa: Economic Performance and Policies*, was heavily weighted towards an analysis of the constraints and potential of the manufacturing sector (Fallon and Perreira da Silva 1994).

Though there was agreement amongst most economists that the key area for policy intervention for growth and employment creation was in trade and industrial policy to restructure and strengthen the manufacturing sector, there was a wide range of suggestions about how best to do it.

Anxiety about dependence on a few agricultural and mineral exports began to preoccupy South African policy makers in the 1970s. Initially the emphasis was on diversifying away from gold, but by the later 1980s, strongly influenced by East Asian successes and international debates, the focus narrowed to manufacturing, narrowly defined.

Why is it necessary to define manufacturing 'narrowly'? Many of the strongest sectors in South Africa are in the business of producing intermediate or semi-manufactured goods. These include products such as basic metals, including iron, steel and aluminium; basic chemicals; wood pulp; and paper. Though there is value added, the production process is usually very capital intensive. The profitability of the output usually rests more on natural comparative advantages such as climate or bountiful mineral resources, than on acquired skills or expertise. The products are generally sold in standardised categories on international markets, with the main competitive levers being price and reliability. In short, these products are essentially commodities. In the standard industrial classification, these items often appear under the 'manufactured' column, but this is misleading. Many countries that export metals and minerals engage in the first stage of manufacturing near the mines in order to cut transport costs. For most intents and purposes, these activities are better seen as final stages in the extraction process, rather than an early stage of manufacturing (see Fine and Rustomjee 1996: 76–90).

The successes in East Asia – essentially Japan, South Korea, Taiwan, Singapore and Hong Kong – showed that there was a powerful connection between economic development and strong manufacturing capabilities. All five countries had grown rapidly and achieved much higher living standards largely on the basis of competitive exports of manufactured products.

Like elsewhere in the world, the interpretation of the East Asian experience, and later the South-East Asian experience, was the subject of a vigorous academic debate in South Africa. One faction explained the success as the result of classical outward-oriented policies by the Asian newly industrialised countries (NICs). These policies included the reduction of protection on trade flows and the implementation of conservative macroeconomic policies. A homegrown statement of what was then the IMF/World Bank orthodoxy came from the economics department of South Africa's Standard Bank:

In an industrial policy framework designed to encourage a
trade orientated modern sector, a core measure must be
the lowering of trade barriers to permit more foreign
competition. In this way the market mechanism will put
pressure on domestic manufacturers to improve their
efficiency. The removal of barriers such as import tariffs
would mean that local and international prices for goods
would converge. There would be pressure to shift funds and
human or other resources into producing goods for export
and/or the local market, where there is a relative advantage
(Standard Bank 1991: 2).

More nuanced orthodox views were put forward by the Industrial
Development Corporation's (IDC's) economic unit, and by Merle
Holden, a leading academic trade policy analyst (IDC 1990; Holden
1990).

A somewhat different approach was offered by those who
believed that trade policy was simply a backdrop for industrial policy.
A report compiled by the government's Board of Trade and Industry
(BTI) suggested that South Africa ought to target industrial sectors
according to suitable measures of existing and potential comparative
advantage, and aid those sectors with specially designed programmes
(BTI 1988). The proposed programmes were, however, rather
complex for government to manage effectively, and vulnerable to
special interests. Government never adopted the report.

Economists working with the ANC and COSATU, who knew
about the BTI report and sympathised with its sentiments, would
not necessarily have proposed the same programmes (Hirsch 1992b:
24). It was not simply a case of bashing down trade barriers and
seeing what came out, or what survived; it was a case of designing
the trade policy reform with certain industrial policy outcomes in
mind, and developing suitable industrial policy tools to support this.

What exactly this meant, we did not necessarily know. The East
Asian experience was not always enlightening or transferable. In
Japan and Korea the state had substantial control over credit and

the interest rate, and tailored both to support industrial development. But, in South Africa, financial markets were too complex and internationally integrated to allow the government as much leverage in this sphere. An exception was the IDC, a government-owned industrial bank, which could apply some lessons from Japan and Korea. The IDC's newly appointed board, in the mid-1990s, instructed the bank to deal with industrial sub-sectors in a more systematic way, rather than operating proposition by proposition.

Other East Asian lessons difficult to apply were the small- and medium-size company character of the Taiwanese system, and the extremely open character of the Hong Kong economy, which, after all, had special characteristics as a very small state. Also, South African policy makers felt constrained in the application of East Asian methods, as they believed that those societies had been both more authoritarian and more blessed with skilled managers than a democratic South Africa was likely to be.

Nevertheless, there was extensive interaction between South African policy makers and interpreters, and theorists and practitioners of the East Asian miracle.[2] Key carry-over themes were the emphases on export promotion, education and training, innovation support, policy-driven economic resource allocation, industrial sector targeting combined with geographic targeting, and public/private partnerships of all kinds.

Within this policy grouping – that saw trade reform as a component of industrial policy that was broadly aimed at exports – there was one significant polarisation. This was whether to focus on extending existing comparative advantages, or to seek new comparative advantages. I will spell this point out briefly, at the risk of caricaturing some arguments. Some policy actors, most notably Zavareh Rustomjee (later to be the Director-General of the Department of Trade and Industry, and later a senior executive in BHP Billiton, a minerals and energy conglomerate) and Paul Jourdan (later Deputy Director-General of the same department, and now President of Mintek – a minerals technology research agency) felt that in order to grow, South Africa should exploit its proven strengths. These strengths, they believed, were largely in industries related to South Africa's natural wealth – mainly mining, cheap energy, and manufacturing of inputs and outputs. Rustomjee and British economist Ben Fine developed the term 'minerals-energy complex' to describe what they saw as the beating heart of the economy (Fine and Rustomjee 1996: part II). The point was not necessarily to invest in more of the same mines or power stations though this was not necessarily a bad thing. The point was rather for the new government to manipulate the experience, power and capabilities of the minerals-energy complex to facilitate new, more competitive investments. Because it was dealing with big businesses, the government could plan very large projects, or large groups of projects.

At the opposite end of the spectrum, within the broad family of supporters of industrial policy for exports, was Brian Levy (see Levy 1992).[3] Levy is a South African who did his post-graduate work in economics at Harvard, taught economics in the United States, and later joined the World Bank. Unusually, in the light of practice at the time, which did not encourage 'nationals' to work on their own countries, the World Bank assigned Levy to cover South Africa during the early 1990s. He had built a reputation analysing small and medium business development in East Asia. Levy's view suggested that the distortions of the apartheid era led to a privileging of large-scale, capital-intensive projects in the minerals-energy complex (though he does not use the term), and that a removal of these distortions, along with appropriate supportive strategies, could lead to labour-absorbing, outward-oriented manufacturing in sectors that did not appear strong before. Levy felt that the underlying potential of the economy to create jobs through exporting was hidden by a legacy of one-sided intervention. The policy implications would be to reduce trade barriers and implement programmes designed to lift the best of new or neglected labour-absorbing industries on a rising tide, especially, but not only, by small and medium firms. The programmes could allow firms to select themselves, as long as they conformed to key developmental criteria such as creating jobs and exports.

Though none of the analysts in the broad 'industrial policy' group discounted the importance of local market growth opportunities, most emphasised export opportunities. There were some writers, though, who focused on inward-oriented development. Patrick Bond, for example, argued that South Africa should focus on producing for basic needs such as 'houses, services (electricity, water, sewage), simple home appliances, clothing and food'. He felt that South Africa would fail if it relied on export markets in the light of an unpredictable and increasingly competitive international environment (Bond 1991: 83). His view of the Asian experience was that it would soon reach its limits, leading to a plunge in exports and prices. The desire to link industrial growth with a growth in demand stimulated by the redistribution of income and social and economic infrastructure was consistent with one variant of the ANC's 'growth through redistribution' slogan that I discussed in Chapter Two. In terms of this approach, growth and redistribution were two sides of the same coin. Other South African economic analysts more or less associated with this position include Trevor Bell and Stephen Gelb.

The 'inward-industrialisation' argument had little initial support in the economic policy community. It was widely accepted that growth in South Africa normally led to imports growing more rapidly than exports (see Kahn 1987; McCarthy 1988). In the absence of sufficient South African savings, it was far-fetched for South Africans to believe that investors would underwrite inward industrialisation, which would reach its limits as a cheap programme after existing industrial capacity was fully used, and manufacturers needed to buy new equipment, mainly from abroad. Inward industrialisation could not sustain growth for any significant period of time, except on the basis of huge multilateral loans, which the ANC would not consider because of fears of threats to South Africa's sovereignty.

Left-wing critics of government sometimes still draw on the

'inward industrialisation' or 'basic needs' approach in criticising government, sometimes even extending it to an argument for resurrecting trade barriers. COSATU, the SACP and left-wing community organisations occasionally fall back on this approach as an alternative to the ANC's approach.

The outcome of the industrial policy debate

So, there were four positions, broadly speaking, on the South African path to growth in the early 1990s. From right to left (economically speaking) they were:

- trade liberalisation and getting the prices right;
- an emphasis on industrial policies with trade reform as a necessary condition, favouring smaller businesses and pre-reform uncompetitive labour-absorbing sectors;
- a similar approach, but with policies designed to exploit existing comparative advantages and bigger projects; and
- 'inward industrialisation', which linked industrial growth directly to domestic demand growing out of redistribution.

The position actually adopted by the ANC was a kind of unresolved compromise between the middle two positions. It accepted that a tariff phase-down was needed; this was reflected in the rather vague references in the *Ready to Govern* document to trade policy reform, and in the Reconstruction and Development Programme (RDP), which refers to the necessity of 'painful adjustment in certain quarters' and the aim to 'reduce and share out the impact of that adjustment while at the same time promoting efficiency'. The RDP mandated the government to 'simplify the tariff structure and begin a process of reducing protection in ways that minimise disruption to employment and to sensitive socio-economic areas' (ANC 1994a: 87–90).

While the RDP refers to manufacturers creating jobs 'through meeting basic needs', it also includes the statement: 'In general, our objective is to enhance our technological capacity to ensure that as a part of the restructuring of industry, South Africa emerges as a significant exporter of manufactured goods' (ANC 1994a: 87).

One of the clearest versions of the ANC's view on industrial policy is found in an unpublished document, prepared by ANC experts in the weeks before the elections on 27 April 1994. The document, entitled 'ANC trade and industry policy guidelines', was developed as a policy reference manual for the new Minister of Trade and Industry and his or her staff, assuming that he or she was an ANC member (ANC 1994b).

The document was drawn up from a collection of contributions from ANC-affiliated experts, some of whom were working in the Department of Economic Planning (DEP) of the ANC, some of whom were trade unionists or politicians, and some of whom worked in universities or research centres. The final meeting of the group took place on the 22 April 1994, five days before the election. Although four future Cabinet ministers – Alec Erwin, Trevor Manuel, Tito Mboweni and Jay Naidoo – were present at that meeting, and though they had overseen the process, the co-ordinator was Zavareh Rustomjee, who was to become Director-General of the Department of Trade and Industry (DTI) within a few months.

Rustomjee approached his task with the precision of an engineer. He had trained as a chemical engineer, had acquired a Masters degree in industrial engineering, and had worked as an industrial engineer in the petrochemicals sub-sector of South Africa's 'minerals-energy complex'. As apartheid began to crumble, Rustomjee decided to interrogate the beast through economic analysis. So in the late 1980s and early 1990s he completed a Masters degree in development studies at the University of Sussex, and a Ph.D. in economics at the School of Oriental and African Studies in the University of London. He then returned to South Africa and took a challenging, if poorly paid, position in the ANC's DEP. His family had long been involved in the struggle against apartheid: his aunt, Frene Ginwala, who also earned a Ph.D. studying in the United Kingdom, was made the first Speaker of the first democratic Parliament. His mother, a medical doctor, was appointed South African ambassador to Italy, and his younger brother joined the Department of Finance.

In 1994, Rustomjee was 37. Like many of his friends in the
ANC, he had decided that, if the opportunity came his way, he
would commit at least the next five years of his life working in the
ANC's economic agencies to build up the democratic state. Of the
23 people at the last meeting of the Trade and Industry Policy
Workshop at a seedy hotel in the inner-city flatland of Berea,
Johannesburg, only three did not end up either in the Cabinet, or
working for a government department or agency.

Rustomjee's summary of the discussion on industrial policy read
as follows:

> Industrial policies will be directed at five objectives, all of
> which are underpinned by the need to create sustainable
> employment in vibrant and growing industries:
>
> 1) To retain and extend the internationally competitive
>   edge held by heavy minerals-based manufacturing
>   industries at the core of the economy.
> 2) To support those light (non-minerals-based) manu-
>   facturing sub-sectors that have the potential to emerge
>   from existing protection with an independent and
>   sustainable dynamic.
> 3) Policies should be directed to bridging the cleavage
>   between the minerals-based core industries and the rest
>   of manufacturing by encouraging forward linkages of
>   further beneficiation as well as backward linkages with
>   industries that can supply consumable and durable inputs
>   to the core industries.
> 4) Growth of the agro-manufacturing sectors should be
>   targeted as these are less capital intensive and can directly
>   and indirectly create formal employment for the most
>   disadvantaged sections of the population. Many of the
>   infrastructure programmes of the RDP, particularly
>   those in the rural areas, will directly facilitate this
>   objective.

5) While pursuing the above objectives, policies within each
   sector should drive industrialisation towards higher value-
   added activities (ANC 1994b: 12).

The wording leaned towards the 'minerals and energy complex'
view of industrial policy, but was broad enough for many to work
within. As the implementation of industrial policy unfolded, the
choice between focusing on the 'natural advantages' derived from
South Africa's bounteous mineral and less bounteous agricultural
wealth, and the orientation towards building comparative advantage in sectors experiencing rising international demand and
rising prices, regardless of South Africa's apparent assets, evolved,
unspoken into a phased approach. For the first few years of
democracy, perhaps the first decade, South Africa would have to
rely on and exploit its 'natural advantages' and would conserve its
managerial resources by focusing on relatively big projects. But,
during that phase, South Africa had to begin to build the capabilities
in human resources, management skills and infrastructure, which
would support diversification into light manufacturing and services
aimed at expanding world markets.

The Marrakech Express: Trade policy reform

On 24 April 1994, Professor Kader Asmal, legal scholar, anti-
apartheid activist and an ANC candidate for the 27 April election,
participated in the signing of the Marrakech Agreement, which
concluded the Uruguay Round of GATT. Asmal was not yet a
representative of any government, and yet he joined South Africa's
Minister of Trade and Industry (and Finance), Derek Keys, in
Marrakech.

Asmal was not in Morocco as a passive observer; he was there
to signify the commitment of the ANC to the conclusion of the
Uruguay Round, and to South Africa's accepted offer. The government and the ANC both knew that the credibility of South
Africa's commitment to this hugely important international
agreement would be very low three days before a general election
that was expected to turn political relations in the country upside-

down. One way to engender belief in South Africa's commitment to the Marrakech agreement was for the ANC to send a senior representative along with the official South African government representative, to endorse South Africa's position.

Professor Asmal was a suitable man for the job. Born in Stanger in the subtropical province of KwaZulu-Natal, Asmal spent 27 years in exile teaching at Trinity College, Dublin, where he specialised in human rights, constitutional and international law. In 1990, his return journey ended in Cape Town where he headed a new ANC-aligned legal research centre at the University of the Western Cape (Harber and Ludman 1995: 3). Though not particularly interested in trade issues, Asmal is a very well-informed and erudite man, with unquestioned credibility in the ANC leadership, and a very sound grasp of international relations. He was soon to be a surprise appointment as Minister of Water Affairs and Forestry in Mandela's first Cabinet, and to bring to that apparently mundane job an aura of competence and excitement.

Asmal and Keys showed the world at Marrakech that South Africans understood that it was important to demonstrate that political history would not stand in the way of national interest in the new South Africa. Their double act at Marrakech (echoing Mandela and De Klerk's double acts in Davos and Stockholm) provided another foretaste of the realism and pragmatism that would characterise the first ANC-led government of national unity (GNU).

But, on what basis was the ANC able to commit itself to the GATT agreement? Two key ingredients combined to create the possibility of effective policy making in the interregnum period of the early 1990s. The first was COSATU's determination to intervene in the policy process, and the second was Derek Keys' strategic vision. Both realised that policy development and implementation were dead during this period, unless a legitimate interim policy-legitimising structure was created. Soon after he was appointed in charge of Trade and Industry, Keys made a speech in which he referred to a golden triangle between labour, business and government. In it, he implicitly acknowledged that he was powerless in a lame duck government (before the 1994 elections) unless he had the support of the best-organised economic constituencies in civil society. After some discussions, all three constituencies endorsed the establishment of a National Economic Forum (NEF), formally as a policy advisory body, but in practice, an organ of policy endorsement.

Though formally the forum represented government, business and labour, the ANC was also present, both through union leaders who were also ANC leaders, such as Jay Naidoo and Alec Erwin, and through participants in the Forum who represented the ANC and no one else, such as Tito Mboweni and myself. But the fact that the ANC was a participant was never formally acknowledged, and the ANC representatives always sat amongst the COSATU delegates.

The NEF discussed a number of policy issues, mostly dealing with trade and industrial policy matters. For example, it endorsed a plan to improve the operations of a leaky customs and excise agency, although the plan failed to have much effect at the time as the organisation needed to be entirely renewed, as it eventually was. Another issue discussed at the NEF was how to phase out the export subsidy called the Generalised Export Incentive Scheme (GEIS) that had been introduced for a limited period in 1990. But the real meat of the NEF, which may have been Keys' intention all along, was South Africa's offer of trade reform in the Uruguay Round of the GATT.

South Africa had submitted an offer in 1990, but because other issues delayed the conclusion of the Uruguay Round, South Africa's offer found itself on the backburner for years. Keys realised that the offer would not stick if labour and the ANC did not support it, and the business community was also anxious as it felt that the consultation process preceding the 1990 offer was shallow and a sham. So Keys withdrew the offer and put the matter before the NEF.

Throughout the period between July and December 1993, members of the Forum toiled over endless reams of spreadsheets of base tariffs (tariff or equivalent in the base year of the Uruguay Round negotiations), applied (actual) tariffs and proposed tariff bindings (ceilings above which new tariffs could not rise). Some spreadsheets also indicated the number of workers employed, imports and exports, and the relative magnitudes and impacts of the proposed tariff cuts. The only government agency with the skills and computing capabilities to act as a secretariat for this process at that time was the IDC. When they met in the panelled IDC boardroom, the NEF members deliberated under the gaze of six stern, white, male, former chairpersons of the IDC board staring uncomprehendingly out of larger-than-life, oil-painted portraits.

All the participants agreed that as a somewhat small and isolated economy, South Africa relied on the multilateral system of trade law to protect itself; they generally agreed that quantitative restrictions should be removed, that the number of tariff lines should be reduced by at least 30% from about 12 800, and that the number of tariff rates should be cut sharply back from about 200. The maximum tariff had to be cut back even more sharply from 1 389%. Not all participants were equally enthusiastic about the 33% average phase-down on all industrial tariffs and the 21% cut on agricultural products. However, the way the IDC chose the base data and calculated the conversion from quantitative into tariff barriers, generally inflating the initial protection levels so that the real cuts were not as bad as they appeared, assured most that the cuts would not be too excessive when phased in over five years.

The industrial tariff was approached in a systematic way. The fact that there had been an industrial policy debate for several years meant that there was a common discourse. The key feature of the new tariff structure was that it would have a cascading structure whereby raw materials would be unprotected, capital goods and intermediates would be taxed no higher than 10 or 15%, and consumer goods would be protected to the extent of 20 or 30% of their value. Where protection was already lower, it would generally not be raised. All duties lower than 5% would be entirely scrapped (Hirsch 1995).

Table 4.2: The level of sectoral protection: average percentage tariff by industrial group.

	1993	1996	1999	2000	2001
Food, beverages and tobacco	14.2	14.4	14.4	9.8	9.6
Textiles	49.1	33.0	25.7	16.0	15.7
Clothing, footwear and leather	59.5	52.9	40.3	21.7	22.0
Wood and wood products	10.9	3.8	3.3	3.1	3.3
Paper and paper products	5.6	5.0	5.9	7.1	7.4
Chemicals	9.1	5.6	4.7	2.5	2.7
Non-metallic minerals	11.0	7.5	6.6	5.2	4.6
Basic metals	7.3	2.8	2.5	2.0	2.4
Metal products and equipment	12.7	2.8	2.3	2.6	2.6
Other manufacturing	20.0	19.0	22.3	5.8	6.2
Total manufacturing	17.7	13.8	13.7	5.2	5.4

Source: Cassim et al. (2003).

There were some exceptions, for sensitive products – products that had very high levels of protection and significant levels of employment. The main sensitive sectors were clothing and textiles, and motor vehicle assembly and component manufacture. In both broad sectors several hundred thousand people were employed (directly and indirectly), but the level of tariff protection was very high – over 100% in some cases if one included the effects of the import surcharge.

With Mandela's intervention with President Clinton (before South Africa's 1994 election), South Africa's industrial offer was accepted in spite of the fact that it required longer phase-down periods and higher terminal tariff ceilings for the two sensitive broad sectors. The industrial offer was exemplary in most other respects.

The same was not true of the agricultural sector offer. There had not been an agricultural policy debate similar to the industrial policy debate, though there had been liberalisation of the domestic agricultural sector since the 1980s. Instead of tailoring the offer in terms of an agricultural strategy, however broad, all that was done was for the base tariffs to be set at very high levels, exploiting the vagueness of the process of converting quantitative restrictions into notional *ad valorem* tariffs, and to make the minimum cuts reach the new tariff bindings. This indulged the South African agricultural sector's resistance to change where it could be avoided, it showed the closeness of the Department of Agriculture to the agricultural status quo, and it demonstrated COSATU and the ANC's uncertainty regarding agriculture. It also reflected the fact that the world market for agricultural products, plagued as it is by preferential systems and subsidies in the major agricultural importing countries, is much less transparent than the market for industrial products – South African negotiators were content to be cautious.

However significant South Africa's GATT tariff reform com-mitments, the biggest single jolt to the status quo was the final removal of all import surcharges in October 1995. The import surcharges had covered about 60% of tariff lines, and ranged up to 40% of import value for consumer products.

Trade reform continued: Export subsidies, guarantees and promotion

The core of the Uruguay Round was a 33% cut in industrial tariffs, a 36% cut in agricultural tariffs and a 21% cut in agricultural subsidies, each over a five- or six-year period. There were other important elements, such as the attempts to establish new world regimes for services trade and for the management of intellectual property rights that South Africa participated in, and an attempt to establish new rules for government procurement, a voluntary code that South Africa declined to join. But the key effect for South Africa of the 1994 GATT agreement, beyond tariff reform, was the end of GEIS.

GEIS was launched in April 1990 amidst a deep economic panic. Foreign capital inflows had practically dried up and commodity markets were in the doldrums, jointly threatening South Africa's balance of payments. Tight money policies and an import surcharge, instituted under the emergency balance of payments provision of GATT, sought to constrict domestic demand. But, the economy was set to plunge even deeper into recession unless a new source of growth and balance of payments strength could be found. It was the culmination of an escalating crisis that began with the slump in the gold price in 1983–85, and the departure of international banks and their credit lines after P.W. Botha's Rubicon speech in August 1985.

The government decided to subsidise exports that were not raw materials. Instead of a complex sector-specific system that the BTI proposed in its 1988 'structural adjustment' report, the government chose a simple export subsidy. The subsidy was a tax-free grant paid to all exporters in proportion to the value of their executed export order. It was divided into four categories, receiving different benefits: primary product exporters (e.g. logs or minerals); beneficiated primary products (e.g. saw logs, billets); material-intensive products (e.g. planed planks, sheet metal); and manufactured products (e.g. furniture, steel cabinets) (Holden and Gouws 1997). Manufactured products got a tax-free subsidy of about 21%, the primary producers got nothing, and the rest got between about 5 and 14%, all modified by a formula that included a factor for changes in the real exchange rate.

The administration of the programme was fraught with fraud and backlogs, and budgeting was always out by hundreds of millions of rand. In the end, perversely, the biggest beneficiaries were the manufacturers of intermediate products such as paper and steel, who now received huge tax-free windfalls on products they would have exported anyway. The beneficiary companies were usually large, capital-intensive processing firms such as Sappi and Mondi (paper and pulp), and Sentrachem and AECI (basic chemicals), which belonged to the giant conglomerates Anglo American and Sanlam, or they were parastatals or privatised parastatals such as Iscor (iron and steel) and Armscor (military weapons) (Fine and Rustomjee 1996: 232). Most analyses of GEIS indicated that it had little effect on exports, especially when compared with factors such as the real effective exchange rate and business cycles (see Holden and Gouws 1997).

GEIS was a headache for government. As soon as he could, early in 1993, Minister Derek Keys removed the tax exemption from GEIS payments. But in 1994 it was difficult for the new government to do away with GEIS precipitously. Firstly, it was concerned that a commitment by the state to continue the programme for a certain number of years (its duration was extended once) had to be honoured, otherwise measures offered by the new government might not have sufficient credibility to influence investment decisions. Also, although GEIS was not cost-effective, most analysts inside and outside of government believed that South African exporters, especially new exporters in small and medium companies, needed encouragement from government, and not much existed beyond GEIS. The new government did not want to send the signal that it did not strongly support manufactured exports.

So, the requirement of the Uruguay Round that unadulterated export subsidies should be removed before the end of 1997 came as a blessing for government. It could blame GATT for the termination of GEIS. Soon, Zavareh Rustomjee, as new Director-General of the DTI, felt that whatever positive influence GEIS had ever had on exports would dissipate with the decision to phase it out, so he accelerated the downsizing of the subsidy, with the very last GEIS commitments made in July 1997. All the same, the programme still cost government about R21 billion in nominal rands over its seven-year history, or about US$5 billion – a lot of money for South Africa. For several years it grabbed the lion's share of the budget of the DTI.

Was there a better and more cost-effective way of supporting new exports? The first new export support programme launched by the democratic government was a credit guarantee programme for small exporters: the first programme to be developed through the Japanese Grant Fund process (see Box 4.1). The scheme was loosely based on a much bigger Korean programme, and was developed in outline for South Africa by Korean consultants working with Yung Whee Rhee, a top Korean industrial policy expert based at the World Bank. The programme took off more quickly than most new South African government programmes aimed at smaller firms, and was fairly effective (DTI 1998a: 90, 1999: 32).

Box 4.1: The Japanese Grant Fund: A novel policy process

Shortly after the 1994 elections, the Japanese government conveyed to the World Bank several million dollars to fund policy research on how to make South African industry more competitive. The World Bank approached the new Minister of Trade and Industry, Trevor Manuel, to ask him how he would like to use the funds. Certain conditions were attached, but the main requirement was a consultative process, and a World Bank indication of 'no objection'.

Manuel handed the project to the NEF, which was later to become the National Economic Development and Labour Council (Nedlac). The NEF set up a Japanese Grant sub-committee chaired by Philip Kotze, who was the Director of Economic Research and a Senior General Manager at the IDC. The IDC would manage the funds on behalf of Nedlac.

The Japanese Grant Fund subcommittee, like all NEF/Nedlac committees, consisted in equal part of representatives of labour, business and government. It approved Japanese Grant Fund research projects (usually proposed at the Trade and Industry Chamber of Nedlac), and appointed project-specific management groups, with between two and four representatives of each of the three constituents. These management teams were called 'counterpart groups'. With the assistance of suitable experts, from the World Bank, or the IDC or the DTI, the counterpart group would finalise a policy research brief, put it out to limited or general tender, and appoint the consultants who would undertake the projects.

The consultants had extensive discussions with the counterpart group in drawing up the final project design and schedule, and from time to time, until a draft final report was ready. The counterpart group then examined the final report, usually asked for improvements, and finally submitted it to the NEF or Nedlac, and to the Minister of Trade and Industry.

Usually the counterpart group prepared a set of policy recommendations based on the project report, not necessarily agreeing with all aspects of it.

Japanese Grant Fund investigations preceded and led to many of the new measures introduced by the DTI, including:

- the pre-shipment export finance guarantee for small and medium enterprises (SMEs);
- the removal of the regional industrial development programme and its replacement with a small and medium manufacturing development programme and a tax-holiday programme;
- a skills development strategy introduced by the Department of Labour;
- the restructuring of the support programme for industrial innovation;
- a competitiveness fund; and
- a wide range of industrial cluster investigations.

The key innovation of the programme was that it knitted agreement between labour, government and business very early in the development or reform of a programme – with external consultants to provide reality checks. The programme was considered so successful that, when the Japanese funds ran out in 1998, the government decided to continue the programme as the Fund for Research into Growth, Development and Equity, or FRIDGE.

The Credit Guarantee Insurance Corporation built the short-term export credit guarantee for small firms on top of an existing government programme to provide export credits. Another important element in the export guarantee portfolio is the Export Finance Scheme for Capital Projects, which is also underwritten by government. This programme is important in supporting South Africa's effort to penetrate developing country markets, especially in Africa, with competitive manufactured goods and project services (DTI 1998a: 90–91).

A second new programme linked with the trade policy reform was the World Player Scheme developed and run by the IDC. The IDC recognised that numerous firms, including several of its own existing interests, could be detrimentally affected by the tariff down phasing programme launched in Marrakech. The IDC offered all firms in industries facing tariff cuts of 15 percentage points or more, discounted loans for projects designed to bring them up to a suitable level of competitiveness. Loans were available at a 3–6 percentage point discount on the normal IDC fixed rate, which itself was usually 3–6% below the prime interest rate. The IDC lent close to a billion rand (about US$250 million) through this programme from 1995–98. Nearly half went to the textile industry and about one seventh went to the motor vehicle industry (DTI 1998a: 73; IDC 1998: 21).

The other key trade policy reform was the major overhaul of an export marketing assistance scheme. When GEIS was finally abolished in 1997, the government and its social partners in Nedlac felt that there should be an additional compensatory stimulus to exports, particularly for smaller, more labour-intensive firms. Instead of developing an entirely new programme, the DTI decided to remodel and upgrade a rather low-level existing programme. The new Export Marketing and Investment Assistance Programme offered seven modes to support firms in their efforts to find markets abroad for their products, and two modes to find foreign investors interested in South African opportunities.

A major new component was the provision for government to support the establishment of sub-sector export councils that could co-ordinate marketing strategies for groups of related firms. The first export councils established, in 1999, were those for structural steel, for capital equipment, and for stainless steel (DTI 1999: 18–19, 31).

Accessing markets
The new government's role in promoting exports was not confined to tariff and incentive programmes – there was also the issue of

accessing and securing markets for South African exporters. Even in a world where the WTO was increasingly influential, special relationships were very important, especially in trade relations between developed and developing countries, and in the trade of agricultural products. Many of South Africa's competitors had such relationships. For example: Canada, the United States, Mexico and Chile entered a combination of free trade agreements; southern European countries were members of the European Union; eastern European countries had special deals with Europe, as did Israel (also with the United States) and much of North Africa; while all African countries other than South Africa, and several Caribbean, Asian and Pacific nations were members of the Lomé Convention with the European Union, giving them quotas and tariff preferences, mainly in agricultural products.

One symptom of this problem was the loss of market share by South African canned fruit exporters during the 1990s that led to damaging job losses and factory closures in the Western Cape. The shift in market share was almost entirely attributable to European preferences and subsidies (Kaplan and Kaplinsky 1998). It was this shift and the fact that South Africa is not located geographically near to any of the major world markets, that persuaded South African politicians and civil servants to focus on the issue of market access – bearing in mind that it was not only market access that was at stake, but also the investment flows that usually accompany strong trading relationships.

South Africa was ill equipped to enter negotiations – the isolation of the previous regime meant there was no legacy of trade negotiation skills. But, negotiations could not be avoided and officials entered an intensive period of on-the-job training.

The highest priority was to secure and deepen relations with South Africa's neighbours in southern Africa collected in the Southern African Customs Union (SACU) and the Southern African Development Community (SADC). One reason was that the new South African leadership felt that South Africa would sink or swim with the region. South Africa's success, particularly as an investment destination, was in part a function of the economic success and political stability of its neighbours. A second reason was that, as sanctions declined, southern Africa (13% of exports) became, as a group, South Africa's third largest export destination after the EU (38%) and the North American Free Trade Agreement (NAFTA) (14%), and the most important market for South Africa's manufactures and services, as opposed to primary products (DTI 1998b). The South African trade surplus with the region grew large and needed regional co-operation to sustain it. Another reason for focusing on the region was that South Africa's policy makers believed that if it could strengthen ties with its neighbours, heading for a free trade area or customs union, both South Africa's and its neighbours' bargaining power with the rest of the world would be enhanced. It should be noted, though, that the sum of the GDPs of all of South Africa's partners in SADC comes to less than half of South Africa's GDP.

South Africa's expectation in reforming SACU was that the relationship between the partners – South Africa, Botswana, Lesotho, Swaziland and Namibia – would become more equal. SACU had a colonial form in that the formula for redistributing the customs revenue inflated the incomes of the poorer members in compensation for having no real control over the customs union. Decisions about adjusting tariffs were South African domestic policy. The other members of the union, which had to go along with the decisions, were paid more than a pro rata share of customs revenue as compensation. But the poorer countries depended excessively on the customs union revenue for their tax base – for Lesotho, customs revenue makes up more than half of the government's annual income – and proved resistant to a major change in the formula. Progress on the democratic form to be adopted by the new SACU was also much slower than expected.

While reforming SACU, South Africa set out to join a SADC initiative to move towards a free trade area – SACU is a subset of the members of SADC. First South Africa had to join SADC, which had originally been set up by South Africa's neighbours as a defence against the apartheid state. Today SADC consists of SACU, plus Angola, Malawi, Mauritius, Mozambique, Tanzania, Zambia, Zimbabwe and the Democratic Republic of the Congo.

Late in 1998, South Africa put the first proposal for a mutual tariff phase-down on the SADC table. It proposed a 12-year period during which first South Africa and then its SADC partners reduce their tariffs, culminating in a free trade area. Like all free trade areas there would be some exceptions for sensitive products but, in line with WTO unwritten guidelines, this could consist of no more than 15% of traded goods. Though a protocol was agreed, the process of ratification and implementation has been very slow. Other barriers to the movement of goods, services and people have also slowed progress in the integration of the region.

The second priority for South Africa was its economic relationship with the EU. The EU had long been South Africa's major trade and investment partner, with the British and German markets being the most important. The urgency of the matter lay in South Africa's concern that its relationships with traditional trading partners were eroding. The EU was becoming enlarged (Sweden, Austria, Finland, former East Germany and, imminently, Poland, Hungary and the Czech Republic), developing new free trade agreements with Morocco and Tunisia for example, and deepening through the European Monetary Union and later the Euro. In relative terms, with all the EU's special relationships, South Africa was losing ground fast.

The EU approached South Africa shortly before the democratic elections in 1994 with an offer of an 'association agreement'. South Africa wanted access to the EU market on the same terms as its neighbours, partly to encourage economic integration in southern Africa, which entailed membership of the Lomé Convention. The EU blocked this, partly because it considered the South African economy too strong for Lomé, and partly because it was trying to steer Lomé towards a set of regional free trade agreements. South Africa found itself engaged in negotiations over a trade and development agreement with the EU, centred on a free trade agreement, and concluded after six years of discussions and negotiations.

By the early 2000s, the focus of South Africa's trade discussions had shifted to the possibility of free trade agreements with India, Brazil/Mercosur, and the United States, and to the Doha Round of WTO-led multilateral trade negotiations where South Africa helped build a coalition called 'the group of 22', which pushed the EU, the United States and Japan towards more significant concessions for freer trade with developing countries.

Investment strategies

Between the Second World War and 1976, total investment grew strongly in South Africa. Most of the growth was attributable to local companies and the public sector, though direct foreign investors played a role in important sub-sectors of manufacturing and the service sector. Gross domestic fixed investment (GDFI) reached a peak at an average of 26% of GDP over the period 1971–76, which was a higher ratio than that of most middle-income countries, such as Mexico, Brazil and Chile, following an import-substitution policy at that time. It was comparable, rather, with countries following export-oriented growth strategies, such as Malaysia and South Korea. Only in the 1980s did these export-oriented economies surpass South Africa in relative size of investment effort (Fallon and Perreira da Silva 1994: 53).

This is part of the tragedy of South Africa – it had so much capacity to invest, and yet the investments reaped such poor rewards. Though private investment was strong, from the 1960s to the mid-1970s investment was led by the public sector. Massive investments were made in roads, dams, railway lines, electrical power, and in 'strategic' industries such as synthetic fuels, nuclear power, iron and steel, and armaments.

Public investment was directed in terms of the perceived needs and desires of the constituents of the minority regime, the whites – and white farmers and business-owners in particular. In addition, distortions in the economy such as negative real interest rates and exchange controls for much of the 1970s and 1980s, and the apartheid restrictions that inhibited investments in human capital, undermined the value of the investments and led to investments that were excessively capital intensive and absorbed little labour. The social and economic returns on these investments were generally low.[4]

With the radical fluctuation of many key prices in the 1970s, the world of the NP slowly came unstuck. Government investment starting falling in the late 1970s, and investments by parastatals followed soon afterwards. After 1985, with the evacuation of foreign banks and their credit lines, the disinvestments of many important foreign-owned businesses (such as IBM, Ford, General Motors and two major British banks), and the privatisation of some parastatal companies, investment fell apart. From 1983-93, GDFI fell from 26.8% of GDP to 15.5% of GDP, while in the period 1986-91, public sector investment growth declined on average by 6.5% per year (SARB 1998b; Fallon and Perreira da Silva 1994: 54).

The old government had several industrial investment promotion schemes. A major theme in the investment support programmes was 'industrial decentralisation'. The main motive was political: to keep black industrial workers out of the major urban centres where they were getting more and more powerful, and to build up a loyal black middle class in the Bantustans. Later still, industrial development in some of the Bantustans was intended to legitimise their putative independence.

The first decentralisation programme began in 1960, but only its successors became really effective in the late 1970s and 1980s. The government poured in subsidies of all kinds, but the vast majority of operations established were destined to survive no longer than the duration of the subsidy programme. Most of the investors were white South Africans, but there were also foreign investors from Europe, Taiwan and Israel.

By the end of the 1980s, the cost of the programme weighed heavily, especially in the light of the growing cost of export subsidies. The report of an enquiry commissioned by the government suggested that the programme should be scaled down with regards the range and depth of the subsidies, but that they should now extend to all new manufacturers anywhere except in the Pretoria-Witwatersrand-Vereeniging area (the PWV). The PWV was deemed not to be in need of such support.

In 1993, a special version of the Regional Industrial Development Programme (RIDP) was developed for smaller firms. This programme – the Simplified RIDP – was effective in attracting more labour-intensive projects than the RIDP, at about R50 000 per job, rather than about R300 000 per job.

In 1996 both programmes were reviewed, using the Nedlac-based Japanese Grant Fund programme. The objectives of the government had shifted, fundamentally. The apartheid government tried to use investment incentives to shape society along lines that would suit its system of political oppression. Investment programmes were essentially nice-to-have add-ons to already satisfactory levels of investment, as far as the rulers were concerned. The objectives of the ANC-led GNU were very different. The level of investment had to be raised from very low levels, to increase the country's wealth, and, equally important, jobs had to be created for the many millions of unemployed.

Also, there were parts of the country that were neglected or even avoided for investment during the apartheid era for political reasons. One example is the eastern Transvaal, now Mpumalanga province, which is located next to Mozambique. Because apartheid South Africa's policy towards Mozambique meant that the latter country's ports were not accessible for South African importers and exporters, the whole region suffered. Another example is the former Transkei littoral, which has tremendous tourist potential, but lacks infrastructure because the apartheid government chose to marginalise the predominantly black region.

The ANC believed that breaking down the politically erected obstacles to development would not be enough to counteract years of neglect. But the national leadership also wanted to avoid the kind of subsidies that could enter the currency of pork-barrel politics, and could further distort markets for no good reason. Other considerations in the ANC's approach to investment included a desire to encourage foreign investors, especially where they brought with them good technologies and/or markets, a desire to increase the 'competitive temperature' in South Africa by introducing new rivals that would challenge old oligopolies, a desire for more labour-absorbing types of investment, and a desire to build up a significant black capitalist class beyond the tentacles of the oligopolies, with real presence in the industrial sector of the economy (not only finance and commerce) (Hirsch 1992a; ANC 1997b: 41–50).

Following a 1995 consultant's report on foreign investment commissioned by the Japanese Grant Fund of Nedlac, the government decided to relocate the marketing programme to attract foreign investors outside of the DTI, where it had languished. There were two main reasons: the intention to instil an entrepreneurial spirit within this organisation, which is more difficult in a government department; and a wish to ensure that the provincial investment promotion agencies truly believed that their seat on the board of the central agency meant that they owned it. The provincial agencies would do most of the work in attracting potential investors and reaching an agreement, but the national agencies could exploit economies of scale in marketing and information management. Investment South Africa was publicly launched early in 1997. Later it took on export marketing responsibilities too, and still later it was reincorporated back into the DTI.

At the same time, the government worked on improving the range and quality of the incentives and instruments to encourage both foreign and domestic industrial investors. It was the firm conviction of the economic policy leadership that frills such as financial incentives were secondary; rather, the overall economic and political conditions were far more important when it came to attracting the right kind of investment (see, for example, ANC 1997a: chapter 1).

The most important government-controlled agency for the development of the real sector, after the DTI, was the IDC. The IDC was set up in 1940 with state funds as an industrial development bank, to invest in strategic industrial sectors. Since the early 1950s it has operated successfully without any further injection of state funds, though until the 1990s it still took advantage of state guarantees of loans to parastatal companies. The legal mandate of the IDC was simple: it should invest in industrial undertakings that benefit the country and also meet the criterion of economic viability. Economic viability really means that the firm invested in should ultimately be expected to make profits and stand on its own. Under the ANC, the IDC's mandate was extended to allow investments in other African countries. The main difference between the IDC and a private investment bank was that with only one shareholder, the government, the IDC was able to take a longer view of investments, and to take some risks that a privately owned bank might not. Nevertheless, the corporation developed a practice and culture of proposition evaluation and economic analysis that made its professionals and its judgements very highly regarded in the private sector.

With its assets worth close to US$3 billion in 1994, and its culture of professional competence, the new government was keen to exploit the virtues and expunge the sins of the IDC as quickly as possible. But what were those sins? The IDC had become quite deeply integrated into elements of what Rustomjee called the 'minerals-energy complex'. Most of the high level work in the IDC was directed towards new 'beneficiation' projects such as steel mills and aluminium smelters. Its integration with the minerals-energy complex also meant that it developed cosy relations with some of the biggest conglomerates, such as Sanlam and Gencor.

Another weakness of the IDC was that it did not devote sufficient resources to black economic empowerment (BEE) and small and medium business development, which are two overlapping but not identical issues. The organisation itself had relatively few black professionals, and none who were in senior positions. Another issue was that, outside of the minerals-energy complex industries, the IDC did not approach investment propositions in the context of sectoral industrial development plans.

The IDC law seemed broad enough to accommodate new parameters. Government economic leaders approached the challenge of reforming the IDC by reconstituting its board and allowing the board to focus on policy issues, and the appointment of senior management. In 1996, the new board members found a new CEO, Khaya Nqula, who had worked for IBM and South African Breweries in marketing, and ran what was then South Africa's fastest-growing unit trust (mutual fund) business. Nqula agreed to a five-year contract, indicating that he had no intention of staying on after that.

Once in position, Nqula moved quickly, first to restore the morale of an anxious organisation, and then to make a string of new appointments, bringing black and female staff into executive management for the first time in the organisation's history. The IDC was turned around, without having to be dismantled and rebuilt from scratch. This was the way the new government preferred to operate: to retain existing assets, in this case the financial assets and the intellectual capital of the IDC, but at the same time turn the agency into an effective organ of reconstruction in the era of democracy.

The RIDP was cancelled after the Nedlac review. The evidence suggested that other methods should be tried to attract significant industrial investments. However, the modified version of the RIDP developed for small and medium firms was retained in a restructured form as the Small and Medium Manufacturing Development Programme (SMMDP). Later this was broadened beyond the manufacturing sector and renamed the Small and Medium Enterprise Development Programme. Its bait is an annual cash grant for investors for up to three years, based on the size of the investment and the audited performance of the firm. It is weighted toward smaller investments and can be used anywhere in South Africa where an enterprise can be established. When the SMMDP was reviewed after 18 months of operation, it had created approximately 26 392 new jobs. At R73 000 (or less than US$15 000) per job, these investments were clearly in labour-intensive sectors (DTI 1999: 15–17).

But for larger industrial investors who had easier access to funds and expected high profits, reduced taxes seemed like the best option. At the time of the RIDP review, in 1996, the government was short of revenue and could not make overall tax reduction commitments. So, a tax holiday programme for larger industrial investments, which was supported in the review, was announced in the GEAR statement in June and launched later in the year. The government wanted to launch the programme as quickly as possible because it wanted to instil confidence that GEAR was being implemented, and because it detected a tailing-off of private sector investment. The tax holiday programme ended up being difficult to implement due to a relatively rushed process of consensus building among all the constituents – in addition to Parliament, these included business, labour, the provincial governments and the government's tax commission. In order to qualify for six consecutive tax-free years beginning in the first profitable year, the enterprise had to be financially discrete (to avoid leakages), had to be located within one of a large number of industrial districts (not excluding the PWV), and it had to indicate a sufficient level of job creation.

Between the middle of 1997 and the end of 1998, 106 tax holiday projects were approved, representing a total investment of R3.1 billion, and 8 854 new jobs (at R350 000, or US$70 000 per job) (DTI 1999: 15–16). The programme had not worked as effectively as hoped, and, in February 1999, before a mid-term review could report, the Minister of Finance, Trevor Manuel announced that the tax holiday window would close, as planned, in September 1999. Simultaneously, Manuel announced a general reduction in the rate of company tax from 35 to 30% of profits (Manuel 1999).

When the DTI pressed for more investment support, two new initiatives were introduced in 2002. The Strategic Investment Programme is an investment allowance provided to large investments that meet a certain set of criteria. So far it seems to be more effective than the tax holiday programme. The Critical Infrastructure Programme provides a subsidy to businesses or public agencies that invest in infrastructure related to a planned private investment project; a railway siding, a harbour terminal or a power line, for example.

Perhaps the most original investment programme launched by the first democratic South African government became known as the Spatial Development Programme. In economic terms, the objective of the programme was to internalise the externalities of public and private investments in targeted regions. Public and private investments could reap higher social and economic returns if they were co-ordinated. For example, if the government was building houses, roads and schools, it would be more sensible to do this where firms were planning to create job opportunities. Some of the risk is removed from the government projects. And vice versa: the public investment could very well lower the cost of the private investment by reducing a firm's outlay on social and economic infrastructure.

In advanced economies, such as the United States, state and city governments would undertake such co-ordination. In South Africa, though, most provincial and city governments did not have the skills or financial resources to make this work. National government and national agency involvement is still essential in South Africa at this stage.

The first Spatial Development Initiative was a kind of exper-imental accident. South African government officials – particularly Paul Jourdan at the DTI – realised that the political settlement made possible significant new investments in the Mpumalanga region and across the border in southern Mozambique. After negotiations and arm-twisting, the South African government agreed to rebuild and extend both the road and rail links to Mozambique's Maputo harbour. Maputo is the closest harbour to much of the mineral-rich interior of South Africa. The Mozambican government agreed to work on its road and rail links, and to upgrade the harbour. In the meantime, firms were being recruited to consider the region for investment, with the active support of the IDC. However, government decided that it would not go ahead unless the private sector saw the whole project as viable, and this signal required public/

private partnerships in some of the infrastructure projects. The positive response to the Department of Transport's tender for a built, operate and transfer (BOT) toll road was the key signal. Public and private investments have since flooded into the region, which is seen as a major example of three key partnerships: between national and provincial/local government; between the public and private sectors; and between three countries – South Africa, Mozambique, and Swaziland (which shares a corner of the region).

As evidence emerged of the success of the Maputo Corridor Spatial Development Initiative, the methodology was extended to other regions that had a high development potential and need. Whereas the Maputo initiative is based on the extraction and processing of minerals, though also on agriculture and tourism, the Wild Coast initiative (in the former Transkei) and the Lebombo initiative (northern KwaZulu-Natal) are primarily tourism-oriented. The West Coast initiative in the Western Cape combines industrial, agricultural and tourist elements, weighted more equally. The key ingredients in successful Spatial Development Initiatives are effective co-ordination at a technical level, and at a political level. A special Cabinet Investment Cluster, which linked Ministers from key ministries such as Transport and Water, chaired by the then Minister of Trade and Industry, Alec Erwin, helped ensure that technical initiatives would get political support. It became an element of the strategy to ensure that a sufficiently prominent national politician, working with a sufficiently prominent regional politician, led each Spatial Development Initiative.

In some cases, no additional government funds were needed beyond the normal budget, though funds were diverted to Spatial Development Initiatives as a temporary priority. In one case, as in the need to build a new port near Port Elizabeth, a bigger public commitment was required. But this was rare. Mostly, no new financial commitments were required, beyond the cost of running the Spatial Development Initiative teams.

The key weakness of the Spatial Development Initiatives is the inevitability, in a democracy, that there will be too many initiatives and not enough effective public and private management skills. All the leadership can hope for under these circumstances is that the best prospective Spatial Development Initiatives get the 'A-team' treatment. In some cases the provincial government has taken over the initiative, such as in the case of Gauteng's Blue IQ initiative, which is essentially a special development plan with strong public support.

Two of the most important lessons gradually learned by the government during the first decade of freedom were that investment dynamics often were not national – rather they were frequently regional and local – and that the manufacturing sector was not ever likely to be a major supplier of jobs in South Africa, though it remained an important dynamo for growth. The result was that the location of investment incentive programmes began to shift away from their traditional location in the DTI, towards other departments, and provincial governments. The Department of Tourism and linked national and local agencies developed an extensive system of incentives for investment in the tourism sector. Gauteng's Blue IQ programme of infrastructure development, aimed at investment in a range of key sectors identified by the province, is another example of this new generation of investment strategy. The eThekwini (Durban) municipality's support for the tourism and conference sectors is another example, and the Western Cape government's support for the development of a major film production centre in Cape Town is another.

Supporting industrial innovation

In general, South African manufacturing firms had no reputation for genuine product innovation. Engineers were known for their ability to modify products and processes, and to find cheap short cuts, but most South African manufactured products were and continue to be made under licence to intellectual property rights holders in the advanced industrial economies. This is not surprising as the nature of South Africa's protectionist regime encouraged licensing and copying for the domestic market, not world-class innovation.

There were a few exceptions in industries that were heavily supported by the government because of their strategic importance in the era of apartheid, sanctions and isolation. Some areas of effort were: oil from coal techniques; nuclear power; military specification electronics and other military products; communications technologies (military and state-run commercial); and systems integration capabilities. The main mode of support was military funding of long-term contracts that would allow for innovation in state-owned or private firms. The government supported science councils, especially the Council for Scientific and Industrial Research (CSIR), would also be contracted to assemble their expertise behind the projects. It was a focused marshalling of nearly all the existing technology innovation talent, and channelling such talent from the universities into a carefully chosen set of missions.

From the beginning of the 1990s, military funding fell rapidly, and the long-term communications contracts came to an end. The focus shifted to commercialisation and cost savings in the context of re-entering the global market place. One unfortunate result was that private sector and public sector innovation expenditure, specifically research and development, fell from just over 1% of GDP in 1991 to under 0.7% of GDP in 1997. By 2001 the effects of new policies and programmes came through and research and development recovered to 0.76% of GDP, and rose to 0.81% of GDP in 2003, but this is still relatively low in an international context (Department of Science and Technology 2005).

Key policy developments were a science and technology white paper in 1996 sketching out the model of the national system of innovation, and laying the framework for incremental policy reform. This was followed by a national research and development strategy in 2001 and specific strategies for biotechnology and advanced manufacturing. An important complementary policy was the 'Integrated Manufacturing Strategy', which emphasised the importance of the development, organisation and transmission of knowledge for the development of a competitive manufacturing sector (DACST 2001a, 2001b; DTI 2002; National Advisory Council on Innovation 2003).

The first new-model innovation support projects were developed in the early 1990s. The Support Programme for Industrial Innovation (SPII) was initially developed by the DTI for the electronics sector, which was seen to be in crisis as demand from the military and the state-owned telecommunications company, Telkom, plummeted simultaneously. Soon it was extended to other industrial sectors. It is a matching-grant programme that supports commercially oriented innovators.

The Technology and Human Resources for Industry Programme (THRIP) was developed at about the same time. Its objective was to link the world of tertiary education in science and engineering with the industrial world. The government added a 50% grant to the contribution by a private firm or consortium to a university- or technikon-based applied industrial research project that had to involve the training of students. THRIP got off to a very slow start, but expanded very rapidly after being remodelled, reorganised and augmented.

These new programmes were designed to combine the knowledge provided by the market with the knowledge developed in public and private research institutions. Several other such programmes were developed to fill evident cracks in the late 1990s. But this did not really solve the problem or challenge of refocusing the science councils.

South Africa's science councils are significant organisations. The CSIR is one of the largest – it receives about R400 million from the government annually and earns a little more than that through contracts with the government and the private sector. By South African standards, this is a lot of money for industrial innovation research. The CSIR is one of a group of 'science councils' that conduct research, develop technology, build information bases and/or develop standards in fields such as agriculture, mining and metals, geophysics, medicine and human sciences. The science councils are partly government funded, and partly funded through contracts and fees through the government and private clients.

In the early 1990s, the CSIR shifted strongly towards the market as it saw that government contracts were drying up, and the 'parliamentary grant' would not grow rapidly. Though this was a logical and sensible thing to do under the circumstances, it meant that the CSIR drew on its existing knowledge resources without building much new intellectual capital through basic and exploratory research. By the end of the decade it was recognised that the CSIR had to balance its commitment to commercial contracts with a strong commitment to technology platform development.

The dilemma over the role of the science councils has three main elements. The first is whether the state has a role to directly supply innovation and technology services, or whether the state should aid innovation through grants or tax concessions directly to the clients. The second is, if the state is going to support the supply side of science and technology, is the general 'council' suitable, or should it focus on smaller, more focused, closer-to-the-client laboratories? The third is, if the council system is maintained, how much of the councils' funding should come from dedicated state funding (the 'parliamentary grant')?

Decisions made so far try to find a sensible path between these choices. Because the science and technology community is relatively small in South Africa at the moment, the councils will be retained for their economies of scale. This allows for long-term investments in equipment and people without expecting instantaneous results. The system will use both supply-side support through the councils and technology stations in higher education institutions and manufacturing advice centres, and support to users through grants or tax concessions, which should rise considerably. And, within 'the science vote' the funds committed to the parliamentary grant slowed in real terms while an increasing proportion of funds were channelled through competitive funds, such as the Innovation Fund, for which the science councils have to compete, and have to form collaborative partnerships with private companies and higher education institutions. Other competitive channels emerged with the creation of Biotechnology Regional Innovation Centres, and are being considered in terms of the strategy for innovation in advanced manufacture, modelled on the CSIR's recently established Automotive Innovation and Development Centre near Pretoria.

However, the biggest underlying concern about the national system of innovation is the constrained supply of people with the skills to innovate. During the 1990s the indicators were negative: a stagnating or declining number of science and engineering graduates; a deterioration in South Africa's relative performance in patenting and publishing in scientific journals; and the average age of South Africa's most productive scientists was rising, and many of them were white males over 50. One of the key constraints was the relatively small number of high-school graduates with suitable maths and science qualifications. The total number of registered professional engineers fell during the 1990s, and though the number of engineering technologists grew, it grew off a low base. These indicators did not bode well for South Africa's future based on competitive innovation (National Advisory Council on Innovation 2004).

The number of registrations in science and engineering degrees began to grow quite rapidly in the 2000s, and, together with the rising percentage of GDP devoted to research and development, this could herald the beginning of a new era of innovation in South Africa.

Strategy development and information programmes

Government support measures should address market failures – where the interests of individual firms contradict their collective longer-term interests. For example, in an economy short of skilled labour, firms are often reluctant to train workers because they expect that competitive firms will poach their trained workers. Without the internalisation of such externalities, firms will often make decisions that are against their own long-term interests and certainly against the long-term interests of the economy as a whole. Government can try to address these conflicts by establishing suitable rules and/or offering appropriate support. In the case of the skilled labour shortage, for example, the government could subsidise firms that offer training to their workers, or it could develop government programmes to increase the supply of suitably skilled workers (see Chapter Five).

Of all markets, one of the most imperfect is the market for information. Imperfect access to information is one of the key factors re-enforcing the inequality between the developed world and the developing world.

In South Africa, political and economic isolation during the apartheid era compounded this problem. South African managers fell behind their counterparts abroad. However, with its sophisticated research, education and communications infrastructure, South Africa should be able to catch up fairly quickly in target areas, with sufficient effort. This was the implicit philosophy behind a series of support measures developed by the DTI, which can be grouped under the heading: strategic and information support.

The first of these initiatives to get a name was the 'cluster programme'. South Africa has a history of industry sector investigations undertaken on the premise that the outcome would consist of a recommendation to government. For example: the import tariff should be increased, and the government should provide additional funds to train workers. In the wake of the Industrial Strategy Project (ISP), the new government's industrial policy leaders believed that, very often, the answer to the challenge of competition was not in the government, but in the firms or group of firms itself: re-engineering, supply-chain management, investment in key inputs, or better training methods, for example. Often the firm or the group of firms did not know what to do because they did not have the capacity to analyse their circumstances; sometimes they knew the answer, but had to be persuaded to do something about it.

More or less simultaneously, influenced by the work of Michael Porter and the Monitor Group, several institutions began to support cluster investigations. In fact, the Monitor Group conducted a study of five South African clusters during 1994, at the invitation of the ANC. The Monitor Group had offered a *pro bono* study, but the

ANC insisted it should be a proper contract. Its findings essentially confirmed those of the ISP – that firms and industries and relationships between firms and industries were inefficient, reflecting outmoded and weak management, poorly trained workers, and a lack of rivalry amongst South African firms. What captured the imagination of South African economic analysts was the Porter methodology, which focused on relationships in addition to the more conventional benchmarking exercises (Porter 1990).

By 1996, about 15 cluster studies were underway, some undertaken by the IDC, some by the DTI, and some under the Japanese Grant Fund of Nedlac. The DTI co-ordinated cluster analysis discussions and training of analysts by international experts from time to time. Not all cluster exercises were the same. The IDC worked mostly with bigger firms and focused on investment opportunities, while some DTI and Nedlac projects tried to bring in smaller firms and look for co-operation opportunities. Cluster studies became 'cluster initiatives', in which the relationships established during the study phase became part of a process of trying to address the problems revealed by the studies. A constant concern of the DTI, though, was to try to ensure that the outcome of the studies or processes was not solely to provide more ammunition for business and labour to lobby government for further support.

The DTI was expected to play a leading role in each cluster process, as well as manage its own. This was unmanageable in view of the weakness of the industrial sector directorates in the DTI and their myriad of other responsibilities. A new mode for encouraging cluster processes was developed – the Sectoral Partnership Fund (SPF). This was a wholly homegrown South African concept, with its roots in the ISP report (Joffe et al. 1995).

The SPF is a scheme to encourage related firms to seek a common solution to a common problem. It is easiest to describe by giving actual examples. A group of South African industrial refrigeration firms recognised that their penetration of the African market was limited not by the quality of their products but by their inferior design – the solution was collaborate on an appropriate design training strategy. A group of wood furniture processors needed to strengthen their bargaining power in relation to timber suppliers, and agreed to set up a purchasing co-operative. The SPF can be used to get such programmes going, if they meet a set of explicit criteria. In the initial version, if the project was approved, the DTI would fund up to 65% of the cost of the project up to a maximum of R3 million.

The DTI launched a similar programme for individual firms called the Competitiveness Fund. Unlike the SPF, the Competitiveness Fund, which pays 50% of the approved cost of consultants, was generated out of a Japanese Grant Fund project, strongly influenced by the World Bank's experiences in Mauritius and Argentina. The two projects were initially financed out of a World Bank loan – the only World Bank loan to the new government. It was a small loan, of about US$25 million, issued in 1998, mainly to allow the South African government to test the waters.

Another 'strategic and information' type support programme was the Workplace Challenge, which was designed at Nedlac to facilitate the joint training of workers and managers in improving productivity in a firm. This was one of the more surprising, successful outcomes of negotiations in the Trade and Industry Chamber of Nedlac. Till then, many workers and unionists had believed that productivity was a synonym for worker exploitation. Many managers probably did too. But, in the context of trade policy reform, and after studying some benchmarking data that showed how poorly South African labour and capital were generally used, workers and managers agreed that they could no longer look away from the harsh glare of competition.

Sharpening the instruments
The debate over competition policy in South Africa is full of ironies. The white business community claimed before and after the 1994 elections to be the upholders of the 'free market' in South Africa. By contrast, the ANC with its socialist background was very sceptical about leaving economic development to market forces alone,

especially after white colonists had used racist policies and violence to establish their economic power in the first place. And yet, when it came to the issue of laws about market structure, the ANC pushed for a tougher pro-competition position than the white capitalists.

Two issues are interwoven in the competition debate in South Africa. The first issue is about the efficient operation of markets. South African capitalism became one of the most highly concentrated and conglomerated forms of capitalism (Du Plessis 1979). The 'mining houses' were so immensely powerful by the 1950s and 1960s that when new gold mine prospects started to dim, they bought up most of the rest of the economy (see Innes 1984). At most, there were six mining houses; some consolidated, and they began to integrate with the major financial institutions. In the 1980s when companies from the United States, Europe and the United Kingdom disinvested their South African holdings, the only available buyers were the already huge South African financial/mining house conglomerates.

The second reason for the anti-monopoly stance of the ANC government is political. The conglomerate empires were built at a time when the majority of the population was excluded from the rights of ownership and wealth. The apartheid government was isolated and needed all the allies it could get, so it was not likely to stand in the way of the conglomerates. The nature of conglomeration in South Africa led to a degree of stagnation in the private sector, and certainly inhibited its response to the new opportunities of the 1990s. Many South Africans believed that there should be a rectification of the legacy of white monopolisation of the economy. In the absence of nationalisation, competition policy was a key tool in this regard.

So, the call to challenge monopolies and oligopolies was powerful rhetoric in the hands of the ANC. The early period of debate was, in retrospect, one of the new South Africa's genuine opportunities for political fun. Then Minister of Trade and Industry, Trevor Manuel, enjoyed baiting the conglomerates. The conglomerates almost invariably dug themselves deeper into a hole whenever they responded.

The chosen spokesperson/victim of big business was Michael Spicer, a senior executive in the Anglo American-De Beers conglomerate. Spicer had come into Anglo specialising in public affairs, and as the personal assistant to Anglo's chair during the 1980s, Gavin Relly. Educated at the elite St Johns College, he attended Rhodes University, unlike many of the Anglo senior executives for whom a spell at Oxford University was de rigueur. By the mid-1990s Spicer had graduated to several Anglo boards, but remained a spokesperson, especially on issues of business-to-government relations.

Conscious of the reversal of ideological roles, Manuel hit out confidently. 'Some of the people who call themselves capitalists in this country would function best in the planned economy of the Soviet Union after 1917,' he said at a business breakfast in Cape Town early in 1995. 'We have capitalists who don't like markets, capitalists who don't want to compete, capitalists who don't want to be capitalists' (*The Argus* 6 March 1995).

'We can't survive like this in the global economy with its high competition and single set of trade rules,' he warned. 'Unless we take an entirely new approach, what's left will die.'

He then promised to introduce a new competition law before the end of the year. The existing law would be 'scrapped and replaced with much stronger legislation, or so substantially amended that it will hardly be recognisable'. Then he emphasised, 'Competition policy must feature very highly in our new approach to the economy' (*The Argus* 6 March 1995).

Another irony was the role played by foreign business in the debate. Local big business argued throughout the early 1990s that South Africa had to implement market-friendly policies in order to attract foreign investment. By 1995, however, prospective foreign investors were telling government and whoever would listen that the key obstacle to direct foreign investment was the defensive behaviour of South Africa's monopolistic conglomerates (*The Argus* 8 April 1995). Manuel could not resist bringing this into the debate from time to time.

The response from big business focused on two main arguments. South Africa's largest firms were not very large by international standards, and South Africa needed big firms to compete internationally. Secondly, they were anxious that ANC politicians should not conflate the issues of economic efficiency and black economic empowerment (BEE) in the competition policy debate. Big business felt that these were two separate issues, and that only the issue of efficiency belonged in the competition policy debate. But even the experienced and articulate Spicer struggled to avoid these arguments sounding like special pleading.

In the event, Manuel could not deliver on his promise to present draft legislation before the end of 1995. Too many other issues preoccupied the DTI to allow it to take on such a major project. Key officials were preoccupied in 1995 and 1996 with implementing the new Small Business Act, and establishing new agencies to support small businesses (see Chapter Six).

Perhaps the delay was fortuitous. By the time the government released its policy document entitled 'Framework for Competition, Competitiveness and Development' late in 1997, much of the hot air had gone out of the debate. Trade and Industry Minister Alec Erwin, his staff, and some skilful consultants piloted a careful course between big business, black business, and labour (which, surprisingly, took up the cause of black business), and delivered legislation to Parliament in May 1998. With some improvements introduced while the bill was before Parliament, it was eventually passed and signed into law in October 1998.

The bulk of the law takes its line from modern competition law, drawing on recent British laws, and on those of some European countries, Canada and Australia, rather than American law. It included several major departures from the old law. It requires for mergers above a certain size to be pre-approved by government. Unlike the old law, it lists anti-competitive practices as possible 'abuses of dominance', which also requires a definition of 'dominance'. Another innovation was the introduction of the concept of 'restrictive vertical practices' in addition to the more conventional 'restrictive horizontal practices'. Exemption provisions allow discretion on the part of the Competition Commission on the grounds of industrial policy considerations, employment considerations, and BEE considerations (Competition Act No. 89 of 1998).

However, BEE is clearly identified as one of the purposes of the law. The other purposes include efficiency, global competitiveness and consumer concerns, employment and welfare considerations, and the desire to build small and medium businesses.

To the surprise of many, and perhaps to the disappointment of the media, the new law was universally acclaimed. In practice it has worked quite well. After some modifications, the merger notification process ran reasonably smoothly. However, those fighting for lower prices, especially for intermediate goods such as semi-processed metals, chemicals, and pulp and paper products, believe that the 'abuse of dominance' provisions of the Competition Act are not effective. The concern is that they fail to address the challenge of import parity pricing – the pricing of goods fractionally under the cost of imports, which allows significant margins when the product has a high weight- or volume-to-value ratio, which makes it relatively costly to transport.

Since 1994 critics of the government, especially on the left, have complained that government has no industrial policy. This is in spite of the numerous measures introduced or considerably modified by government, such as the various investment support, innovation support and strategic and information support programmes developed since 1994, as well as the small business programme discussed in Chapter Six and the competition strategy. The complaint continued even after the launch of the Integrated Manufacturing Strategy in 2002.

Government could easily point to numerous successful interventions – certainly some of the innovation and strategic and information programmes have passed the test of stringent policy reviews. In addition, the Motor Industries Development Programme and the concerted effort to strengthen the tourism sector were notable successes of the late 1990s and early 2000s.

Nonetheless, when compared with successful strategies in East and South-East Asia, South Africa's industrial strategy successes seem modest and few and far between. In the early years after 1994, policy managers felt that government did not have the capacity to engage in sophisticated Asian-style interventions. Government focused instead on broad-brush programmes intended to allow the cream to rise to the top – to reward competence and commitment. Occasionally, such as in the tourism and motor sectors, government did engage effectively with its social partners in efficient development programmes.

It is probably fair to say that government is haunted by the nagging feeling that we could and should be doing more. Surely we know enough to be able to identify some key sectors that can grow faster with effective policies – interventions such as focused innovation support, dedicated training programmes, concerted marketing programmes, or some form of investment support? Why have we not done more of this? Could we not have grown faster than 2.94% per annum in the first 10 years of democracy?

There are several reasons – lack of confidence, a shortage of skilled management, opposition to 'targeting' in some parts of government, lack of suitable modalities with business and labour in some sectors and a range of related institutional factors. The issue has come round again after 10 or more years of democracy as part of the question: how can we sustain a higher level of investment by the private sector? How can we afford not to focus resources on high potential growth and/or employment sectors? These are some questions about industrial policy being posed in the second decade of South Africa's democracy.

Notes

1. Development economists in this tradition would include Raoul Prebisch, Hans Singer, Albert O. Hirschman and Hollis B. Chenery, whereas the economic history evidence is usually traced to Alexander Geschenkron or Simon Kuznets. Singer had contact with numerous South African graduate students at the University of Sussex, whose alumni include many senior civil servants and politicians in South Africa, including the current President, Thabo Mbeki.

2. Some key interpreters or practitioners of the East Asian miracle who have worked with South African policy makers are: Alice Amsden, Sanjaya Lall, Ha-joon Chang, Lin-su Kim, Duck-woo Nam, Daim Zainuddin, Yung Whee Rhee, and economists directly linked to South Africa such as Martin Fransman, Raphael Kaplinsky and Brian Levy.

3. Levy was not alone. Anthony Black's work has a similar perspective. Most World Bank economists working on South African trade and industry followed this position, as did I, to an extent, in my own report 'Trading up: trade policy for industrialization in South Africa' (Hirsch 1993). The Industrial Strategy project synthesis shared key assumptions with the Levy approach (Joffe et al. 1995).

4. See Fallon and Perreira de Silva (1994: chapter 3) for a discussion on the quantity and quality of investment in South Africa until 1993; and Nattrass (1990a) on profits.

CHAPTER FIVE

Jobs and skills

Remaking the labour market

How the jobs crisis tested the governing alliance

Early in 1998, the Congress of South African Trade Unions (COSATU) fired a shot across the bow of the ANC. It demanded that, in return for continuing to support the ANC election alliance, it, and the other alliance member, the South African Communist Party (SACP) wanted to enter into 'bona fide' negotiations on 'fundamental policies' (*Mail and Guardian* 16–22 January 1998).

Zwelinzima Vavi, then Deputy Secretary-General of COSATU, announced the confrontation. Vavi is a tall, well-built man, with a forthright demeanour. He singled out the Growth, Employment and Redistribution (GEAR) strategy as the unions' target. 'Any macroeconomic programme that fails to deliver jobs and decent salaries to the poor is wrong,' he said. '[I]t would be immoral for COSATU not to speak out' (*Mail and Guardian* 16–22 January 1998).

After growing well during the first three years of the new government, the economy slowed down. While exports still grew, the job market stagnated and unemployment rose. In spite of this, the government continued to pursue a fiscal policy that COSATU saw as contractionary. It sought to bring the deficit down by re-engineering government, which included cutting back on government employment, holding government wage increases to low real levels, and privatising or restructuring a range of state-owned companies.

The government promised a Jobs Summit during 1998 – where

its leaders would meet with those of business and labour and 'the community' to attempt to agree on strategies and programmes that might deliver sufficient new jobs. But the role of the summit was still unclear; visions ranged from a wide-reaching wages and prices pact, to little more than an opportunity for grandstanding by unreconciled social partners.

In spite of the uncertainties, government did not shrink back. President Mandela chose his state of the nation speech early in February 1998 to endorse the 'leaner government' strategy. The opening of Parliament speech is the equivalent of an American presidential state of the union address, or the Queen's speech to the British Parliament. It sets the parameters for the legislative year. Mandela spoke of the need to shed some of the 1.2 million public sector jobs as a key strategy to eliminate government overspending. Minister of Finance, Trevor Manuel, underlined the message. 'There is no room for equivocation' on public sector employment, he said. 'We've got our battle orders to get this thing in line' (*Sunday Times: Business Times* 8 February 1998).

The South African Municipal Workers' Union (SAMWU) replied angrily. The union's 'anti-privatisation co-ordinator', Maria van Driel, slammed the ANC's endorsement of GEAR at its December 1997 three-yearly national conference as 'immoral'. Van Driel portrayed GEAR as a tool of financial capitalists who promote neo-liberal policies to allow them maximum freedom to make profits. As business taxes are cut to boost profits, fiscal pressures force government to privatise. Privatisation leads to the fragmentation of the working class, and to inferior conditions for workers. So, SAMWU called on COSATU, its federation, to 'maintain its convictions regarding the rejection of GEAR', and not to 'pander to the ANC' (*Sowetan* 16 February 1998).

Had the economy been growing strongly, SAMWU's appeal might have been seen as special pleading. But the economy was cooling off fast. The onset of the Asian crisis in 1997 had encouraged the South African Reserve Bank (SARB) to maintain excessively high interest rates, and then raise them still further.

This attracted a growing pile of short-term foreign credit that was soon to lead banks and ratings agencies to view South Africa as an investment risk. A growing fear that the Asian contagion would not spare South Africa meant that growth rate projections of 2–2.6% early in the year were soon edging downwards. There was no silver cloud. Vavi's contention that the poor could not wait 20 years for delivery began to resonate.

Shortly before Trevor Manuel presented the 1998–99 budget to Parliament, COSATU's Vavi struck again, this time with a critique of the role of Parliament in the formulation and implementation of fiscal policy. He both appealed to the populist sentiments of the ANC parliamentary members to engage with the fiscal process in order to produce a 'People's budget', and chided them for not doing enough. 'Parliament's role is limited to symbolic comments, and the holding of hearings that will not make any difference to the Budget,' he mocked (*Cape Times: Business Report* 6 March 1998).

During the pre-budget assault, the union and SACP theme was that the GEAR budget deficit target was 'arbitrary' and 'too tight'. Trevor Manuel could not resist reminding his left-wing critics that 'while balanced budgets are the stuff of market orthodoxy now, Karl Marx warned against public debt in *Das Kapital*' (*Business Day* 9 March 1998).

But COSATU was not convinced. The next day it announced that it was withdrawing from the parliamentary hearings on the budget. Normally, COSATU, like other interested parties, would submit its views to the parliamentary committee that was responsible for taking the bill to Parliament. It would also expect the former COSATU union leaders amongst the ANC parliamentarians to promote the cause. This time it decided to boycott the committee process to convey its anger about the perceived inability of the committee to have a 'real impact on Budget decisions' (*Cape Times* 3 March 1998).

In truth, the committee was not entirely powerless. As is the case for all 'money bills' in South Africa, the committee could not amend the budget bill, but could only return it to the drafters in the government. To some degree, then, COSATU was protesting at the party unity and discipline of the ANC parliamentary caucus. Some bills, even money bills, have been blocked or amended by ANC-dominated parliamentary committees. But for the ANC-dominated parliamentary committee to challenge the budget would have been tantamount to a vote of no confidence in the Cabinet and the ANC leadership.

Union anger continued to smoulder in the run-up to the COSATU and SACP congresses in mid-year. Sometimes this was reflected in documents that were circulated in preparation for the Jobs Summit. For example, the first labour input to the Presidential Jobs Summit called on government to sustain current levels of public sector employment by 'lower(ing) interest rates, restructuring the taxation system and reducing the burden of apartheid debt'. It also called on government to reverse trade policy reform, and to pass further laws to regulate the labour market (COSATU et al. 1998a).

Tripartite meetings between the ANC, COSATU and the SACP failed to reduce the temperature of the debate. In draft resolutions prepared for a mid-year central committee meeting, COSATU reaffirmed 'its rejection of GEAR and the government's macro-economic practices'. COSATU revived its own pet obsession saying: 'We reject the obsession around deficit reduction' (*Financial Mail* 19 June 1998). (The government had proposed a gradual reduction of the fiscal deficit from 5.1% in 1996 to 3% in 2000.) The SACP documents for its July congress adopted a similar tone. Commenting on these developments, political reporter, Justice Malala, wrote in the *Financial Mail*: 'The divisions over GEAR are the deepest that the tripartite alliance has ever experienced' (*Financial Mail* 19 June 1998).

In his speech to the COSATU meeting, Deputy President Thabo Mbeki, who had been elected President of the ANC in December 1997, acknowledged the perilous state of the alliance: '[W]hen we speak of this strategic alliance, are we speaking of something that continues to exist, or are we dreaming dreams of the past?' he asked. 'Does a Congress movement still exist[?] Do we have the right to call one another Comrades signifying a commitment to our being fellow combatants for liberation . . . or are we calling one another Comrade simply because we are no longer used to calling one another Mr, Mrs or Miss' (Mbeki 1998b: 2).

President Mandela was equally challenging at the SACP meeting a week later. Mandela departed from his prepared text when he heard SACP leader, Charles Nqakula, and a COSATU representative criticise the GEAR programme. Mandela thundered: 'GEAR, as I have said before, is the fundamental policy of the ANC. We will not change it because of your pressure. If you feel you cannot get your way (then) go out and shout like opposition parties. Prepare to face the full implications of that line' (*Business Day* 2 July 1998).

Then Mandela called on the SACP to 'choose a role you want to play'. After a polite comment from the chairperson of the session, the hall sat in stunned silence as Mandela slowly departed (*Business Day* 2 July 1998).

One reason for Mandela's anger was the fact that the Asian contagion seemed to entail potential danger for South Africa. Standard and Poor's risk study in July 1998 placed South Africa second riskiest, after Indonesia, on a list of 10 emerging economies (*Business Day* 17 July 1998). Though this was soon shown to be rather inaccurate by the Russian and Brazilian crises, it demonstrated the vulnerability of the South African economy. In this context, the posturing of COSATU and the SACP seemed like disloyalty to the ANC.

The looming Jobs Summit took on an added significance. Not only did it need to come up with feasible strategies to address the unemployment crisis, it also had to show the world that South Africans were not fragmenting, but were working together for the future of the whole country. This was how the ANC leaders and the government increasingly saw the Jobs Summit.

To achieve this objective would require two necessary conditions: firstly that the parties agree on some more or less significant policies or programmes that could make a dent on unemployment, and secondly, that the ANC and its alliance partners patch their wounds through some symbolic re-engagement. It also required a degree of agreement amongst the social partners about the causes of the unemployment problem, an issue that had long been the subject of an acrimonious debate.

In the end there was a Jobs Summit in October 1998, with a set of agreements. But the limited nature of the agreements and the poor follow-through after the summit showed how far apart the major economic actors were, both in their analysis of the causes of unemployment and on the appropriate solutions. Trade-offs to reach agreement left the country with a lowest common denominator outcome. For example, business agreed not to raise questions about labour laws and regulations, and labour agreed to lay off its criticism of the GEAR strategy. One of the few substantive outcomes was an agreement to develop a programme to support the purchase of locally made products and services that ultimately became the Proudly South African campaign, but even this took years to implement because of residual disagreements about the orientation of the programme.

What did the Jobs Summit achieve? One important achievement was that it showed that when it came down to it, business, labour and government could at least achieve a show of unity to the rest of the world. Another achievement was that it encouraged business to come up with a novel and exciting programme to establish a business trust to support economic development programmes, but the trust was not a formal outcome of the Summit.

A similarly indirect outcome of the Jobs Summit was that its mediocrity suggested to then Deputy President, Thabo Mbeki, that new channels of communication should be opened up between the major economic stakeholders. One of the weaknesses of Nedlac was that it was becoming a meeting point for middle-level leaders from business, labour and government – especially the business contingent. These were often representatives with vague mandates and no authority to improvise. The senior leadership of business, government and labour seldom met, and when they did they focused on procedure rather than substance. Mbeki established channels of communication directly with leaders of business and labour – eventually four economic 'working groups' were established under Mbeki after he became president in 1999. They are: a Big Business Working Group, a Black Business Working Group, a Trade Union Working Group and a Commercial Agriculture Working Group (for black and white farmers). Each of these groups of leaders meets with the President and an appropriate group of Cabinet Ministers and Deputy Ministers, plus some senior staff, usually twice annually. Twice a year there is usually a Joint Working Group meeting where all four groups meet together with the President, ministers and a few top officials.

The meetings are essentially opportunities to exchange views and voice concerns – they are not sites for negotiation, and they are private. This has allowed for unusually free and frank exchanges. The *Towards a Ten Year Review* publication of the government remarked that one of the constraints on investment and growth in South Africa was the lack of trust between the economic and political elites because of the historical reality that most business leaders were white and most political leaders were black, and that they shared very few experiences (Policy Co-ordination and Advisory Services, The Presidency 2003). This was one of the key reasons for the establishment of the working group system. The other, related reason for the working groups is that the President clearly believes that there are structural impediments to growth and development that can only be confronted in frank exchanges between the major economic stakeholders. One of the slogans of Mbeki's ANC in the 2004 election campaign was 'A people's contract for growth and development'. Mbeki and his party clearly believe that in order for the ceiling on growth to be breached, more and deeper mutual commitments are required between the social partners. This is why Mbeki called for a Growth and Development Summit, which took place in June 2003. The key targets of the Growth and Development Summit, like those of the Jobs Summit in 1998, were to roll back unemployment and poverty.

How bad is the unemployment problem?

South Africans believe that the biggest economic problem in South Africa is unemployment. Opinion surveys show an overwhelming and still rising consensus that not 'poverty', 'low wages', 'housing' or 'inequality', but specifically 'unemployment' is South Africa's key challenge. The unemployment rate is very high in South Africa.

Unemployment is generally seen as a synonym for poverty. Certainly, poverty surveys in South Africa have shown that the poorer you are, the more likely you are to be unemployed, and that poorer households have a higher percentage of members who are unemployed (May 1998: 81–86). So, unemployment and poverty have become almost indistinguishable in South Africa.

Just how large the unemployment problem is, is not a simple question. An International Labour Organisation (ILO)-sponsored study proposed 14 reasons why employment estimates produced by the South African government might be wrong – mostly under-estimating employment levels (Standing et al. 1996: 68–71). Unemployment statistics were a terrain of political debate during the apartheid years, and remain politically charged.

In response to this challenge, the South African government's revamped statistical agency – Statistics South Africa – overhauled the employment measurement machinery in the late 1990s. Household surveys were introduced to compliment the census data and the firms-based surveys. The October Household Survey (OHS) was introduced in 1995 and became the Labour Force Survey (LFS) in 2000. The estimate of unemployment for September 2004 was 26%, which is considerably worse than the level of about 17% recorded in 1995. This is according to the 'official definition', which uses the convention that a person is unemployed if he has not worked in the previous seven days, was available to take up work within a week of the interview, and had sought work or self-employment in the past four weeks. If one uses an 'expanded unemployment rate' that does not require that the person sought work in the past four weeks, the rate rises to 40%, compared with 27% in 1995 (Statistics South Africa 1998; LFS, various).

Unemployment is very unevenly distributed. A very high proportion of young people are unemployed – 75% of the unemployed are under the age of 35. This is partly a result of queuing, poor, young people slowly making themselves employable or finding self-employment, and partly a result of the likelihood that more people over 35 no longer seek work, though they are unemployed. Unemployment weighs more heavily on 'African' South Africans, compared with 'coloured', 'Indian' and 'white' South Africans who have respectively increasingly lower levels of unemployment. Historically, unemployment has been higher in the rural areas of South Africa. This was an anomaly by all standards, the result of the influx control policies of the apartheid government. Part of the purpose of apartheid was the removal of black unemployed people from politically vulnerable urban centres to remote rural areas. Many, especially the poorly educated, still find it very hard to escape what are effectively rural poverty ghettos. The remoteness and backwardness of the former 'African reserves' raises the costs of job seeking to a level that many poor households can barely afford. This situation rapidly adjusted in the post-1994 period, though there is still an unusually high level of unemployment in South Africa's rural areas (Statistics South Africa 1998, 2003).

Does this mean that South Africa experienced jobless growth? Growth has averaged about 3% in the post-1994 era, but what happened to employment? This is a matter of some controversy, as the employment data doesn't offer definitive answers. The definitive employment series, the bi-annual LFS, began in 2000. Though it picked up where the OHS (1995–99) left off, there are discontinuities in some definitions. For example, the definition of employment in the informal sector changed a little with the LFS, and some analysts argue that the early OHSs undercounted employment in some sectors. There are also weighting issues, but these are relatively easy to accommodate.

The alternative measures are not any better. The Survey of Earning and Employment, a firm-based sample survey, deteriorated during the 1990s, and when the sample was re-based in 2002 to accommodate structural changes in the economy, the index of employment increased by 40%. The population census has very limited questions on employment, and, in this respect, is seen by the statistical service as no more than a way of roughly verifying the employment data of the LFS.

The lack of a consistent employment series going back beyond 2000 made the issue of employment statistics politically controversial, both between the ANC government and the opposition, and between the ANC and its ally, COSATU.

According to various OHS/LFS surveys, about 9.5 million people were employed in 1995, with about 8.3 million in the formal sector. By 2003, about 11.5 million people were employed in South Africa, with about 8.2 million in the formal sector. The increase in employment came largely from the domestic workers (0.3 million), subsistence farmers (0.4 million), and the rest of the informal sector (1.4 million). However, as subsistence farmers were not counted in 1995, this number should be discounted as a trend. Within the formal sector there were significant shifts, with commercial agriculture falling from 1.1 million in 1995 to 0.9 million in 2003, the public sector falling from 1.7 million to 1.6 million, and the private non-agricultural sector rising from 5.5 million in 1995 to 5.8 million in 2003. About 20% of employees were temporary, casual or had fixed-term contracts.

In short, according to the OHS/LFS surveys, the number of employed people rose by something in the vicinity of 2 million people, but it could be as high as 2.2 million, or as low as 1.5 million. Most of the new jobs in the 1990s were in the informal sector, and, especially after 1999, a rise in formal non-agricultural employment compensated for a fall in farm workers and public servants.

Though it is not desirable that so many of the new jobs came from the informal sector, at least growth in private sector non-agricultural jobs compensated for the fall in farm employment and public servants – the latter a result of the belt-tightening exercises of the late 1990s. Another important trend is the revival of the private sector job market after the pain of restructuring in the 1990s. While private formal sector non-agricultural jobs fell from 5.5 million in 1995 to 5.0 million in 1999–2000, they then grew to 5.8 million by 2003. By contrast, almost all of the growth of informal sector jobs took place before 2000, after which this sector was virtually stagnant.

The mean rate of overall job growth was about 2.1% per year – with a mean economic growth rate of about 2.8% per year. This suggests a coefficient of 0.75 between the rate of growth and the rate of job creation. This is a relatively elastic employment response. Assuming that elasticity is in fact 0.75, a steady growth rate of 4% would yield a job creation rate of 3% per annum, or about 345 000 net new jobs per annum (Bhorat 2003). There are substantial differences in the employment elasticity of different sectors, so the sectoral composition of growth would be significant. Also, a significant proportion of these new jobs may be in the informal sector, and some may be temporary, casual or fixed-term contracts.

Even though employment grew between 1995 and 2003, the number of unemployed and the rate of unemployment grew steadily. How is this possible? How can it be that unemployment grew in spite of the fact that job creation grew faster than the population growth rate?

The answer is that the economically active population (EAP) grew at an exceptionally fast rate over the same period. The EAP consists of those people who are either employed or who are seeking employment, and are aged between 15 and 65. The EAP grew from 11.4 million in 1995 to 16.8 million in 2003. This represents a growth rate of about 5% per year, which is well above the population growth rate (about 1.6% in 2003). Why should the EAP have grown so exceptionally fast over this period? Studies suggest that the main factor is that many African women, who defined themselves outside of the job market in 1995, now define themselves as employed or seeking work. This is a result of migration from the rural areas, a degree of social liberation of women, and the fact that a very significant proportion of the new jobs created since 1995 were open

to and attracted African women. Another factor could be the rising
education levels (Posel and Casale 2003).

So we have a paradoxical situation. Because of the very rapid
growth of the EAP (people defining themselves as employed or
seeking jobs), the fact that we have had job growth has not prevented
the unemployment rate from rising rapidly to over 30% in 2003
before falling back to 26% in 2004.

What this suggests is that the social and demographic changes
we have experienced since the mid-1990s have made the task of
reducing the rate of unemployment even more difficult than we
expected. A key question for which there are no definitive answers
yet is: will the labour force participation rate continue to rise, and
if so how quickly? The trend-line for labour force participation seems
to have flattened in the 2000s at around 68%, but it is still relatively
low compared with developed countries.

What causes unemployment in South Africa?

We should explore the 'market clearing' approach first. It dominates
international perceptions of South Africa for those influenced by
the Bretton Woods institutions – in a sense the economic policy
elite.

The inflexible labour market

It has been argued for a while now that the labour market in South
Africa is less flexible than it should be, as a result of political and
institutional factors. Some of these factors, such as racial and gender
prejudice, are relics of the past. Some, like revised labour laws and
the role of trade unions in economic management through Nedlac,
are products of the political transformation. The leading role of
trade unions in the struggle for democracy meant that they won
victories that sheltered the determination of wages for black workers
from the unforgiving heat of the markets.

South African trade unions have a strong egalitarian streak,
and tend to strive for the narrowing of wide wage gaps, so that
unskilled workers got the most benefit. The new government

followed suit by raising the wages of the lowest ranks of government employees most rapidly. So, the loss of 'flexibility' or responsiveness to markets became most significant for the unskilled sector.

Peter Fallon of the World Bank and Robert Lucas from Boston University reviewed the evidence of market clearing problems in a 1998 study. They did not blame unemployment simply on the inflexibility of the labour market, but they saw it as a key factor.

Fallon and Lucas showed that the wages of white workers were more responsive to changes in labour market conditions than the wages of black workers. In other words, if the wage employment of Africans and whites each fell by 1%, real African wages would fall by only 0.22–0.27%, but white wages would fall by between 0.93–3.18%. This shows, they argued, that white workers' wages react more efficiently to changes in labour market conditions. The data also showed that unskilled wages adjusted most slowly to changes in market conditions. The rise in unemployment levels from 1980–94 should have led to wages falling for African workers, but they rose by 20% (Fallon and Lucas 1998: 12–14).

The main reason for African wages reacting perversely in relation to levels of unemployment is the strength of the black trade unions, argued Fallon and Lucas. This argument is supported by the finding, according to one survey, that a unionised unskilled worker would be paid a remarkable 71% more than an non-unionised worker with the same lack of skills (SALDRU 1993).

It is not really a matter for dispute that unskilled and semi-skilled workers in the formal sector in South Africa are paid relatively more than their counterparts in some other parts of the world, including the surrounding countries of southern Africa. There is evidence of this in all the major studies drawn on for this chapter, whether written by or for the left or the right (Fallon and Lucas 1998: 12–14).

In my own work in the 1980s I found that workers employed in Bantustan factories outside of the South African wage bargaining system, were paid around half as much as workers in similar employment in a nearby town lying outside the Bantustan, and around one quarter of the average wage for Africans in the relevant sector in South Africa (Hirsch 1987: 268–271).

In an informal survey in 1994, I found that basic operatives in the textile and metal working industries were paid about 15 times more in South Africa than in Tanzania. But the wage level did not mean that South African workers had a standard of living 15 times better than their counterparts in Dar es Salaam – apartheid led to excessively high living costs for workers in South Africa, especially transport costs as a result of population location policies, as we shall discuss shortly.

The big question, though, is whether, and to what extent, the high level of unemployment amongst unskilled workers can be attributed to labour market inflexibilities and distortions. One example of the explanation of unemployment that emphasises the inflexibility of labour markets for the unskilled is found in the 1996 South Africa Foundation *Growth for All* document, and in several iterations of the International Monetary Fund's (IMF) annual Article IV South Africa staff report (for example, IMF 1998: 19–21).

The South Africa Foundation's *Growth for All* document gave the impression, deliberately or accidentally, that the main cause of unemployment was the distorted labour market resulting from union pressure and government regulation. For this reason, the report emphasised the need for restructuring the labour market as a 'two-tier market' and seemed to underplay other possible corrective actions (South Africa Foundation 1996: chapter 6).

This was an analytical and a political error. Political, because it set up a conflict between other social forces and the unions which, with their backs rubbing up against the proverbial wall, linked arms and marched forward. It forced the ANC, if temporarily, into the arms of the unions. It led to damage in the social fabric that was only partly patched up nearly three years later at the Jobs Summit.

But why was it an *analytical mistake*? The main problem is that it ignored the history of South African unemployment. According to Charles Simkins, an authoritative analyst of the history of unemployment in South Africa, unemployment probably began to escalate in the 1960s, during an economic boom, and in a period when black trade unions were banned and black workers were severely oppressed. Simkins found that black (African) unemployment, broadly defined, already stood at about 12% in 1970 and rose to slightly more than 2 million, or 21%, by 1981 (Simpkins 1982). According to the official Current Population Survey, narrowly defined unemployment was already as high as 13% in 1977, and another official government report put broadly defined unemployment at 30% in 1980 (Archer et al. 1990: 166–167).

Structural unemployment
Black trade unions only began to re-emerge in the mid-1970s, after being crushed by the apartheid government in the early 1960s. Trade unionism for Africans was only re-legalised in 1979, having been excluded from the bargaining system in the 1950s. Therefore black trade unions cannot be blamed for the emergence of high levels of unemployment in modern South Africa. It is even hard to blame high wages, as black wages in the 1960s, when unemployment emerged as a significant phenomenon, were at historically low levels.

This realisation led to South African analysts resorting to a concept of 'structural unemployment' that differed from the inflexibility argument. 'Structural unemployment' explained David Lewis, 'refers to a deep-seated disjuncture between the growth and structure of the national workforce on the one hand and the growth and structure of economic activity on the other hand' (Lewis 1991: 246).

One explanation, used by Alec Erwin before he left academia for the trade unions, and many years before he became a Cabinet Minister, was that capitalism in South Africa was incomplete – it was a stunted, colonial version of capitalism that could not generate balanced growth or adequate employment (Erwin 1978). The implication was that South African production should move into fields controlled by the advanced capitalist countries – that South Africans should not be confined to mining and exporting gold and making consumer products for the domestic market only.

A later version was that South Africa was unable to make a transition to a more modern form of capitalism than stunted 'racial fordism' because of the nature of white racist political rule (Gelb 1991a). Black progress in the job market, into skilled, professional and managerial roles, was incompatible with white minority rule. This had elements in common with Erwin's approach, in that both suggested that the anti-colonial struggle had to be completed for South Africa to make the transition to a healthy growing economy.

White rule and its opposition to the development of a competitive black middle class in the modern urban sector set up obstacles to black business (see Chapters One and Six), demolished black education, and decimated industrial training systems as white artisans moved into managerial positions. A reasonably good apprenticeship system for whites was virtually destroyed, and not replaced. The result was that an annual global survey of competitiveness placed South Africa last in 'investment in people' virtually every year since 1994 (*Cape Times: Business Report* 18 September 1998; Garelli 1998).

Another approach was to show how the incentive structure of the South African economy favoured capital-intensive investments in the 1970s and 1980s. The structure of protection, subsidies on investment, and low or negative interest rates conspired against the employment of unskilled workers. As Merle Lipton put it:

> This distortion of relative factor prices (making capital artificially cheap and labour dear) led to a costly and inefficient development path. It encouraged capital intensity, thus increasing the demand for scarce resources such as capital and skill, while discouraging the use of what by the 1960s had become a surplus of unskilled labour, so contributing to growing unemployment (1986: 244).[1]

Certainly, South Africa experienced very low or negative interest rates (tilting investment towards capital-intensive projects) for most of the latter half of the 1970s and most of the 1980s. One could extend this argument into a critique of certain investment incentives that encouraged capital-intensive projects, such as Section 37e of the Income Tax Act in the early 1990s, or of the investment priorities and organisational bias of the Industrial Development Corporation (IDC).

Trade unions and a government that was soft on workers did not create the unemployment problem. Apartheid's social and economic policies were the main cause. However, there is a risk, identified by not only business, the World Bank and the GEAR strategy, but even by the government's own study of poverty and inequality in South Africa, that emerging rigidities in South African labour markets could block investment and employment opportunities.

The GEAR strategy pointed to the need for 'a more flexible labour market'. It indicated that wage settlements and agreements should 'be sensitive to regional labour market conditions, the diversity of skills levels in firms of varying size, location or capital intensity, and the need to foster training opportunities for new entrants to the labour market'. Industrial agreements 'which reach across diverse firms, sectors, or regions should be sufficiently flexible to avoid job losses and should be extended to non-parties only when this can be assured'. The GEAR strategy also argued against the establishment of a national minimum wage, but rather that minimum wages should be set appropriately for sectors and areas and should take into account 'the potential for employment creation and the alleviation of poverty' (Department of Finance 1996: 18–19).

The GEAR report pointed to three key problem areas: the peri-urban and rural regions where unemployment is high; small firms, which cannot yet support top-class conditions; and the never-been-employed youth. As the Poverty Report notes, a more flexible labour market will help draw in the unemployed, though it must be tempered with as much job security as possible, and through government improving the social wage – improved access to public services and facilities for the poor (May 1998: 90).

Perhaps the most important regulatory issues in this respect concern: the capacity to extend bargaining council agreements to non-parties (for instance, to small towns); the powers of the Employment Conditions Commission (for workers not represented in bargaining councils); and the wage-setting example of the government sector. All three should be carefully managed so as to avoid bidding unemployed people out of the system.

Trade liberalisation and unemployment

There was heated debate over the effects of the trade liberalisation programme on employment. In an early submission for the Jobs Summit, the trade unions urged:

> Stop the damaging effects which trade liberalisation has on employment. Where South Africa has lowered individual tariffs to below GATT commitments and these have resulted in job losses, these must be increased up to the GATT binding rate (COSATU et al. 1998a: 2).

But the evidence on the relationship between trade liberalisation and employment is hard to evaluate, especially on a sector-by-sector basis. Johannesburg-based economist Simon Roberts noted that there is no workable 'general explanation' on the effects of the tariff reform programme on growth and employment, and that 'recent developments can only be understood through an examination of sub-sector specific factors together with industrial structure'. His sectoral study failed to establish consistent results. In some sectors exports and employment increased, in others both decreased, while in some, exports grew but output and employment stagnated or declined. For manufacturing overall, exports grew steadily, but employment stagnated or declined (Roberts 1998: 26).

A trend that has been noted is that much of the strength in manufactured exports has come from the more capital-intensive sectors of manufacturing, while a significant proportion of the increase in imports is in labour-intensive sectors (Bell and Caettaneo 1997). However, another broad trend, detected by an ILO study, is that jobs have generally been gained in the non-tradable and import-competing sectors, and lost in the export sectors in spite of output and export growth in these sectors. It also found that sectors with significant tariff cuts performed best with regards production, exports, employment, wages and productivity. Part of the explanation is that export sectors have been forced to streamline in the light of a higher competitive temperature and the disappearance of export subsidies. More recent academic work has come to similar conclusions (Hayter 1999: 2–6; Edwards 2001: 40–72).

It is possible to come to two alternative policy proposals. One would be to suggest that liberalisation is a mistake if your economy is not sufficiently competitive in labour-absorbing industries – the problem is that only capital-intensive sectors are reaping the export benefits of greater efficiency (Bell and Caettaneo 1997). The alternative would be to address the problems in the labour market, to improve the supply of cheaper, sufficiently skilled labour, and to remove obstacles to investment in the labour-intensive sectors so that efficiency gains could be exploited in employment-absorbing sectors (Nattrass 1998; Tsikata 1998).

Bear in mind that some of these studies misunderstand the main purpose of trade reform, which is to remove price distortions in the domestic market. As Minister Alec Erwin argued in his presentation to the Jobs Summit, the tariff reform programme is 'designed to induce previously protected enterprises to become more efficient and to reduce domestic cost levels so that they are closer to general world cost levels' (Erwin 1998: 5). This makes the economy as a whole more competitive, and will encourage investment and job creation, but will not necessarily produce predictable results on a sub-sector by sub-sector basis, unless the analyst is able to account for all the particularities that frustrated Simon Roberts in his study. There will also be lags between negative and positive effects in some sectors. A U-shaped labour demand curve should be the anticipated outcome of a significant trade policy reform.

The floor price of labour in South Africa

But there is an underlying and rather obvious point that must be made. There are very few labour-intensive manufactured tradables that South Africa is likely to be competitive in. The competitive labour-intensive sectors will be those where South African producers are able to exploit an underlying advantage, such as cheap or special access to natural resources, or a preferential market arrangement. To put it another way, no matter how much the labour market is made more flexible or the currency is depreciated, South Africa will never have tens of thousands of workers making Nike shoes for export, like Vietnam or Thailand.

Why is this? One reason is the strength of the trade unions combined with the country's human rights culture. Tables 5.1 and 5.2 indicate the growth of worker rights, and the continuation of worker militancy in democratic South Africa. Another reason for relatively high wages is the high cost of living in South Africa. Apartheid raised living costs for all South Africans, especially the poor, one of the main costs being apartheid-determined residential locations (Department of Transport 1998). The working poor were located miles from their potential places of work, and often equally far from commercial and public services. Public transport systems had practically collapsed by 1994, and some of the new distant locations were not served at all by public transport. Though public transport services have begun to improve under the new democratic government, pressures to reduce the government deficit forced it to reduce subsidies that might have helped the poor and working poor use public transport. The deterioration of access to public services such as education, heath, and social security for Africans under apartheid meant the diminution of the social wage.

Table 5.1: Key new labour laws since 1994.

Name of law	Main purposes	Signed
Labour Relations Act	Framework for collective bargaining, rights of unions, right to strike and lockout, introduction of voluntary workplace forums, resolution of disputes.	1995 & 1996
Basic Conditions of Employment Act	Provides framework for applying minimum standards for workers not covered by the LRA, and sets overall minimum standards for hours of work, leave conditions, dismissal procedures, overtime pay, and restrictions on exploitation of children.	1997
Employment Equity Act	Framework for reporting plans for and the implementation of the removal of race and gender discrimination in larger firms.	1998
Skills Development Act and Skills Development Levies Act	To institute a compulsory training levy of 1% (starting at 0.5%) of a firm's annual wage bill, which can be reclaimed if the firm reports equivalent spending on training approved by an independent certification authority, or it is used to train other workers or potential workers.	1998 & 1999

Moreover, in South Africa the earned wage represents a much higher proportion of most households' income than is the case in some surrounding African countries, where many workers have non-wage incomes often deriving from their rural land-holdings. In South Africa the expulsion of Africans from the land was far more complete under a vicious form of settler colonialism than it was in most African countries where settler interests were weaker. South Africa has neither significant agricultural subsistence income nor a sufficient social wage for worker households. If living standards were actually 15 times higher in South Africa than in Mozambique and Tanzania, illegal immigration would be much higher than current high levels.

It will take time to bring down the cost of living and raise the social wage for the poor and working poor in South Africa. Trade liberalisation has already helped to reduce the cost of living of the urban poor, and there is further downwards potential for the price

Table 5.2: Person-days lost in strikes in South Africa, 1990–2002.

Year	Person-days lost
1990	2 200 000
1991	1 000 000
1992	3 100 000
1993	2 400 000
1994	2 500 000
1995	870 000
1996	1 700 000
1997	650 000
1998	2 300 000
1999	3 100 000
2000	500 000
2001	1 250 000
2002	945 000
2003	700 000

Source: According to labour consultants,
Andrew Levy and Associates,
extracted from various issues of the
Mail & Guardian; ww.finance24.co.za
30 March 2004; *Andrew Levy Strike
Report* 30 June 2003.

of wage goods in southern Africa. The social wage is improving as the poor and working poor get better access to health and education services. In the future new urban residential and transport policies could help too. As the cost of living and the social wage of the working class improves, and as the number of suitably skilled workers increases, competition for employment should prevent the cost of employment from rising too fast. In the meantime, though, it is important to ensure that opportunities for employing the poor from what President Mbeki calls the second economy (the marginalised poor) are not forgone due to inappropriate regulatory constraints.

The skills challenge
The skills crisis in South Africa in some ways resembles the

challenges facing many other countries, but in several important ways it is unique. What it has in common with the rest of the world is that the structure of the economy has changed more quickly than the institutions that impart education and skills. The decline of employment on the mines and farms, and in some other sectors, and the rapid rise of employment opportunities in the service sector and more skilled jobs in the manufacturing sector, was as dramatic in South Africa as in any other country. Employment in mining fell by about 40% in the 1990s, while employment in the financial services sector rose by 300%, to illustrate the shift (SARB 2005: table S-138).

More specific to South Africa are the historical reasons for the weakness of the supply of skilled workers. The damage to the general education system done by apartheid is briefly described in an earlier chapter. The system of industrial training was equally damaged by apartheid. The job colour bar meant that there was no point in training Africans as artisans or professionals. It was illegal to award apprenticeships to Africans. In addition, the system of industrial training was falling behind modern industrial trends. This was recognised by training experts in the old regime, and was detailed in reports commissioned by the National Manpower Commission and the National Training Board published from the early 1980s to the early 1990s. The problem was that the continuation of apartheid meant that the reforms proposed by the Commission were difficult to implement. The education system was fragmented, the training system was decentralised and un-integrated, and the colour bar still ruled (Kraak 2004a).

The result was that the number of people trained in enterprise training programmes fell dramatically, by more than 75%. Whereas in 1986, 736 581 people were exposed to industrial training, of whom 29 826 were apprentices in training, by 1998 the total number of industrial trainees had fallen to 152 870, of whom only 16 577 were trainee apprentices. The system of industrial training was disintegrating, and was not yet replaced by a more modern and non-racial system (Badroodien 2003).

The result is what is now widely termed a mismatch between the supply of labour (unskilled) and the demand for labour (skilled) in South Africa. Iraj Abedian, then chief economist at the Standard Bank, estimated that 300 000 vacancies remain unfilled in South Africa because of the shortage of suitably skilled labour (Abedian 2004). It can also be speculated that South Africa would have received considerably more domestic and foreign investment had there been sufficient numbers of suitably skilled people.

The government's response had its origins in COSATU policies that sought industrial training to support multi-skilling, and the broader development of workers. The driver of the Skills Development strategy in the Department of Labour after 1994 was Adrienne Bird who, before 1994, led the discussion on industrial training in COSATU as an official in the Metal and Allied Workers' Union (MAWU). A human resources green paper surfaced in 1996, followed by a Skills Development strategy green paper in 1997 and a Skills Development Act in 1998. Finally, in 2001, the Minister of Labour launched the national Skills Development strategy (Kraak 2004b).

One reason why the process was so extended (Adrienne Bird published a paper outlining the proposals in 1991) was because of the deeply consultative mode of policy development adopted by the labour department. All stakeholders had to commit themselves to the policy – unions, employers, government and training providers. Another factor was the reluctance of the National Treasury to agree to a levy-grant funding system. But, eventually the plan was ready to roll out.

The funding system eventually agreed to by all was a payroll levy of 1%, of which a small amount goes to administration, about a fifth goes to a 'national skills fund' for training for SMEs (small and medium enterprises) and the unemployed, and the remainder can be returned to the employer as a grant on completion of accredited training programmes. Hence the use of the term: 'grant/ levy'. Clearly the grant is intended as an incentive to encourage employers to mount suitable programmes. The National Treasury added a small additional tax incentive for the training of unemployed potential workers.

Accredited programmes include 'learnerships', which are an evolved form of apprenticeship aimed at new employees or the unemployed, and skills programmes, which are shorter and focus on specific skills. All programmes are required to combine theory with practical experience in the workplace. All programmes must be accredited by the South African Qualifications Authority in terms of the National Qualifications Framework. The system is administered by 23 Sector Education and Training Authorities (SETAs), while the training programmes themselves can be undertaken by employers or other accredited training providers.

The annual income of the system from the levies paid was about R4 billion in the 2004/05 financial year. It is an ambitious and complex programme. It required the establishment of a large number of new institutions with huge responsibilities. The national Skills Development strategy is undoubtedly the most ambitious and complex of all of the new South Africa's social development programmes. It is not surprising that the system took a long time to implement. Initially the programme has been more successful with larger firms and in higher skills bands, and has not been very successful with smaller firms and illiterate, unskilled or unemployed workers. The tax incentive has not had a significant effect, possibly because it was set at too low a level. Some of the new institutions have functioned well, but some of the SETAs have failed badly. The Labour Department was forced to amend the skills law in 2003 to give the Minister of Labour more power to intervene in under-performing or failing SETAs.

But the Labour Department and the Minister have worked hard to get support for all aspects of the programme. In the context of high levels of unemployment, the issue of learnerships for the unemployed was emphasised, with the ambitious target of 80 000 people in learnerships by March 2005. Government sought and won the commitment of business and labour to support the achievement of this target, and an intermediate target was written into the Growth and Development Summit agreement.

The way forward: A real social contract?

There are a host of underlying reasons for high levels of unemployment in South Africa. One was the colonial form of capitalism which, for a lack of democracy, was not impelled towards full employment. Strong national industrial unions, which steeled themselves in the struggle against apartheid, seized and defended their turf vigorously. The lack of a bond of trust between the political and economic elite is a further key element of the political economy of uneven or incomplete capitalist development in South Africa. On top of this, poor economic policies, isolationist strategic decisions, and the effects of globalisation on the worldwide distribution of investment resulted in a kind of dual economy in South Africa, not based on the long-term expansion of the domestic economy, the spread of employment, or the rise of incomes.

President Thabo Mbeki has used the metaphor 'two economies' to describe this situation (ANC Today, weekly e-mail newsletter 24 August 2003). One part is the modern, globalised, industrial sector; the other is the place occupied by the households without a breadwinner in full-time employment, or without productive assets who live on the margins of the first economy. When measured for the year 1999, 3.7 of 11.4 million households fell below the poverty line, about one third of households.[2] The degree of inequality, before social transfers are included, remains very high, with a Gini co-efficient of about 0.59 in 2000 (Policy Co-ordination and Advisory Services, The Presidency 2003: 91). The extent and deep entrenchment of this inequality is an obstacle to development.

Overcoming this legacy required more than the half-hearted 1998 Jobs Summit. It required a concerted and united social effort. This was why in his state of the nation address in February 2002, President Mbeki called for a Growth and Development Summit (GDS). The idea was to move beyond the lowest common denominator outcome of the 1998 Jobs Summit. Perhaps he believed that the relationship-building processes of the intervening years would support a more substantive outcome.

The date for the summit was eventually set for 7 June 2003. As in the case of the 1998 Jobs Summit, Nedlac convened the GDS, but there was a subtle difference – as the President had initiated it, this became a 'presidential' summit or 'the President's summit'. This had the effect of keeping the initiative with government, rather than with Nedlac, partly because of the disappointment of 1998, and because Nedlac's performance in some recent industry sector summits suggested that it was not as effective an organisation as it had been in the 1990s.

In the negotiations process, but particularly at the Summit itself, it was evident that there had been some positive shift of tone in the relationship between government, business and labour since 1998. The culmination of several months' intensive negotiations was an agreement that differed from the Jobs Summit agreement mainly in terms of its breadth. The lengthy agreement focused on four major themes: 'More jobs, better jobs, decent work for all; addressing the investment challenge; advancing equity, developing skills, creating economic opportunities for all and extending services; and local action and implementation' (Department of Labour 2003b: 26). In each of these areas broad and detailed commitments were made implicating one or several parties. The two largest and most concrete agreements were support for an expanded public works programme driven by government, and for the learnerships being rolled out by the Department of Labour and the SETAs. On the learnerships, specifically, government and business agreed specifically to register 72 000 learnerships by May 2004.

Supervision over the implementation of the agreement became the responsibility of Nedlac's executive council. Initially the pace of implementation of most of the agreements was disappointing. It is possible that the election scheduled for April 2004 could be blamed for distracting the parties, but this may not be a sufficient explanation. The only programmes where clear progress was evident were in the learnerships effort, and in the government's Expanded Public Works Programme (EPWP).

The EPWP was developed by government in response to the jobs crisis in the second economy. The philosophy behind it was that there were unemployed people in the second economy, usually younger and more educated, who had the chance to migrate from the second economy to the first economy, and that they lacked experience, information and skills. The EPWP has four elements: labour intensive construction projects; conservation programmes; social service programmes; and economic sector interventions. One reason for getting support for the EPWP from the GDS was that government wanted an arrangement on employment conditions that did not comply with the outcome of regular national agreements, first agreed to at the 1998 Jobs Summit, to be extended to beneficiaries drawn in under the EPWP.

The first element, labour-intensive construction, essentially earmarks a small but increasing portion of the government's growing infrastructure programme for implementation through labour-intensive techniques. The Department of Public Works identified categories of projects that are suitable for manual labour rather than using 'yellow machines', and developed suitable implementation protocols. Projects are suitable for manual labour implementation when the manual labour system produces quality outcomes similar to mechanised systems, and at no extra cost.

In order to access a portion of their Municipal Infrastructure Grant (MIG) or Provincial Infrastructure Grant (PIG), the relevant agency has to assure National Treasury and the Public Works Department that it will adopt these suitable manual labour techniques. The initial portion of the MIG and PIG earmarked for labour-intensive construction is quite small, but it will grow over the five-year duration of the current programme. It is expected that by the end of the five-year period, over 700 000 people will have been employed in such labour-intensive projects, for a period averaging four months. During this time, the beneficiary, who will be drawn from the locality of the project, will also receive formal training, not necessarily specific to construction, and will be supplied with labour market information. As this programme is inspired by an existing successful provincial project, expectations of success are high.

The conservation programmes are similar to the labour-intensive construction programmes in many ways, but they are usually of somewhat longer duration. They are also based on existing successful projects.

Perhaps the most innovative element of the EPWP is the extension of the idea of public works to social services. It was recognised that people in the second economy are greatly in need of certain social services such as early childhood development (educare for pre-schoolers) and home-based health care, especially with the burdens of AIDS, TB and malaria. Government could not afford to extend these services as part of the formal public service, so the idea emerged that such services could be extended through semi-skilled health and educare workers, employed by sub-contractors to government. Again, this is not a new modality in South Africa, but one that could be significantly expanded. In this case, the duration of contracts would be up to two years, and the training support would aim at producing a strong group of proto-nurses and proto-teachers who might later be absorbed into formal teaching and nursing.

The economic component of the EPWP is essentially various forms of support for micro-enterprise development including credit and training.

In all, the EPWP was planned to include one million direct beneficiaries in the five-year period between 2004 and 2009, for durations between four months and two years.

In spite of the fine words spoken at the GDS, in spite of the comprehensiveness and sophistication of the agreement, and in spite of the really significant major learnership and EPWP projects, the GDS remains an unfinished project. Most of the detailed decisions were not implemented a year later, and some of the really big issues around employment have not yet even been discussed. Perhaps it was frustration regarding the impact of the GDS that led President Mbeki to structure the ANC's 2004 election campaign around the theme of confronting poverty and unemployment.

Notes

1. This argument is extended in Brian Levy's 1992 paper, 'How can South African manufacturing efficiently create employment?'.
2. The poverty line used was computed by Haroon Bhorat for a 2003 paper prepared for The Presidency's Ten Year Cabinet Review. It indicates an annual household income of R12 982.50 as the poverty line level.

CHAPTER SIX

Reaching for the economic kingdom

Black economic empowerment and small and medium business development

Black economic empowerment and small business development

The most unfair, damaging and destabilising feature of the South African economy is that a very small proportion of skilled workers, professionals and proprietors are black.[1] It is unfair for obvious reasons: black people were not allowed to fulfil their personal potential, unlike most whites. It is damaging, because it cut off the economy from its lifeblood – the talents and entrepreneurship of four fifths of the population. It is destabilising, because if it were not put right it would eventually lead to an assault on the state by the emerging black elite. At worst, failure to redress racial economic inequities could re-ignite damaging conflict between black and white. At best, this could result in the state being used to put right the economic wrongs of apartheid, not as an agent of general reform but as an instrument of accumulation on behalf of an elite. This is what happened in some African countries where market-driven capitalism was unable to redress the economic inequities of colonialism. State capitalism benefited only the bureaucratic elite and their associates. The state frequently degenerated into nothing more than an instrument for enrichment for those who controlled and occupied it. This path of accumulation sometimes, misleadingly, called itself 'African Socialism'.

Another very damaging feature of the South African economy

has been the very high degree of concentration of economic power, especially during the late apartheid era. This made conditions very difficult for independent smaller businesses. In turn, this had detrimental effects on the rate of economic growth and, particularly, employment creation.

The project to bring racial equality to the economy and the project to reduce the dominance of monopolies and oligopolies and grow small businesses in South Africa are not the same thing. Black economic empowerment (BEE) is about more than ownership of the economy; it is also about skills, management and income. Similarly, small business development is not necessarily about black-owned small businesses; white-owned small businesses can benefit from and contribute through effective small business development. But these two very important challenges in South Africa have enough in common to make it convenient and appropriate to address them in the same chapter.

Ownership concentration and monopoly power in South Africa

Ownership concentration and monopoly power are both high in South Africa, and were exceptionally high at the time of the transition in 1994. Ownership concentration is about economy-wide power, the domination of the economy as a whole by a small number of very powerful owners. In South Africa's case, the form of ownership concentration has been locally based, white-owned conglomerate companies. Monopoly power is about the control of particular markets, for example the market in chemicals, or the retail consumer goods market. The monopolies and oligopolies, except where owned by the state, were generally under the control of the white-owned conglomerates.

Ownership concentration
It is commonly known that the South African economy is highly concentrated. It is not widely known how concentrated: 'In 1992, the top six conglomerates controlled companies accounting for

85.7% of the market capitalisation of the Johannesburg Stock Exchange (JSE). These are . . . the Anglo American Corporation (with 33.7%), the Rembrandt Group (14.6%), Anglovaal (2.9%), the Liberty Group (4.7%), SA Mutual (14.2%), and Sanlam (15.6%)' (Lewis 1995: 149).

Note David Lewis's careful wording: 'controlled companies accounting for', not 'controlled X% of the market capitalisation of the Johannesburg Stock Exchange'. Why these words? In South Africa, companies can gain control of other companies through a cascading series of subsidiaries called pyramids: 'If company A owns 51% of the voting stock of Company B, which in turn owns 51% of Company C, then A will have acquired control over C but will, through its 51% commitment to B, have contributed some 25% of C's equity capital. If C now acquires 51% of D, then A will acquire control of yet another company, but this time with an effective capital commitment of only 12.5%.' Control is retained, though there is a progressively smaller 'claim to dividends' (Lewis 1995: 153).

How did this extent of ownership concentration come about? Firstly, it happened when the financially powerful mining houses, which were assembled to finance costly deep-level mining, began to run out of mining certainties. In the context of a growing and protected domestic market, they saw manufacturing and banking as attractive propositions. A wave of acquisitions began in the late 1950s and continued into the 1960s, spurred on by exchange controls imposed in 1960 (see Innes 1984).

The second wave occurred during the 1980s, when many foreign companies sold their South African subsidiaries and affiliates to local buyers. The mining houses were joined as buyers by the insurance-based financial services companies: Liberty, Mutual and Sanlam.

What was the result of this enormous concentration of economic power in a small country? Was it, on balance, positive, through international market power and shared domestic resources, or did it stifle competition and entrepreneurship? Most writers believe that the latter was true. The South African conglomerate was sluggish and conservative. As Derek Keys, former Finance Minister, and both previously and subsequently conglomerate executive manager, put it – the investment behaviour of the South African conglomerate, including large manufacturing groups, is akin to that of a trustee, reluctant to invest in large projects with long payback periods, or in risky small ventures. As David Lewis has shown, they generally added little value to their subsidiaries and affiliates (Lewis 1995: 160).

This deadening effect of conglomerate ownership and the fact that it had no effective countervailing power in South Africa means that it could quite credibly be said to threaten both competitiveness and democracy in South Africa. Within the ANC alliance, once the option of nationalisation had receded into the distance, there was disagreement about whether the new government's competition authorities should directly address the issue of corporate structure through forced dismantling/unbundling, or if they should manage the conglomerates by challenging their anti-competitive behaviour. While Trevor Manuel was Minister of Trade and Industry, he certainly gave the impression that new competition law would be 'anti-trust law', and would be drafted to confront 'an unacceptably high concentration of ownership' in South Africa (*The Argus* 6 March 1995).

In response initially to threats of nationalisation from the ANC, later veiled threats of forced dismantling from ANC ministers, and the more amorphous threat of rising foreign competition in an increasingly open economy, the conglomerates began to restructure their businesses. Several companies combined unbundling of non-core assets with BEE by ensuring that black South Africans made up a significant proportion of the new owners (see later in this chapter). The result is that the holdings of the big five groups – Anglo, Sanlam, Mutual, Liberty and Rembrandt – slipped from control of companies accounting for 85.7% of the market capitalisation of the JSE in 1992 to 54.7% by 1998, though they rose again to 59.8% by 2002. A really significant proportion of the unbundled assets went not to new black business people, but to relatively new, entrepreneur-led Afrikaans groups such as the Rand Merchant Bank group and Christo Wiese's retail and banking empire, 4.8% and 3.4% respectively by the end of 1998, while Rembrandt grew from 7.8% in 1995 to 13.7% in 2002 (*Sunday Times: Business Times* 13 June 1999; Chabane et al. 2003).

In the end, the approach embodied in the 1998 Competition Law leant towards an emphasis on behaviour rather than structure. But forced unbundling could be imposed by the Competition Tribunal as a last resort against repeated anti-competitive behaviour (Competition Act No. 89 of 1998).

Market concentration

Not only has there been a very high level of concentration in the ownership of South African firms, there are also very high levels of market concentration – dominant large firms in particular sectors. As the chair of the Competition Tribunal put it (some years before he was appointed): 'The paper and pulp industry, the various sub-sectors engaged in minerals beneficiation, cement production, the furniture, footwear, poultry and wine industries, basic chemicals, and the production of white goods are all highly concentrated' (Lewis 1995: 136).

To be a little more precise: the market share controlled by the top five companies in broad industrial markets (3-digit ISIC) averaged 36.7% in 1988, up on 34.2% in 1972. The same data reflected an inequality coefficient of 0.844 in 1988, up from 0.782 in 1972. For Gini inequality coefficients, 1 is absolutely unequal, and 0 represents equality (Fourie 1996).

While ownership concentration declined somewhat, market concentration generally has not. Chabane et al. have used the term 'unbundling, rebundling' to describe a process whereby, during the 1990s, South African conglomerates unbundled and rebundled into sector-focused industry powerhouses. One of the results of this process is the exceptionally high mark-ups that remain in key sectors. Several of these rebundled industry powerhouses became international players in their field, such as Anglo American and BHP Billiton in the resources sector, SAB Miller in beer and Standard Bank Liberty in financial services (Chabane et al. 2003).

The average South African factory employed twice as many workers as did their British counterparts in the mid-1980s, not only at the aggregate level, but also at the sectoral level. For example, while British furniture factories employed 15.6 workers on average, South African plants averaged at 31.3 workers. In Italy, in the same mid-1980s period, the average furniture firm had less than six employees (Kaplinsky and Manning 1998: 142–144).

Not surprisingly, this reflected a situation where small and medium enterprises (SMEs) were far less significant in employment and output terms than SMEs in comparable countries.

When researchers Raphael Kaplinsky and Claudia Manning tried to find reasons for these patterns using the South African furniture industry as a case study, they found that the explanation did not lie in anti-competitive relations between larger and smaller furniture manufacturers. Rather, it lay in the relationship between the manufacturers and their suppliers, the retail sector and the financial sector. Kaplinsky and Manning pointed to similar relationships in the clothing and footwear sectors. The suppliers, retailers and banks all seemed to favour large manufacturers of standardised furniture products – the stock in trade of a middle-income country like South Africa. Kaplinsky and Manning felt that preferential relationships might be traced to the fact that the conglomerates owned key players in each sector; for example, Anglo American owned three of the largest retailers, the largest manu-facturing group, one of two dominant wood suppliers, and major financiers in the furniture sector, while Sanlam owned a parallel collection of companies (Kaplinsky and Manning 1998: 144–154). Indeed, before unbundling, there was not much left of the South African furniture industry once you deducted Anglo and Sanlam's interests.

Kaplinsky and Manning were reluctant to recommend policy measures. The Industrial Strategy Project (ISP), which they had both contributed to years earlier, was more forthcoming. After considering evidence of the dominance of inter-sectoral groups of large firms, often owned by the same conglomerate, ISP co-ordinator David Lewis concluded: 'The weakness of SMEs in South Africa is strongly attributable to the highly concentrated industrial structure, and provides a powerful argument for a vigorous competition policy directed at market power' (Lewis 1995: 140). ISP proposals included monitoring and penalising preferential relationships in vertically integrated ownership structures and supply chains, prohibition of anti-competitive vertical mergers and acquisitions, reserving markets, for example for government contracts, for SMEs, and permitting inter-firm co-operation between SMEs that might be frowned on if pursued by bigger firms (Joffe et al. 1995: 74–75).

When the new government's competition law was finally drafted, it prohibited restrictive horizontal and vertical practices (between similar firms, and firms above and below each other in the production chain, respectively), and it also outlawed the abuse of a dominant position. Both sections emphasised a ban on unfair discrimination between firms. Seven years after legislation, it may still be too early to say whether these measures will hit their targets and result in reduced prices and the economy's increased competitiveness. It is, however, fair to say that, so far, abuse of dominance measures have not proved very effective in diluting or redistributing market power.

Competition strategies

When Alec Erwin, Minister of Trade and Industry, presented the Competition Bill to Parliament in 1998, it was the conclusion of many years of detailed research, heated debate, pompous posturing and careful negotiation. In retrospect, it was amazing how easily the bill eventually passed through Parliament, and how it gained universal acceptance.

In the early years of the democratic government, the ANC knew that it had to do something about the huge imbalances of economic power. The Reconstruction and Development Programme (RDP) promised to introduce 'strict anti-trust legislation to create a more competitive and dynamic business environment . . . to systematically discourage the system of pyramids where they lead to the over concentration of economic power and interlocking directorships, to abolish anti-competitive practices such as market domination and abuse, and to prevent the exploitation of consumers. Existing state institutions and regulations concerned with competition policy [would] be reviewed in accordance with the new anti-trust policy' (ANC 1994a).

Late in 1997, the government published a set of proposed guidelines on competition policy for public debate. The government is only obliged to negotiate labour law in Nedlac, with other relevant laws discussed but not negotiated in the forum. However, it decided to take the competition policy document into Nedlac for extensive negotiation. In this way it could try to get a high level of agreement amongst government, business and labour, and also limit the right of labour, and especially business, to reopen issues for debate when the bill got to Parliament. Issues agreed to within Nedlac cannot be reopened in Parliament by the Nedlac parties, as long as the law is drafted within the terms of the agreement.

The approach of business was to focus the law on carefully defined issues of 'behaviour' or 'conduct', to try to limit the powers of the tribunal or the Minister to intervene in business structures. The business constituency was unhappy about the use of competition law as a means of wealth redistribution, arguing that competition law should focus on market efficiency. Evidently, the business delegation represented big established businesses. Business South Africa – the Nedlac business caucus – ostensibly represented all of business (Nedlac 1998b).

The labour contingent at Nedlac confounded some participants in the negotiating process. Instead of trying to defend workers from competition by smaller firms, labour acted as advocates for the entrepreneurs who had been prejudiced by apartheid. Labour believed that the law should have strong powers to enable government to break up and restructure big business in favour of black businesses (Nedlac 1998b).

All this worked in government's favour as it could occupy the middle ground, comfortable in the knowledge that this was its chosen position, anyway. The law, when it was finalised, acknowledged the objective of wealth redistribution, but did not build in instruments to enable competition law to be a primary tool of redistribution. It gave the government divestiture powers, but only in response to recalcitrant behaviour (Competition Act No. 89 of 1998).

The parties in Nedlac achieved agreement on the policy and the draft bill sooner than expected. The bill had to be revised in Parliament, but eventually got through less than a year after the government published its policy document. After years of building the issue up – exploited by the ANC when it was in a populist mood – the law went through with remarkably wide support. Only the salivating financial journalists were disappointed.

Strategies for small business development

Long before the competition debate was concluded, the new government made a substantial commitment of people and resources to small business development. In fact, this was the first high-profile new programme of the Department of Trade and Industry (DTI) under ANC management. It was prominent because it fitted into the ANC's view that the economy was unbalanced in favour of the giant conglomerates, and that small business development was a key strategy for the economic advancement of historically disadvantaged individuals and communities (ANC 1994a: 94–96).

A widely publicised Presidential Conference on Small Business in March 1995 was followed by a white paper, a new small business law, and four new major institutions – all this less than two years after the democratic government was elected. The institutions were: the Centre for Small Business Promotion (a policy unit at the DTI); the Ntsika Enterprise Promotion Agency (to provide non-financial assistance to small entrepreneurs, mainly through local sub-contractors); Khula Enterprise Finance Ltd (to provide loan funds and loan guarantees through intermediaries); and the National Small Business Council (to represent regional councils of small business to advise national policy makers).

Creating these agencies from nothing took time. It was one thing to draft laws and found institutions, but quite another to make them function effectively. The government was criticised for not trying to re-orient the Small Business Development Corporation (SBDC) – instead it decided to withdraw the government's shareholding and use the funds to capitalise the new Khula. The remainder of the SBDC (there were private shareholders too) was driven into the private sector. The government believed the SBDC was discredited in its dealings with very small and black borrowers, and that it could not be reformed to fit in with the needs of the new government.

The new implementation agencies had serious teething troubles. Khula battled to persuade banks to use its funds and guarantees; most of Khula's prospective clients came in for less than R50 000, what banks claimed was the minimum break-even loan size, even if it was partly guaranteed. Ntsika struggled to find reliable contractors to run its Local Business Service Centres, and had three CEOs within the first two years of its operation. The National Small Business Council, though set up after exhaustive and exhausting consultations, battled to persuade its constituents that it represented them. Then it foundered into forced dissolution by government when executive officers misused its funds.

By making small business its initial BEE focus, the DTI was unknowingly jumping in at the deep end. The challenge of building new institutions to support a constituency as weak, politically and economically, as small black business, stretched the capabilities of a small, if energetic, policy unit. As a business consultancy later put it, 'The small and medium enterprise (SME) sector was the hardest nut to crack' (Cargill 1999: section three, introduction).

In spite of this there were some successes. Several of Ntsika's Local Business Service Centres and the Manufacturing Advisory Centres ran successfully, supported by a sophisticated information and referral web-based network called BRAIN (Business Referral and Information Network). Also, both Ntsika and Khula were developing stronger relationships with key private sector players through projects and products of mutual interest.

In the short term, though, some of the more effective interventions were achieved by making existing small business programmes sensitive to BEE demands. The DTI's export centre offered marketing support and loan guarantees on special terms for small exporters. Its regional investment promotion unit developed a Small/Medium Manufacturing (later 'Enterprise') Development Programme (SMMDP) with tax-free grants for proprietors of new small factories. The DTI's innovation support programmes were embellished with empowerment devices to tilt them towards black professionals and small black-owned businesses (DTI 1998c). Its Spatial Development Initiatives built in reserved opportunities for small- and medium-firm development, whether as infrastructure contractors, suppliers of components or services, or manufacturers of niche products. The Industrial Development Corporation (IDC) and the Land Bank – two institutions designed with very different missions in mind – also refocused towards small business development. Under new boards and senior management, they developed unevenly effective facilities for small and black entrepreneurs.

In 1998/99 a review of the regulations affecting small business was carried out, and a strong report was produced for government. However, possibly affected by the reassignment of the Deputy Minister of Trade and Industry after the elections in 1999, as Minister of Minerals and Energy, there was no real follow-through on regulatory reform. By 2005, some of the problems in the small business sector were still awaiting remedy. Two major reforms only completed in 2005 were the establishment of an Apex fund to support very small loans to micro-businesses and poor households, and the merger of the less successful Ntsika into the more successful National Manufacturing Advisory Centre (NAMAC) programme to form SEDA – the Small Enterprise Development Agency.

One lesson of the small business development process was that it is easier to succeed relatively quickly if you built on existing institutions rather than build new ones. Another lesson was that when a government department establishes semi-independent executing agencies, the government should remain deeply involved in overseeing the establishment of integrity and effectiveness in the agency. A third lesson is that there are distinct and very different types of small business sector, in need of very different types of support from government. A recent government report divided the small business sector into three different and distinct segments for policy purposes: micro-enterprises; small businesses in high growth sectors; and black-owned and managed small and medium enterprises (DTI 2003b). Government programmes, sometimes under indirect political pressure, did not always successfully target the small business programmes effectively towards these three distinct target markets.

A brief history of black people in business in South Africa

It was not because black people had no inclination for business in South Africa that the black business class was so poorly developed. It was because, for 100 years and more, black entrepreneurs were harassed and systematically beaten down by government. At the same time, giant white-owned corporations emerged that exhibited the characteristics of black holes, obliterating everything within reach.

Holding back the tide

In spite of being relatively new to the cash economy, African South Africans seized emerging business opportunities in 19th-century South Africa. They opened stores, established mines, and entered the world of commercial agriculture. But their entrepreneurial instincts were soon dampened. Laws and regulations increasingly forced Africans out of the proprietorship of businesses. Cecil John Rhodes as Prime Minister of the Cape Colony pushed through legislation that destroyed the basis of African commercial farmers in the Eastern Cape. Historians believe his main motivation was to weaken Africans economically so that they would be forced to work on his diamond and gold mines, which were short of cheap labour (Bundy 1979).

In 1913 the Land Act of the Union of South Africa banned Africans from owning land outside areas scheduled for them – eventually less than 14% of the land area of South Africa. Almost all of the 14% was restricted to communal ownership, further inhibiting the development of African commercial farmers. Many African farmers managed to operate for years as sharecroppers or labour tenants on what had become white farms, but they were gradually squeezed out as the whites became more wealthy and powerful.[2] White mining companies benefited through access to migrant workers whose work options narrowed dramatically, while white farmers gained through their virtual racial monopoly of commercial farming, and through cheap wage labour.

Black traders and manufacturers were not otherwise restricted by general statute before 1923, which did not prevent white local governments from hindering their development. The 1923 Native (Urban Areas) Act confined African residents in urban areas to 'Native Locations' and undermined their right to permanence. It also specified that urban local authorities could allow African traders to operate in the African rural 'villages' and urban 'locations'.

The Minister of Native Affairs was empowered by the Act to override local authorities where they tried to block African entrepreneurs, but this proved to be a dead letter in the Orange Free State province, where African entrepreneurs were effectively banned. The Orange Free State municipal association provided two reasons for banning African traders: firstly, to deny the recognition of 'Native Locations . . . in the urban areas as (permanent) townships'; and, secondly, 'that the interests of White traders should be protected' (cited in Hart 1972: 100).

Elsewhere in South Africa, local authorities were not quite so blunt or quite so harsh, and even the Orange Free State softened its stance in the early 1940s. But African traders could never doubt that their right to trade, like their right to residence, was limited by the perceived interests of whites. Things were destined to get far worse after the National Party (NP) came to power under the banner of apartheid in 1948. The same was true for Indian and coloured entrepreneurs – the key law applicable to them was the Group Areas Act of 1950, which removed their right to own or run businesses outside of 'their own group areas'. This was the first national legal assault on the commercial rights of coloureds, though Indians had already suffered statutory economic discrimination.

In 1955 the whites-only government explicitly excluded African traders from operating outside of the African reserves and locations, while those with businesses already in 'white areas' (86% of the country) were warned to look for alternative sites for their businesses in the locations. Two years later, even African entrepreneurs in African locations or reserves had to seek permission to run a business from the local 'Native Administrator'. The Minister of Native Affairs explained: 'Some Natives abuse their presence within the white urban area to trade in competition with the White traders ... That is not something which I am prepared to tolerate' (cited in Hart 1972: 103).

From then on it was downhill, fast. The Afrikaner *Sakekamer* (business chamber) complained that Africans were allowed to have trading licences in the locations/African townships. The Minister promised to do something to 'make it clear to intending traders in the locations that their trading facilities are temporary; that they must go and continue their business in their own homeland areas' (cited in Hart 1972: 104).

The Minister kept his promise in a circular minute he issued in 1963 to local authorities. Its provisions are too Byzantine to summarise completely, but these are some notable elements: firstly, Africans could assume no right to trade in the urban areas, even in African locations; secondly, Africans could not own commercial property in the locations or anywhere else in the urban areas; thirdly, each entrepreneur was allowed to run only one business, and not even any branches thereof; and, fourthly, the only businesses permitted were those confined to 'the provision of the daily necessities of the Bantu' (the official name for Africans in 1963), which excluded 'dry cleaners, garages, and petrol filling stations' let alone banks or factories (cited in Hart 1972: 105). This restriction assumed that Africans did not own or operate motor vehicles, or wear dry-cleaned clothes, or if they did, that these were not necessities for 'the Bantu'.

In 1968 the restrictions were tightened further to ensure that African business people did not have more than one physical business outlet, to stop them from expanding their business premises without permission, and to ban them from selling or delivering goods 'to a non-African person who lives outside the urban Bantu residential area' (cited in Hart 1972: 106).

Meanwhile, the apartheid government made half-hearted gestures towards supporting the establishment of African commerce and industry in the Bantustans/homelands. This was meant to keep alive the fiction of 'separate development' – the rationale for apartheid. As the infrastructure and the people were poor in these remote regions, and trading opportunities were already controlled by white-owned wholesalers and retailers, this gesture could never remotely compensate for the unbridled assault on African entrepreneurs in the urban areas.

So, for Africans, the capitalist path to progress through accumulation as an entrepreneur was erased by the apartheid regime. Simultaneously, the whites-only government blocked African advancement through companies they did not own. It placed a cast-iron legal ceiling on the advancement of Africans through firms as wage earners.

The 'job colour bar' began as protection for white workers in skilled occupations on the gold mines around the beginning of the 20th century. In the 1920s, it extended into a 'civilised labour policy', which gave preference to white skilled and unskilled workers in the public sector, while the private sector was persuaded to comply. Under the apartheid government, the job colour bar rigidified to the point that the government issued list after list of occupations

that Africans were not allowed to have, and imposed minimum
white-to-African ratios on some industries. The government also
attacked working-class solidarity across colour lines by defining
African workers out of the formal system of industrial relations.[3]

With the advent of Bantu education policies, Africans were
excluded from schools that taught scientific and technical subjects,
and from universities that trained scientists and engineers. School
attendance was made discretionary, not compulsory for Africans,
and the standard of Bantu education plummeted under the
approving gaze of the apartheid government. More and more
explicitly, the apartheid government simply said that no Africans
could be trained or employed as skilled workers.

Even those African workers employed as unskilled workers lost
ground in the era of rampant apartheid. After their trade union
rights were crushed, many African workers in the urban areas were
made temporary migrants – none were allowed contracts of more
than one year, and all had to 'return' to their putative homelands
once a year. In 1968, the Deputy Minister of Bantu Administration
and Development declared that of the six million Africans in white
areas, only two million were economically active. The rest were
'surplus appendages' who should be deported to the Bantustans. It
was the object of government policy 'to rely on migratory labour to
an increasing extent' (Lipton 1986: 35).

The tide flows in
Perhaps the most important reason for the apartheid government's
turnaround on the economic rights of Africans was its recognition
that it had lost the war against the urbanisation of Africans. No
doubt, apartheid had slowed down the influx of rural Africans into
the urban areas – though the rural areas were generally poor and
contributed a tiny proportion of national income, more than half
of all Africans still resided in the rural areas in the 1980s. The
stream to the cities, if not an engulfing torrent, was strong, steady
and inexorable. While thousands of poor African people were
deported daily to the homelands, thousands more would return.

Along with this, the NP had undergone something of a conversion away from a highly regulated economy, which had helped it enrich its supporters, towards a version of free market economics, to protect its newly rich supporters from intervention. Influenced by Thatcherism, the government began to consider the virtues of privatisation, deregulation and small business development – small businesses even for Africans, coloureds and Indians, and even in the urban areas.

Policy changes included the establishment of the SBDC in 1981, which was allowed to lend to some 'non-white' business people, and a series of government economic reports, which increasingly emphasised the importance of the small business sector in wealth and job creation, and in political stabilisation (Rogerson 1987). As one critic points out, the enthusiasm of the government about the informal sector may have also reflected its desire to hide already massive unemployment figures in questionable informal sector employment figures (Nattrass 1990b).

By the end of the 1980s, it was estimated that there were at least 500 000 African-owned businesses in South Africa, including 100–120 000 taxis, 150 000 hawkers and vendors, 50 000 small shopkeepers, and 70 000 backyard manufacturers in South Africa (Khosa 1990; Nattrass 1990b). By another estimate, possibly 40% of all liquor retailed in South Africa was sold in 'shebeens', or speakeasies, in the black townships (Rogerson 1987: 416). Though this seemed like progress, most of these enterprises did not constitute a sound basis for real capitalist accumulation. As the 1990s progressed, their limitations became more and more evident.

The apartheid government also changed tack on the labour market. Black trade unions were legalised in 1979, Africans were allowed permanent urban status in 1986, and job reservation began to melt away in the late 1970s. Gradually, Africans were permitted to progress to skilled, supervisory and managerial positions in enterprises they did not own. But progress was slowed down by prejudice, racial bias and the problem that black schools and colleges changed little for the better; in fact, many deteriorated.

Black Economic Empowerment strategies
BEE policy in the ANC

The slow pace of black advancement in the white-dominated economy made BEE a major factor for the new government in 1994. Strangely enough, ANC economic policy documents before the *Reconstruction and Development Programme* document in 1994 barely recognise BEE as a significant policy thrust. The earlier documents refer to affirmative action in the workplace, to the correction of past inequalities in training, to the dismantling of the monopolistic conglomerates, and to the promotion of small businesses. In *Ready to Govern*, ANC economic policy included: 'Democratising the economy and empowering the historically oppressed' (ANC 1992: par. D1.1.2). But it stopped there. Unlike issues such as trade policy, minerals policy and foreign investment policy, for example, there were no concrete ideas about the implementation of empowerment programmes.

Why was there a blind spot? This was probably because, until the 1994 elections, the drafting of economic policy documents was left to academics, professional researchers and other intellectuals. BEE had become a corporate buzzword, and perhaps the intellectuals were reluctant to be seen to be pandering to business. Another factor might be that empowerment was a broad issue that cut across the economy, whereas policy groups were narrow and focused on traditional subjects such as trade, public finance, mining, agriculture, or industry. Also, black business remained a fragmented and weakly organised interest group, while the left in the ANC alliance seemed even more wary of black capitalism than white capitalism. The economic policy drafters may have assumed that BEE was implicit in notions of bringing about equality. They certainly failed to realise its political importance. 'Political' in two senses: first, in the narrow sense of the ANC communicating effectively with its existing and potential constituency; secondly, in the broad sense of the importance of a strong black middle class to underpin democracy. As Bheki Sibiya, CEO of the united business umbrella organisation, Business Unity South Africa (BUSA) put it: 'Political democracy would not be sustainable without BEE. What is happening in Zimbabwe is less political than economic, because black empowerment was not introduced there' (*Engineering News*, online daily newsletter, 28 May 2004).

As its first election manifesto, the RDP was the ANC's first post-1990 social and economic policy document in which the political leadership played a key role in drafting – not only an approving and amending role. In this sense, even the 1992 *Ready to Govern* document, with all the razzmatazz of the national conference in Johannesburg, was still largely drafted by specialists. The economic debates at the 1992 conference focused on a few high-profile issues such as nationalisation and relations with the World Bank and the International Monetary Fund (IMF) – while numerous potentially controversial, technocratic formulations went unnoticed.

The RDP recognised that monopolistic white corporate ownership of the land and economic wealth creates 'social and racial tension' and damages economic potential. It committed the ANC to 'democratise the economy and empower the historically oppressed'. More specifically, it indicated that a 'central objective of the RDP is to de-racialise business ownership completely through focussed policies of black economic empowerment'. Financial institutions would not be allowed to discriminate on the basis of race, state agencies and public corporations would provide capital and tendering procedures to facilitate BEE, and there was a reference to 'training' and 'upgrading' of black business people and their firms. The RDP was only specific on BEE in the case of small business development where the highlighted issues were access to credit, access to markets, skills, and supporting institutions (ANC 1994: par. 4.1.5, 4.2.2.6, 4.4.6.3, section 4.4.7).

So, while the RDP recognised the political and economic importance of BEE, it failed to anticipate the immense challenges that would emerge when government attempted to implement the BEE policy. Or maybe it just avoided the issue. When the ANC took the reins of power in the government of national unity (GNU), its BEE thrust was fragmented and uncoordinated, and worked within an extremely vague set of common guidelines as articulated by the RDP.

Even at the ANC's major congress at the end of 1997, where it set out a policy framework to inform the 1999 elections and the coming Mbeki government, the ANC leadership could only point to the need for a coherent BEE strategy (ANC 1997b). It was still unwritten.

BEE and government procurement

One important route for BEE was through procurement – the allocation of public contracts. In 1995–96, an interim strategy called the '10-point plan' was developed within national government for smaller contracts. If the tendering company was fully black-owned and women-owned it could get a bid-price advantage of 13.64%, less if only one of the criteria was satisfied (Cargill 1999: chapter 16).

The strategy had several limitations. The criterion of black ownership was not always effective – some white-owned companies hid behind black front-companies for bidding purposes, and some black-owned companies were less progressive than white or foreign companies in their hiring and training programmes. Tender boards learned to avoid some of these pitfalls, but the system remained less than perfect.

Another limitation was the fact that many public tender authorities were newly established after 1994, especially the nine provincial tender boards. They did not fall under the jurisdiction of the national 'State Tender Board' or the 10-point plan. In the absence of an accepted nationwide framework, the policies and practices of the public contract bodies differed widely.

In 2000, the National Treasury's Preferential Procurement Policy Framework Act was passed, accompanied by regulations in 2001. This law established a common framework for procurement for all organs of state. For smaller contracts, 20% of the evaluation could be allocated to specific goals – either to cater for contracting with people historically disadvantaged by unfair discrimination, or to further the goals of the RDP. Larger contracts could allocate 10% of the evaluation score to these goals. The Act has not proved easy to implement – some state organs were concerned that it did not give them sufficient flexibility to achieve empowerment objectives, while the private sector indicated that the Act and regulations placed too much emphasis on equity ownership, and not enough on capacity-building and the promotion of local content. Public corporations are not bound by the Act, and continue to maintain a variety of empowerment procurement systems (BusinessMap Foundation 2003: 17–20).

In spite of the continuing lack of uniformity of empowerment procurement systems, bidders for government contracts learned that they had to have a strong BEE component. There is no doubt that black proprietors and partners in the construction sector, the information technology business, and in legal, auditing and consulting firms benefited considerably from even the haphazard adoption of BEE in government tenders.

Empowerment or enrichment, or is that the wrong question?

One of the most significant BEE exercises began in 1993 when Sanlam, the giant Afrikaans insurance-based conglomerate, unbundled a significant asset into black hands. This was also a pioneering foray by the state-owned IDC, which helped to finance the deal. The IDC was one of the first finance companies to support the larger kind of empowerment projects – the transfer of ownership of privatised or unbundled (the private sector form of privatisation) companies into black ownership. There were various ways to participate: warehousing shares while black buyers were found; financing the transfer of ownership; or taking a minority shareholding in a firm being transferred to black owners.

The IDC became involved in BEE in a tentative way in the early 1990s. One form of involvement was to support the establishment of some small and medium black businesses, even though they were outside of the IDC's usual field of industrial development.

One instance was when the IDC agreed to finance the expansion of a medical clinic in Soweto owned by medical doctor, Nthatho Motlana. Dr Motlana had been a hero in the parents' response to the schoolchild-led revolt in Soweto in 1976, and in subsequent conflicts. He ably conveyed the community's demands, and negotiated with dignity and courage. He had been associated with ANC leaders before the banning of the organisation in 1960, and retained these links. Dr Motlana strove to serve Soweto effectively as a committed community doctor, and built up a clinic over many years. In the early 1990s when the IDC began dipping its toes in the unexplored waters of BEE, Dr Motlana's clinic made a good pilot project.

Sanlam had begun a more general unbundling exercise in response to market pressures for stock market value. The South African conglomerates had grown large, bloated and inefficient in the 1980s, after picking up assets discarded by foreign firms that were disinvesting under political pressure. (Elsewhere in the world, the 1980s were characterised by wide-scale unbundling and repackaging of conglomerates.) Sanlam anticipated the competition that was to come after the lifting of sanctions, and began to restructure. The fact that it chose to dispose of Metlife, a substantial and profitable life assurer, was probably more influenced by Sanlam's view that this would be a political investment for the future.

Sanlam sold a controlling share of Metlife to Dr Motlana's new company called New African Investments Limited, or NAIL, with the help of finance from the IDC. A year later, NAIL was floated on the Johannesburg Stock Exchange, and it grew rapidly. It acquired new assets regularly, mainly in the financial services sector, but also in telecommunications, the media and in the industrial sector. NAIL's acquisition path seemed to depend more on what assets made themselves available, rather than a focused strategy. In this respect, the behaviour of some new BEE conglomerates has been uncannily similar to the behaviour of the old white conglomerates picking up sanctions disinvestments when they became available. Another resemblance was in the pyramid control structures, which in South Africa allow holding companies to control the boards of their subsidiaries' subsidiaries.

NAIL's executive directors soon resembled a kind of political aristocracy within black business. Motlana and his (non-black) partner Jonty Sandler were first joined by advocate Dikgang Moseneke, who had been Deputy President of one the ANC's rivals, the Pan- Africanist Congress (PAC) during the pre-1994 negotiations. Moseneke decided to leave politics before the 1994 elections. Then they were joined by Cyril Ramaphosa, outgoing Secretary-General of the ANC, lawyer, and former leader of the black National Union of Mineworkers (NUM). Ramaphosa was a senior ANC negotiator in the pre-1994 period, and was seen as the chief rival to Thabo Mbeki for succession to the leadership of the ANC once Mandela left office. When Mbeki consolidated his claim to succession, and all parties agreed to the country's final (rather than interim) Constitution in mid-1996, Ramaphosa decided to leave politics for the private sector. He entered NAIL with a group of investors called the National Empowerment Consortium, including several trade union funds, which helped NAIL buy industrial conglomerate Johnnic from the giant Anglo American Corporation.

Last executive director on board was Zwelakhe Sisulu, son of Mandela's friend and mentor Walter Sisulu. Zwelakhe Sisulu had been a brave journalist, editor, publisher and media union leader in the apartheid era, and was selected to run the national public broadcaster, the South African Broadcasting Corporation (SABC) after its new board was appointed by the new government. Perhaps worn out by the mammoth task of transforming the public broadcaster, which was largely accomplished under his management, he joined the private sector in 1998. NAIL's significant media interests may well have attracted Sisulu.

In the meantime, NAIL had grown and become one of the largest black-owned publicly traded companies, known in South Africa as 'black chip' companies. By the end of 1998, following a serious correction in the Johannesburg Stock Exchange during the third-quarter, NAIL had a market capitalisation of nearly R6 billion, or US$1 billion (*Financial Mail* 11 December 1998).

NAIL symbolised the rapid accumulation of wealth that several black-controlled companies enjoyed after 1994. Soon, comparisons came to be drawn between the rise of black capitalism after 1994, and the rise of Afrikaner capitalism after the NP came to power in 1948 (*Financial Mail* 7 February 1997). Afrikaners had previously been economically subordinate to English-speaking South Africans who had controlled almost all of the country's wealth. Afrikaners used insurance companies such as Sanlam as their main accumulation vehicles. With 60% of the white population being Afrikaans speakers, and with an Afrikaans-controlled government, Afrikaner financial services companies had a major market base they could win over with nationalistic marketing.

The moment when Afrikaner capital truly came of age was when Federale Mynbou acquired General Mining from Anglo American, the bastion of South African English-speaking capital. Harry Oppenheimer had chosen to draw the upstart Afrikaners into the fold of the establishment. As business historian J.G.F. Jones wrote in 1995, 'the arrival of the Afrikaners into the Chamber of Mines had the important consequence of defusing the ruling Afrikaners' [unfavourable] view of the mining industry' (cited in *Financial Mail* 7 February 1997). Federale Mynbou/General Mining grew into Gencor, a Sanlam-linked company that ranked second only to Anglo American in the South African mining sector, and now, as BHP Billiton, is a leading world player.

The echoes of Anglo American's pre-emptive move in 1963 in Sanlam's gesture 30 years later is hardly accidental or coincidental. There can be little doubt that Sanlam's executives recognised both the political significance of their 1993 sale of Metlife, and its echoes of the 1963 precedent.

Sanlam set a trend, and NAIL was a beneficiary when other conglomerates followed suit. But NAIL soon found that good assets and political credibility were not enough. At the end of its financial year in September 1998, NAIL's ordinary (voting) shares were trading at a 23.6% discount to the net value of its underlying holdings, while the low voting N shares were trading at a 41.6% discount (*Financial Mail* 11 December 1998). There are various explanations, including the same explanation that was applied to the white unwieldy conglomerates in the early 1990s: that the holding company's management was not adding value to its assets.

Early in 1999 things began to turn sour at NAIL. First, Cyril Ramaphosa resigned his position as Executive Deputy Chairman. Ramaphosa has not revealed his reasons for leaving NAIL, but one factor may have been differences over the restructuring of Johnnic, where Ramaphosa was chairman of the board (*Enterprise* Vol. 131, April 1999). Or it may have been because he anticipated a storm that was about to break over NAIL and wanted to distance himself from its cause.

The storm broke in mid-April 1999 when the *Financial Mail* drew NAIL's minority shareholders' attention to the fact that 'next week they will be asked to approve a R100 million bonanza for four of their executives' (*Financial Mail* 16 April 1999). The board was asking shareholders to approve the transfer of share options in NAIL's dynamic subsidiary African Merchant Bank, to the four remaining executive directors: Motlana, Sandler, Moseneke and Sisulu. The options were worth about R136 million, or R34 million (US$6.5 million) per executive director.

If the performance of NAIL had reflected strong management, shareholders might not have been outraged, but they were not grateful for the discounted value of their shares. The outcry forced the NAIL board to withdraw this and two other controversial resolutions before the shareholders' meeting. Sandler resigned – portrayed by some as the fall guy – and Motlana joined him, motivated partly, it seems, by weariness brought on by his advancing age (74). The publicly available evidence does not indicate whether any of the executive directors was more culpable than the others of what was a presumptuous rather than an illegal act (*Financial Mail* 7 May 1999).

What conclusions can we draw? Firstly, BEE is of course riddled with temptations for enrichment, which may be legal, but not entirely ethical. In this regard the new black companies learned the tricks of the trade from the directors of established South African companies whose incestuous world is somewhat obscured from public scrutiny. A second and more positive lesson, though, was that with South Africa's less-than-perfect company law, and even with its often-somnolent financial press, inappropriate actions can be stopped before they happen. There is some significant degree of transparency, and a reasonable supply of shame. Thirdly, and perhaps most importantly, it pointed to dissatisfaction with the nature of some BEE holding companies and the way they are managed.

For NAIL this was the beginning of the end. Under a new management team, NAIL attempted to focus itself as a media powerhouse, but was thwarted by unfavourable decisions made by the regulator of broadcasting and telecommunications – the Independent Communications Authority of South Africa (ICASA). Rules designed to prevent the emergence of excessive control by a company of the media in particular markets prevented NAIL from accumulating the assets its board believed would make it a viable media company. Since the decision, NAIL has gradually unbundled its portfolio on the path to a complete dismantling of the NAIL empire. Once the black chip amongst black chips, NAIL is limping along the path to dissolution.

Financing BEE: How special were 'special purpose vehicles'?
How are the big empowerment deals financed? Most of the black owners have little wealth, or collateral in any other form. They have to raise finance with relatively little to offer except that there may be a discount to the ruling price of the transferred shares, and that the cachet of black ownership will be a credit in dealings with the South African government. Since the introduction of BEE charters more recently, the incentive to share equity with black owners has grown considerably.

The early form of a BEE deal used the redeemable preference share in conjunction with the creation of a type of company known as an SPV, or 'special purpose vehicle' (see Stassen and Kirsch 1999).[4] Once a deal is struck, the financier provides funds to the SPV in exchange for a combination of equity and debt preference shares, the combination depending on the size of the discount on the original sale (usually at least 10%). The BEE company gets the voting rights, but the financier enjoys the performance of the underlying shares, up to a certain hurdle rate. The hurdle rate is usually expressed as a percentage of the prime lending rate. Over the hurdle rate, the returns go to the BEE company.

In essence, in exchange for the cachet of black ownership and a chance to participate in a big share transfer in a relatively illiquid market, the financier gave up a notional half of the upside of the share and took all the downside risk. This was fine in a bullish market, but when markets turned bearish and interest rates rose rapidly, as in the second half of 1998, the dividends from the underlying investment failed to cover the debt preferences hurdle rate. The additional debt was added to the loan capital of the SPV, forcing the BEE company to raise cash or give up some of the underlying shares to the financier to relinquish debt. Several weakly capitalised empowerment companies and consortia collapsed under this kind of pressure in the late 1990s and in 2002–03.

This raises questions about the SPV system. The 'good times' scenario of returns without risk for SPVs had encouraged passivity in the BEE companies, and even carelessness about the way they assembled and organised their holdings. They had little incentive to add value to their assets in any significant way. But their returns were also constrained.

The problem became very obvious in early 1999, in the aftermath of the mini-crash of the second half of 1998. BEE companies had to scramble to avoid mounting debt to their financiers, leading to some significant shake-ups, such as the partial separation of Johnnic from NAIL (*Enterprise* Vol. 131, April 1999). But it went much deeper. With many of the new BEE holding companies trading at really significant discounts to their underlying assets, black business leaders sometimes became frustrated and embarrassed about their lack of involvement at the operational level of the firms they owned.

As black business leader, Ruel Khosa, put it in the wake of the NAIL crisis: 'Our empowerment agenda is driven by the corpor-ations that seek to do business with us, along with the assorted advisors and financiers who in fact stand to benefit more from these initiatives than ourselves. Often we bring to the table nothing more than the pedigree of blackness and expect this to do the magic for us. We bring little by way of strategy, a plan, capital, expertise of skills to the deals that we get involved in' (*Sunday Times: Business Times* 25 April 1999).

Initially many BEE deals resulted in a transplanted head that had to get to know its body better, but did not always show the inclination to do so. It's hard to measure the extent to which this was a result of the specific form of BEE SPV, and the extent to which it was a predictable outcome of the adoption of 'pyramiding South African style' by the black business community.[5]

These problems were ignored for a long time because the BEE deals were so lucrative to the successful merchant banks – deal flow overwhelmed everything else for a while. But the merchant banks and the BEE companies were forced to look for ways for the new black owners to share more effectively in the risk, returns, and obviously in the management of the assets being transferred. Some of the financial companies sought out those black companies that emerged from the ground up. Black businesses with an operational track record became increasingly well placed to benefit even from top-down BEE deals vis-à-vis those that only had political connections.

The problem – the main problem – is that there were not enough of these successful ground-up black companies to facilitate continued fast-paced BEE. This was a key challenge for government.

The BEE Commission, the broad-based Black Empowerment Act and the National Empowerment Fund

In November 1997 the Black Management Forum (BMF), an association of black senior managers formed in the 1980s, proposed the establishment of a Black Economic Empowerment Commission. As the BMF explained, 'The motivation for the establishment of the commission is that the notion of true empowerment as defined by black people does not exist, nor does a common definition or benchmark' (BEECom 2001: 4). There were no accepted standards or criteria for empowerment. Organisations were making it up as they went along, which created ideal conditions for all kinds of opportunism.

Society as a whole needed a systematic approach. A month later at its congress in Mafikeng, the ANC endorsed the position of the BMF and the mandate of the commission, which became known as the BEECom. Cyril Ramaphosa, former organiser of mine workers, and senior ANC official and negotiator, who had left Parliament and entered business in 1996 was appointed Chair of the Commission, with several other senior black business people on the Commission.

Three-and-half years later, after extensive discussions with politicians and the business community, the Commission published its report. The BEECom adopted a 'broad-based' approach to BEE – it was about training, small business development, economic growth, and access to financial services, in addition to the issues of ownership and procurement. As President Mbeki once put it, part of the task of the BEECom was 'to answer the question – how do we promote the formation of a black bourgeoisie which will itself be committed and contribute to black economic empowerment?' (Mbeki 1999).

The ANC picked up the theme of broad-based empowerment in its detailed and substantive resolution on BEE at its five-yearly congress in December 2002. The government was at last ready to launch a comprehensive BEE strategy. The DTI published a policy paper in March 2003; in April the Minister of Trade and Industry appointed an advisory committee to help him finalise a draft law; and in September 2003 the Broad-Based Black Economic Empowerment law passed through Parliament to almost universal acclaim. President Mbeki signed the bill into law in January 2004.

The broad-based concept evolved into the idea of a balanced scorecard to rate the performance of industry sectors and firms with regard to a wide range of empowerment objectives (DTI 2003: appendix A). While most opposition parties supported the bill, the conservative Democratic Alliance (DA) opposed the bill on the grounds that it was aimed to encourage cronyism and patronage politics by the ruling party (*Business Day* 5 September 2003).

Some deals raise the question of the ease with which senior government officials and politicians glide through a revolving door to powerful positions in the private sector, often in businesses closely related to their portfolios in government. The path of the former Director-General of the Department of Communications into a major information technology business, and then his role as leader of a consortium to buy a parcel of shares in Telkom raised some eyebrows during 2004. This was not an isolated event – many former top officials and politicians have moved into the private sector. This should not be surprising – as in any democratic revolution, the struggle against apartheid drew many of the best and the brightest people, who in normal societies would have been professors, business leaders or professionals. When the Afrikaner nationalists won power in 1948 in a less democratic regime change, for many Afrikaners, politics or the civil service was a path into the private sector. There would be more cause for concern if this path were not followed in South Africa – the clear distinction between the province of political power and the province of economic power is now well entrenched, unlike the situation in many African countries with weak private sectors. The ethical issue is, more precisely, the manner of the passage from public to private sector, a debate not yet concluded in South Africa.

Though not quite as wide-reaching as the BEECom proposal, influenced particularly by trade union supporters in its ranks, the BEE law entailed a powerful streak of egalitarianism in the description of the law's objectives. The concrete elements of the law had four main elements: the establishment of a Black Economic Empowerment Advisory Council chaired by the President that would review the implementation of the law; a commitment that the Minister of Trade and Industry would issue a strategy document to define the parameters of the policy; the empowerment of the Minister to publish codes of good practice for the implementation of the policy; and the Minister was obliged to publish in government gazettes the transformation charters agreed to in industrial sectors (Broad-Based Black Economic Empowerment Act No. 53 of 2003).

It was not expected that there would be an empowerment charter for every sector. Only major sectors (such as mining), those with a significant commercial relationship with the government (such as information technology), or those that operated under significant government regulation (such as the liquor sector) would develop transformation or empowerment charters. A charter is essentially an agreement covering an industrial sector that commits the firms in the sector to achieving over a specified time period a range of objectives, usually including the main elements of the BEE scorecard: equity ownership levels, management composition, employment equity, skills development, preferential procurement, enterprise development (usually black-owned contractors), as well as industry specific goals.

The first charter to be launched was the Liquid Fuels Industry Charter signed in Johannesburg in November 2000. This was followed by the Mining Charter in October 2002, but not before an early government draft of the charter was leaked leading to a sudden and significant loss of confidence in South African mining equities. The Minister of Minerals and Energy had to lead an intensive communication campaign on the charter and the BEE strategy in general to begin to restore confidence in South African shares. The next major charter was the Financial Sector Charter, released in October 2003, though the implementation details had to be firmed up over the next year or so. Several other charter processes got underway in 2003 and 2004; indeed the charter process proliferated more widely than originally anticipated by the government. What this seems to reflect is the desire of each

industrial sector to have clear and pertinent BEE rules and objectives, rather than operating within the broad scope of the law.

The charter experience taught government and the private
sector that it was not only necessary to devise industry specific
charters, but that the process of charter development varied
considerably from sector to sector. In some sectors, the government
took the lead; in others, the black and white industry players sought
to do most of the charter work themselves, and only brought the
government into discussions when they had already progressed quite
far along the road to charter development.

One of the key ingredients of a successful BEE programme is
finance. How do you transfer ownership and all other kinds of
economic assets to black people who have not been able to
accumulate marketable assets as a consequence of the apartheid
system? SPVs have obvious limitations, and the sponsorship of
empowerment deals by the companies being shared out destroys
value and therefore has to be limited. In some cases empowerment
partners bring value to the firm being shared and this may be
considered to legitimise a discount of the equity issued to empowerment partners, but even taking this into account, there is a huge
amount of financing outstanding.

In the Metlife case, and in numerous other transactions, the
IDC helped to finance the deal. But with net assets of about R25
billion and a range of other responsibilities in its mandate, the
capacity of the IDC to finance BEE is limited.

Late in the Mandela government, legislation for a National
Empowerment Fund (NEF) was finalised. The idea behind this Fund
was that the government needed an instrument to enable ordinary
people – historically disadvantaged people to be specific – to benefit
from the fruits of privatisation, and to benefit from economic
empowerment opportunities.

Privatisation had three main goals in South Africa, goals that
sometimes proved to be mutually incompatible. The first was to
help to reduce the national budget deficit. The bulk of the proceeds
of privatisation (about R26 billion of a total of R36 billion by the

end of 2004) went straight into the Treasury, not without some skirmishes between the Minister of Finance and ministers of portfolios affected by the privatisation (for example, Transport or Communications) who believed that the funds should be reinvested in that sector. In many cases, though, the privatisation contract was conditional on the new owners or shareholders contributing to significant new investment in the field for which the privatised company was responsible. The semi-privatised national tele-communications company, Telkom, was required to lay down two million new telephone lines as a condition for the successful bidders. The new services or infrastructure were generally aimed at the poor – the redistribution of services and infrastructure being the second goal of privatisation. The third goal of privatisation was to improve the efficiency of the economy. So, for example, the semi-privatisation of Telkom was accompanied by the removal of the Telkom monopolies over fixed line and overseas telecommunic-ations, but delayed by five years to give Telkom an opportunity to prepare for competition and to meet the redistribution require-ments. In practice, regulatory uncertainty has led to Telkom being allowed to maintain its monopoly longer than originally planned.

In addition to those three goals – paying off the national debt, extending services and improving economic efficiency – a fourth goal emerged that was more specific to the South African experience. It was that the historically disadvantaged individuals and communities could use the opportunity of privatisation to get access to some of the wealth they had been barred from. Privatisation had to include the redistribution of wealth in South Africa. But what did this mean? Did it mean that individuals would be given equity, and if so, how would shares be distributed to avoid criticisms of favouritism? And what about the small entrepreneurs who needed capital to grow their companies rather than supplement their income or pension? Finally, who was going to pay for it: the new owners, consumers, or the taxpayer?

In the end a rather complicated solution was found. Those

fractions of privatised companies that were reserved for the historically disadvantaged (usually about 10% of the portion sold) would be sold to a trust, which would draw on state funds (taxpayers' money) to pay for the shares. Shares set aside by early 1999 were: 10% of Telkom at R1.8 billion; 15% of Sun Air at R7.5 million; 10% of the Airports Company at about R400 million; and 15% of Aventura (a holiday resort manager) at R13 million (Cargill 1999: chapter 17). The trust was set up by specific legislation in 1998 (National Empowerment Fund Act No. 105 of 1998). The trust would share this wealth in three ways: firstly there would be a portfolio management trust, which would manage rare large parcels of shares that would eventually be sold to black companies or consortia; secondly, some of the shares would be included in a venture capital fund, where the assets would be used to support capital injections into emerging smaller black companies; and, thirdly, some assets would be transferred to an investment trust/ mutual fund, which would encourage smaller black investors to buy units at a significant discount, not tradable for a period of time to encourage habits of saving and investment. In the case of the latter two funds, the portfolios would clearly have to be diversified in order to give them greater stability and balance. The venture capital fund could become a joint-venture company with private partners if it proved adept at picking high-potential prospects.

In practice it did not work out exactly that way. The only shares transferred to the NEF were 1.5% of MTN (the second cell phone operator), transferred at a value of R171 million. The government provided an additional R14 million as part of the NEF's R100 million commitment to a venture capital fund called NEF Ventures Trust, which is a joint venture between the NEF and the IDC.

The remaining shares were not transferred to the NEF for a variety of reasons, but mainly because even after several years of operations it had failed to convince anyone that it could make a serious contribution to empowerment. A new CEO was appointed in October 2003 to turn it around. The new CEO was Sydney Maree, a black athlete who during the apartheid era immigrated to the United States to compete as a middle-distance runner. One of South Africa's greatest-ever athletes, Maree held the world record for the 1 500 metres in the early 1980s. Maree returned to South Africa in the 1990s and held several jobs in the financial sector, and by 2003 was a senior officer in the JSE, and was a special adviser to the Minister of Trade and Industry, Alec Erwin.

After Maree was appointed to the CEO post, the government committed itself to re-capitalising the NEF with a R2 billion injection. This was part of R10 billion that the Minister of Finance indicated in his 2003 budget speech would be set aside for BEE. The new NEF would have four main product areas: accreditation and advisory services to improve standards and information for BEE; the 'generator' venture capital fund for small firms; the 'accelerator' venture capital fund for medium firms; and the 'transformer' fund, which is designed to invest in BEE enterprises that seek a listing on the JSE. Sadly, Maree was suspended from his position, accused of being complicit in some irregular transactions, only six months after his tenure began – yet another sorry episode in the history of the NEF.

In addition to the NEF, the Minister of Finance announced the expansion of the Isibaya Fund of the Public Investment Corporation (PIC). The PIC is responsible for the investment of over R400 billion on behalf of the government, most of which belongs to the government employees' pension fund. The Isibaya Fund was created to invest up to 3.5% of the PIC funds into socially responsible investments, including the financing of BEE deals. Initial reports indicate that about R2 billion will be invested in BEE small and medium businesses between 2004 and 2007, but the fund has been slow to find its feet (*City Press: Business* 13 June 2004).

The challenge of financing BEE deals is a very serious one. EmpowerDEX, an empowerment consultancy, estimated early in 2005 that it would cost about R389 billion in financing to advance black ownership to 25% of the JSE (EmpowerDEX 2005: 3). Competing for the use of funds are the growing investment plans of the public sector and the private sector. Symptomatic of this conflict was an extended argument within the Financial Sector Charter process about the allocation of funds set aside by the financial institutions in terms of the charter for investment – how much of the money should be used for investment in housing for the poor, how much for infrastructure investment by the public sector, and how much for empowerment? Yet, even if the entire amount set aside by the Financial Sector Charter had been allocated to empowerment, it would have amounted to less than a third of the amount estimated by EmpowerDEX needed to finance the purchase of only a quarter of the JSE.

BEE outcomes
It is not easy to measure the outcomes of the BEE policies and programmes. Many of the outcomes are not necessarily measurable in straightforward terms. One can examine objective measures such as the number of black managers recorded by the Department of Labour and the extent of black ownership of companies listed on the JSE. But this would be a representative number, not a complete account. For example, in the petroleum sector most of the firms are not listed in Johannesburg, so the 25% stakes of each of Caltex, BP, Shell and Total South Africa sold to empowerment partners would not be reflected in the outcome of a survey of the JSE.

In addition, measurement can be influenced by the range of interpretations of what BEE is. For some analysts (e.g. EmpowerDEX) BEE control over the JSE is measured through an account of all BEE-held shares, while for others (e.g. BusinessMap Foundation) only BEE-controlled companies count. In addition, the passing of the BEE Act in 2003 and the emergence of the escalating BEE charter trend has meant a new wave of BEE deals beginning in 2000 with the signing of the first charter, and this is likely to continue for a decade. An analyst for Nomura Securities perspicaciously said in 1998 that BEE was likely to dominate the Johannesburg Stock Exchange for the next 10–15 years. The pace continues to accelerate – the BusinessMap Foundation indicates that 2003 was a record year for BEE deals, valued in excess of R30 billion (*BBQ*, Vol. 7, No. 1, 2004: 101). Measuring BEE in South Africa is like trying to hit a rapidly moving target.

Nevertheless, the extension of black ownership in the economy has been progressing fairly slowly. In terms of direct ownership, black people still only owned about 1.6% of the JSE by September 2003, and held another 14.1% through institutional investors (*Financial Mail: Top Empowerment Companies* April 2004: 10).

Over 90% of BEE wealth in the market is held indirectly through institutions, and the PIC (the agency responsible for investing government financial assets such as pension funds) holds 58.8% of that. The majority of BEE investment – 68.9% – is invested in the resources and financial sectors. This is in line with the fact that these two sectors constitute 70% of market capitalisation on the JSE (EmpowerDEX 2003).

If we look at the boards of the JSE's top 100 companies, there were only 14 (1.2% of total) black directors in 1992. By 2002, there were 156 black directors – 13% of total directors. In 2002, there were 24 black executive directors, that is 5.2% of total executive directors compared with one executive director (0.2%) in 1992. Of the top 100 companies, 71 had black representation on their boards (EmpowerDEX 2003).

If we look at the JSE as a whole, there were 435 black directors in September 2004 compared with 432 in 2003 – 16.6% of the total. Only 7.7% of executive directors were black. Only 3.2% of all directors were black women, and only 0.8% of executive directors. Only 4% of boards had a majority of black directors, and 64% of boards had no black directors at all (EmpowerDEX 2005).

For affirmative action in the workplace, the history of the measuring tool is short – launched with the Employment Equity Act of 1998, data is only available for the period since 2000. Steady progress is being made on employment equity in the private sector whilst the public sector is becoming representative of the population. In the public sector, 72.5% of employees were African, 3.6% Indian, 8.9% coloured and 14.7% white, as of 31 March 2003. With regard to gender, 52.5% of public servants were female and 47.5% were male. At senior management level, 56% were African, 8.2% Indian, 10.1% coloured, and 25.6% white. The gender breakdown for senior management was 22.1% female and 77.9% male. As the data show, great strides have been made in employment equity within the public sector, although the gender bias in senior management is still skewed in favour of males.

State-owned enterprise board composition by late 2003 was 63% African, 2.5% Indian, 9.9% coloured and 24.7% white. Regarding gender, 76.5% were male and 23.5% female. At senior management levels, 56.5% were white and 43.5% were black with a gender breakdown of 75% male and 25% female. Again it would be fair to say that the boards and senior management of state-owned enterprises are becoming more representative, with the caveat that gender equity lags.

If we look at the top levels of occupation categories as defined in the 2001 census, we find that black South Africans constituted 61% of all professionals, technicians and associate professionals, and 44% of managerial positions in the economy (Statistics South Africa 2003).

Looking at the private sector on its own, progress is being made, in that 22% of all new managers in 2000 were African and 47% of all new promotional opportunities went to African managers. However, progress is slow. By 2001, only 13% of top managers were black, and only 16% of senior managers. Moreover, each category had only improved by 1% since 2000. At the middle management/ professional level, progress is even slower.

Progress towards gender equality is similarly slow in the private sector, with only 11% of top management being female in 2001, and 18% of senior management. For both categories and for middle managers/professionals, the annual rate of progress is very slow, at between 1% and 1.7%.

Notes

1. In general, I use the work 'black' to mean other than white. All 'non-white' people were economically discriminated against. But economic discrimination was more severe for black Africans, compared with 'coloureds' and 'Indians'.

2. This story is vividly told through the eyes of one African farmer in Charles van Onselen's *The Seed is Mine: The Life of Kas Maine, a South-African Sharecropper, 1894–1985* (1996).

3. See Davies (1979), for a class analysis approach; Horwitz (1967), for an economically conservative but anti-Afrikaner account, and for something in between, Lipton (1986).

4. I am greatly indebted to Chapter 1 of Stassen and Kirsch (1999), and Cargill's (1999) publication as a whole, for this section of Chapter 6.

5. See earlier in this chapter, and the anticipation of this problem in Lewis (1995: 172).

CHAPTER SEVEN

The two economies and the challenge of faster growth

The persistence of two economies

On 24 August 2003, President Thabo Mbeki wrote the following lines in his weekly letter published in the ANC's electronic newsletter:

> It is sometimes argued that higher rates of economic growth, of 6 percent and above, would, on their own, lead to the reduction of the levels of unemployment in our country. This is part of a proposition about an automatic so-called trickle-down effect that would allegedly impact on the 'third world economy' as a result of a stronger 'first world economy'.
>
> None of this is true. The reality is that those who would be affected positively, as projected by these theories, would be those who, essentially because of their skills, can be defined as already belonging to the 'first world economy'.
>
> The task we face therefore is to devise and implement a strategy to intervene in the 'third world economy' and not assume that the interventions we make with regard to the 'first world economy' are necessarily relevant to the former.
>
> The purpose of our actions to impact on the 'third world economy' must be to transform this economy so that we end its underdevelopment and marginalisation. Thus we will be able to attend to the challenge of poverty eradication in a sustainable manner, while developing the 'third world

economy' so that it becomes part of the 'first world economy' (Mbeki 2003a).

This was not the first time that the ANC had recognised the extent of poverty and inequality in South Africa and argued that without government action these problems would remain. But it was the strongest form of articulation of this position since the Reconstruction and Development Programme (RDP) had been written nearly 10 years earlier. The effect of the introduction of the 'two economies' paradigm in mid-2003 was to refocus the attention of the government and the ANC on the persistence of poverty and inequality. What more could be done to address this social and political challenge, and how did addressing this challenge fit into a coherent overall approach to economic and social development?

The approach taken by the ANC to the April 2004 elections was unusual for a ruling party. While the organisation missed few opportunities to celebrate the achievements of '10 Years of Freedom' in 2004, it was not afraid to highlight the socio-economic disappointments of the freedom era. The party leaders spent much of the campaign identifying with the needs of the disadvantaged. President Mbeki even focused attention on the plight of the growing numbers of white people who were poor and unemployed.

The manifesto of the ANC highlighted the plight of the unemployed:

> The economy has created 2-million net new jobs since 1995. But the number of people seeking work has sharply increased; many workers have lost their jobs; and many have been negatively affected by casualisation and outsourcing. As a result many, many South Africans do not have jobs or decent self-employment; poverty is still a reality for millions as many do not have appropriate skills, while many cannot get credit to start or improve their own businesses (ANC 2004).

Similar points were made about the quality of services delivered to the masses, about the challenges of crime and disease, and about the circumstances of the youth and women.

The organisation sought a mandate to increase and improve the interventions of government. It believed that its successes over the first 10 years would give it sufficient credibility to remain the popular choice of the disadvantaged. As it won an increased majority of nearly 70% of voters, its strategy was obviously successful.

The targets the new government had set for itself included halving the rates of poverty and unemployment, improving skills delivery, improving the quality and accessibility of government services, rolling back diseases including HIV and AIDS, TB and malaria, and reducing corruption and the number of serious and priority crimes. Priority crimes identified by the Minister of Safety and Security include hijackings; cash in transit robberies; and crimes involving violence like murder, rape and child abuse.

The economic achievements of the first 10 years

The achievements of the first 10 years were considerable. Macro-economic policies stabilised a very unsteady economy. The fiscal deficit came down from a giddy 9.1% in 1993, to 2.5% or less in the 2000s. Public sector debt came down from 64% of GDP (gross domestic product) in 1994 to about 50% of GDP in 2004. The management of public finances improved to the point that the Finance Minister now has room to embark on relatively ambitious expansionary strategies without causing alarm, or even concern, amongst financial commentators; and he is able to raise debt at far more favourable rates because of the considerable improvements in South Africa's sovereign credit ratings.

Monetary policy has had considerable successes too. In 2004, the inflation rate fell to its lowest level since 1959, and the Governor of the South African Reserve Bank (SARB) was able to bring nominal interest rates down to their lowest level since the early 1980s. Moreover, an overhang of US$25 billion in the forward book was completely eliminated, and the central bank's reserves are growing steadily, with gross reserves at about US$15.1 billion by January 2005, and net reserves US$3.5 billion less.

In addition, a major trade reform has been accomplished with average non-agricultural tariffs declining to less than 5%, and imports and exports have diversified far beyond raw and semi-processed mineral products. The result appears to have had a considerable positive effect on total factor productivity, and hence on the capacity of the economy to grow (Cassim et al. 2002). It also contributed to the fight against inflation, as some imports cheapened and some domestic suppliers met real competition.

In sectoral terms the story is mixed. Some of the more successful sectors have been the automobile sector where exports have grown from virtually nothing to between 120 000 and 180 000 vehicles annually (depending on the exchange rate); the wine industry; and the tourism sector. Platinum mining has boomed, but this has been a response to the market rather than the result of policy interventions.

In the field of skills development, a new, very ambitious national system has been established with gradually mounting successes. The national innovation system turned round a declining trend in research and development. Black economic empowerment (BEE) has made considerable advances, and some restructuring of public enterprises has been completed.

As a result of better policies and a more favourable environment, the growth performance of the economy improved from averaging 1.4% growth and negative per capita growth in the decade before 1994, to averaging 3% GDP growth per annum and positive per capita growth since 1994.

The commitment of resources to the delivery of social services and social transfers has resulted in these aspects of government activity rising from about 44% of government expenditure in 1994 to over 56% of expenditure in 2003. In addition, the extension of infrastructure services such as water, sanitation, housing, electricity and communications has been considerable. For example, the number of housing subsidies approved since 1994 reached 2 million in 2004, while the proportion of households with access to electricity rose from 32% in 1994 to over 70% by the early 2000s (Policy Co-ordination and Advisory Services, The Presidency 2003: 24–25).

There is no question that both the performance of the economy and delivery to the poor have both improved considerably. The problem is that growth remains modest in international terms, the rate of unemployment has risen, and poverty remains an inescapable reality for about one third of the population. The government's own *Ten Year Review* report warned that, in spite of the positive advances, 'if all indicators were to continue along the same trajectory, especially in respect of the dynamic of economic inclusion and exclusion, we could soon reach a point where the negatives start to overwhelm the positives' (Policy Co-ordination and Advisory Services, The Presidency 2003: 102).

Major challenges

The first problem is the rate of growth. Though President Mbeki agued against a trickle-down approach, he was not under the illusion that one could address poverty and inequality without at the same time fuelling the engine of growth. In the same weekly letter in which he pointed to the intractability of poverty and inequality, he also wrote about the need to raise the rate of growth: '. . . the economy is growing at rates that are lower than those we need and desire . . .' (Mbeki 2003a). It is worth looking at the growth challenge in more detail.

South Africa's growth performance did improve after 1993. When we look at it in comparative terms, though, it is evident that the rate of growth is still less than impressive.

Figure 7.1 shows that the growth performance has moved strongly beyond the very poor performance of the early 1990s. Growth is much steadier than before, and the consecutive quarters of growth since 1998 represent a more consistent performance than ever before in South Africa's recorded economic history. However, the rate of growth is pedestrian. It is consistently below the rate of growth of developing countries in general (of course, strongly

Figure 7.1:   Comparative GDP growth rates.

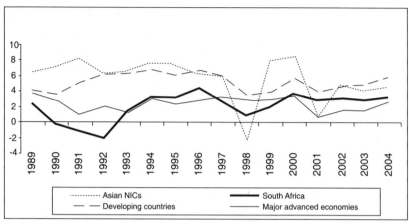

Source: IMF (2004).

influenced by the performance of China and increasingly India)
and below the rate of the newly industrialised countries (NICs) of
Asia. South Africa's rate of growth is similar to the pattern of the
major advanced economies – the difference being that their per
capita income is six or seven times as high as South Africa's, on
average.

An improvement in South Africa's per capita income at a rate
of around 1% per year is not nearly fast enough to roll back poverty
and unemployment. One recent study of the performance of the
South African economy estimated that it would be possible to halve
the rate of unemployment if the economy grew at 5% per annum
on average until 2014 (Texeira and Masih 2003: 15).

The underlying reason for the lukewarm rate of growth has
been a long-term decline in the rate of investment. As Figure 7.2
indicates, the rate of investment declined sharply in the 1980s,
which coincided with a decline in the rate of growth. Though
growth stabilised at an improved level in the mid-1990s, the low
rate of investment has constrained a significant increase in the rate
of growth. As it is, the ability of the growth rate to recover with a
low rate of investment suggests that the efficiency of investments

improved during the 1990s, a postulate that is supported by a range of evidence on total factor productivity (for example, Texeira and Masih 2003: 12). What Figure 7.2 also shows is that the economy was capable of investment rates over 25% of GDP in the past, as well as growth rates of 6%. This was not only true in the early 1980s, but also for periods in the 1960s and 1970s.

Figure 7.2: Fixed investment as a percentage of GDP.

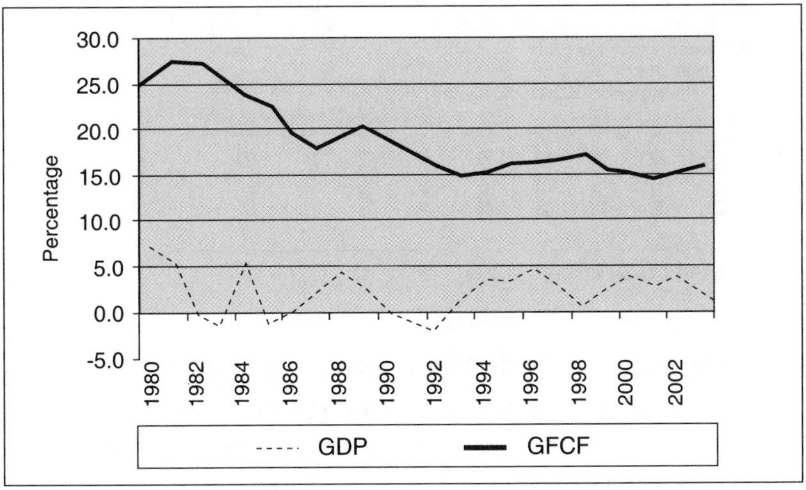

Source: SARB *Quarterly Bulletin*, various.
Note: This graph was compiled before the 2004 adjustment in the post-1998 GDP data, but this does not affect overall trends.

Figure 7.3 takes the investment and growth story a little further. It shows that it was not only private sector investment that declined – in fact, public sector investment declined more dramatically than private sector investment. Public sector investment declined from a peak of about 16% of GDP in the late 1970s to around 4% of GDP since the mid-1990s. Part of that decline is a result of two important companies leaving the public sector in the late 1980s – Sasol and Iscor. But if you study the graph carefully you will see that the damage was already done.

Figure 7.3: Gross fixed capital formation as a percentage of GDP.

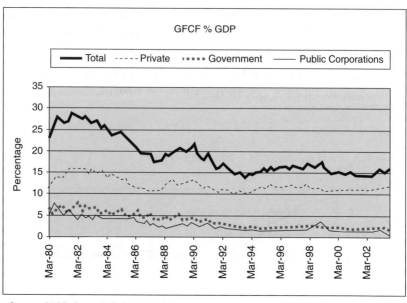

GFCF % GDP

Source: SARB *Quarterly Bulletin*, various.

When you compare South Africa's performance to other countries over the same period, the deterioration in its investment performance becomes even more obvious. In the early 1980s, and before, South Africa's investment performance was similar to Australia and South Korea – between 20 and 30% of GDP. Subsequently South Africa's performance fell dramatically, stabilising in 1994 at around 16% of GDP, while Australia continued to maintain an investment performance above 20% of GDP, and Korea never fell below 25% of GDP.

Why this dramatic deterioration in the investment performance of the economy, and what are the policy implications of the answer to that question? One of the obvious reasons is the declining appetite of private investors for the South African economy in the 1980s because of its political instability, and in the 1990s because of uncertainties about the redistributive policies of government, high interest rates and a high crime rate (Gelb 2001). The government lost much of its capacity to invest in the 1980s, as the growth rate

Figure 7.4:   Fixed investment in comparative international terms.

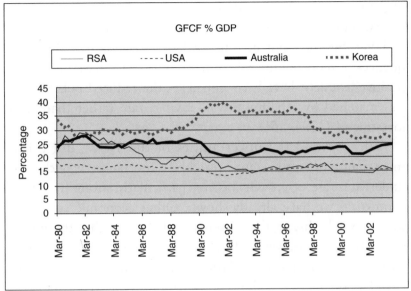

declined and the tax collection system weakened, and its attention drifted from building the apartheid system to desperately defending it.

When the democratic government took over in 1994, it recognised that another key constraint on investment was high nominal and real interest rates. These had risen as a consequence of mounting government debt, almost entirely raised domestically in rand-denominated bonds, and because of the tight monetary policy pursued by the central bank as part of the fight to bring the inflation rate down. The new government felt that conservative fiscal and monetary policies would ultimately raise the rate of investment through reducing the cost of capital. This was a key part of the rationale of the Growth, Employment and Redistribution (GEAR) strategy. Indeed, GEAR did succeed in lowering the cost of borrowing as South Africa's investment rating steadily improved, the risk premium declined, and the interest rate followed the rate of inflation's downward trend.

One thing that GEAR did not really reckon on was that most of the response of the private sector to lower inflation and interest rates would not be to invest more, but to consume more. As Davies and Van Seventer put it, 'The evidence suggests that the consequences of reducing the role of the public sector have not been as positive as might have been hoped ... the reduced public deficit was matched by a falling private savings rate rather than rising investment' (2004: 151).

Why, beyond the uncertainties of the 1990s, did private investment not grow more quickly? One factor was that the underlying rate of growth was not particularly strong in a global context, as we have already shown. Other economic constraints were the volatility of the currency and the fact that the interest and inflation rates were still relatively high. Moreover, the South African and the southern African regional market are not very large in global terms at about one sixth of the Mercosur trade pact in Latin America.

But the constraints on investment in South Africa were not limited to objective economic conditions. A new untried government – an African government at that – continued to invoke suspicion and mistrust amongst local and international investors, sometimes clouded by ignorance and prejudice. Accurate or inaccurate interpretations of the government's ability or willingness to address issues such as crime, HIV and AIDS, and the Zimbabwean impasse, as well as founded or unfounded concerns about the inflexibility of the labour market and the implications of affirmative action and empowerment, all added grist to the mill of pessimists. Some observers were concerned that the deep inherited inequalities could not be effectively turned around, which risked rising social conflict and instability.

Most of these negative factors could only be countered in the passing of time with the growing reputation of the ability of the South African government to deliver effectively and consistently.

Another important factor influencing the rate of investment was the role of the state. In the high period of apartheid, public investment reached 16% of GDP, which was unrealistically and inappropriately high. But its rapid decline to 4% of GDP was a severe shock to the system. One of the objectives that the RDP shared with GEAR was to eliminate government dissaving (public borrowing exceeding public investment) and to increase the rate of public investment as a proportion of government spending. It was a constant concern of the National Treasury that public spending, especially by the provinces, was so heavily weighted towards social transfers and salaries, and so little was devoted to investment expenditure. It is a notable fact that in spite of all its macroeconomic successes, government has not yet been able to completely eliminate dissaving.

There are several reasons for this. One stems from the inexperience of management in national, provincial and particularly local government, which has hindered its ability to develop and implement capital projects. The restructuring of the system of local government in 2000 added to discontinuities, even if temporarily and for good reason. Another limitation on public investment has been the cautious conservatism of the ANC government – a reluctance to incur debt where the outcome of the expenditure was risky or speculative, deriving from a fear of losing sovereignty as a result of indebtedness. Besides, beyond some obvious social infrastructure programmes, there were few very good public projects on the table for the first several years of the democratic era. Another constraint on government investment was the pressure on provinces to employ teachers and health-care workers, and to increase social transfers – at the expense of capital projects.

All these issues were recognised by government. As soon as the deficit was reduced to a manageable level and the revenue system was delivering due to better management and more optimal tax policies, the Treasury shifted to a strongly pro-investment stance. The 2001 budget introduced a renewed focus on infrastructure investment with targeted allocations to national departments and a supplementary infrastructure grant to the provinces (National Treasury *Budget Review* 2003: 130). This was extended in subsequent budgets with the establishment of the Provincial Infrastructure Grant (PIG) and the Municipal Infrastructure Grant (MIG). These are conditional grants to provinces and municipalities that have to be spent on capital projects within defined parameters. Public enterprises were also encouraged to review their investment patterns, and in 2004 government announced that it would review both the investment plans and the financing mechanisms for public enterprises.

The initial response to this shift in stance was slow. Most of the government and provincial departments, municipalities and public enterprises have taken time to gear up to higher rates of investment. But Treasury continues to press forward, and in some key areas such as provincial spending on roads, hospitals and schools, investment spending is growing fast. Total public sector investment plans for the three-year Medium Term Expenditure Framework period 2004/05–2006/07 totalled R267 billion according to Treasury estimates early in 2004 (National Treasury *Budget Review* 2003: 131). If this level of spending were realised, public sector investment would rise from 4% of GDP to over 6% of GDP.

But, even if the rate of growth increased as a result of higher public and private sector investment, would this directly offer improvements for the lives of the marginalised poor in South Africa? Not to a great extent directly, because the location of the marginalised poor in the society has tended to trap them in a state of poverty and dependence on remittances and social transfers. President Mbeki introduced the metaphor of two economies to highlight this challenge.

The challenge of the second economy
The second economy does not exist at a certain place, and it does not consist of an integrated economic system as such. It is essentially a condition – the condition lived by millions of people on the margin of the modern, industrial economy. They are linked to the industrial economy, but are not in it. They are people without a steady income based on their own economic activity. In other words,

they are households with no members in steady employment, whether in the formal or informal sector, and without a significant income-generating asset of their own. Such people mostly live in the informal settlements clustered around our towns and cities, in rural slums, and in poor, remote rural communities. For analytical purposes, the second economy is a metaphor for 'the marginalised'.

This [second] economy is a product of the colonial and apartheid economy and society created by successive minority regimes, during a period of three centuries. More recently, the process of global integration has exacerbated certain features of the divided economy in that competition from countries with cheap, relatively skilled labour makes it more difficult to find employment for unskilled South African workers in the tradable sector (Mbeki 2003: 2).

It is not easy to measure the number of people or households that we can classify as part of the second economy. As unemployment is a key indicator of poverty, one approximation would be to measure the total number of employed people as a proportion of the economically active population: 74% (Statistics South Africa 2005). But many households have more than one member in full-time employment. A more accurate measure would be to take the number of households falling below a poverty line. A 1999 measurement indicated that 3.7 million households out of 11.4 million households were below the poverty line, based on the poverty line developed in the 1998 Poverty Report prepared for The Presidency (Bhorat 2003: 23).[1] These measures suggest that about 30% of the households in South Africa are marginalised households.

International studies have shown that highly unequal societies are generally not able to roll back inequality without some significant interventions by the state. They have also shown that where inequality is reduced, risks of instability are reduced and the economies tend to grow faster (Birdsall and Londono 1997; Fields 2000). There is a very powerful case for carefully designed and properly managed interventions to build a staircase between the two economies, and to meld them together.

One form of intervention is through direct transfers to the needy. South Africa has developed a substantial social security system, with a social pension, a disability pension, a foster care grant, and a child support grant for children under 15 living in indigent households. Work undertaken for the *Ten Year Review* showed that our social security programmes are well targeted, are radically reducing poverty and may soon virtually eliminate extreme poverty (HSRC 2003).

However, there are two concerns in government about social security. One is that the government does not want to build conditions of dependency, or entitlement attitudes. South Africa cannot afford to become a 'granny' state. The other is that the cost of social security transfers is rising rapidly as the child support grant and disability payment systems roll out, which is sounding a warning bell regarding the allocation of government resources. Figure 7.5 shows that while social investments – education and health – have reached a plateau as a percentage of GDP, social transfers – the grants – are rising fairly rapidly as a percentage of GDP. The rate of growth should even out when the child support grant is fully rolled out by the end of 2006, but the potential danger that the social security system could grow beyond the means of government is already clear.

After announcing that the social security system already covered 7.7 million beneficiaries and that 3.2 million more children beneficiaries would be added by 2006, President Mbeki said, during his address to the first joint sitting of the third democratic parliament in May 2004:

> . . . a society in which large sections depend on social wel-
> fare cannot sustain its development. Our comprehensive
> programme to grow the economy, including the inter-
> ventions in both the First and Second Economies, improving
> sustainable livelihoods and creating work is meant precisely

Figure 7.5: Social transfers and social investments as a percentage of real GDP.

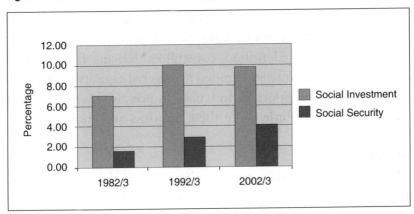

Source: National Treasury, *Budget Review*, various.

to ensure that, over time, a smaller proportion of society, in particular the most vulnerable, subsists solely on social grants (Mbeki 2004: 8).

What this means is that both policies designed to address the plight of those consigned for the present to the second economy, and policies for the development of the modern industrial economy must aim at reducing levels of dependency on the state in the medium to long term. Nevertheless, the number of South Africans receiving social transfers rose to 9 million by the end of 2004.

Priorities and choices

Addressing the challenge of growth and the challenges of rolling back poverty, inequality and unemployment simultaneously is not easy. While some policies do address both challenges simultaneously, it would be unrealistic to believe that all measures that support growth will be optimal for poverty alleviation and unemployment, or that anti-poverty or pro-equality strategies are necessarily optimal for growth. Though policy makers might strive for complementary strategies, not all optimal strategies are complementary and not all complementary strategies are optimal. However, in a vigorously democratic yet still extremely unequal society such as South Africa, one does not have the choice of focusing on growth challenges first and poverty and inequality later. So, when a range of relevant strategies has been identified, constraints deriving from limited capacity to raise finance and limited managerial capacity force policy makers to establish priorities and make choices. In this final section we need to think a little about these priorities and choices.

Macro

The successes of macroeconomic policy in South Africa are evident. Lower inflation, lower fiscal debt and deficit, lower interest rates, financial stability, and a more stable and predictable economic performance are some of the products of strong macro policies. Some of the key ingredients are monetary discipline and inflation targeting, effective medium-term budgetary planning, a stronger revenue service, liberalisation of the trade regime, and a better competition regime. All this is a huge advance on 1994.

But there are gaps in macroeconomic policy. Why do administered prices – health, education and infrastructure services – remain resistant to attempts to reduce inflationary expectations? Why is it so hard to achieve currency stability at a level that is reasonable for importers and exporters, and supports faster growth? Why is it so difficult to lift the rate of investment significantly above the mediocre level of about 16% of GDP? To some extent these issues will be addressed in the passage of time, but not without some key policy choices being highlighted.

Some of the key questions to be asked are:

- Is it possible to fix the regulatory and governance environment in the administered prices sectors? Should there be more competition or better governance and regulation? And how does the recipe vary from sector to sector, for example from electricity to telecommunications?
- In achieving relative currency stability at a suitable level, what combination of exchange control reform, foreign

reserves management and interest rate management tools
is optimal?
- And stemming from this question, while inflation
targeting is now widely accepted and endorsed, to what
extent should monetary policies take other factors such
as growth and employment into consideration, and should
this be built explicitly into the monetary policy mandate?
- Regarding fiscal policy there are two key questions. How
should government finance the much-needed revival in
public sector investment: rand- or foreign-denominated
bond issues, project loans, privatisation sales, sacrificing
other spending priorities? At the same time, can the cost
of capital for the private sector be lowered further,
especially for smaller businesses?

These are difficult questions to answer. Yet it is no small consolation
that they are entirely different questions from the macroeconomic
questions we were asking in 1994, such as: how do we reduce the
excessive public deficit and debt, how do we bring inflation down,
and how do we introduce responsible public financial management?

The macroeconomic approach must be to complete the victory
over inflationary expectations so that we can put to bed the domestic
triggers that exacerbate the effects of prices beyond our control.
Once inflationary expectations are subdued, we will have removed
a key constraint on the employment of monetary policy in support
of growth, in conjunction with other policies. In the meantime,
the combination of growth-oriented fiscal strategies in combination
with a lower nominal interest rate than South Africa has experienced in more than two decades should underpin a steady
improvement in growth performance.

Micro
The questions have also shifted for microeconomic policy. In 1994
we were asking questions such as: how quickly should we lower tariff
barriers, and how do we get South African producers to adjust to

the harsh glare of international competition? Though the productive sector has not quite sparkled, and though the level of value addition to inputs is still lower than some hoped it would be, South Africa has managed to pass through a severe restructuring of the economy without huge restructuring costs.

Exports grew and diversified in the 1990s, helped by a weakening rand. Some sectors transformed themselves from mundane domestic suppliers to world-class international competitors – with more or less assistance from government. For example, the automobile assembly and component sectors were strongly assisted by a well-designed Motor Industry Development Programme. For the tourism sector, government support certainly helped, but was perhaps not as crucial as in the case of automobiles. The wine industry relied largely on its own resources and its natural advantages, which catapulted it into international markets.

While parts of the mining industry, especially platinum, grew strongly as a result of favourable prices, especially in the last few years, the growth of the metals-processing sector, mostly steel and aluminium, is in no small part attributable to government involvement, through encouraging Eskom to offer cheap electricity or supporting the Industrial Development Corporation (IDC) taking a major stake in the metals beneficiation sector.

What is disappointing though, so far, is the relatively poor performance of many of the more labour-intensive sectors. Clothing, textiles, agro-processing, and similar labour-intensive sectors have performed without distinction. One reason is the lack of consistent and persistent public/private strategies; another reason is that global conditions did not support the rapid growth of these labour-intensive sectors in South Africa.

As President Mbeki suggested in a passage cited earlier in this chapter, global competition from labour-abundant countries has made the traditional path of development through cheap labour industries much more difficult. Adrian Wood's work suggests that it would not be wise for land-abundant economies in Africa to attempt to emulate the labour-abundant economies of Asia by entering the field of mass production (Wood 2002). But even if there was no intention of frontal competition, we expected that South Africa would be a strong niche competitor in some fields of manufacturing.

One missing piece is strong sectoral strategies – not necessarily entailing high-handed intervention, but including strong public/private co-operation. Another gap is that some infrastructural services are not sufficiently competitive – telecommunications is a strong sector with a reliable product, but regulatory uncertainty has led to a persistence of monopoly pricing for data transmission and international telecommunications. The railways suffered years of poor management and under-investment, and the ports were cash cows, milked by an embattled Transnet to keep its head above water. Clearly, the regulatory, governance and investment strategies for some key infrastructure sectors need urgent review.

The lack of competition and competitiveness affected other sectors too. South Africa's relatively great distance from competitive industrial economies means that producers of products with high weight-to-value ratios – where shipping costs are significant – remain relatively protected in South Africa. Mark-ups in products such as paper, steel and basic chemicals remain relatively high. Food prices are also affected by the ability to expand margins at critical points in the value chain. It is a tough challenge to simulate competitive conditions in sectors prone to import parity pricing. It probably requires some rethinking of competition law, and possibly other mechanisms too.

Some other persistent challenges for microeconomic reform are to get small business support and micro-finance institutions working better, to address the huge challenges of BEE, and to find ways to ensure that it complements the other goals of economic development strategy.

Nevertheless the productive sector has been resilient, even under unfavourable currency conditions. Partly this is because of the growing buoyancy of domestic demand as disposable income grows and consumers become more confident. But it is also in part a reflection of the success of some of the support systems for business. The skills strategy is slowly taking off – its next frontier is effective integration with the formal education system. The national system of innovation is well managed, though it could be better resourced. Empowerment has entered a bright new era of rapid change, but by mutual agreement. And even though the support networks are not yet perfect, small businesses are flourishing with the steady economic growth that the new millennium brought.

The bottom line for government is that there are two key driving strategies. The first is to ensure that the medium- to long-term cost structure of the economy improves. Regulation and competition are important, and so are public investment strategies. The second key strategy is to ensure that, at least for a selected set of industrial and service sectors, the private and public actors agree on long-term strategies, and work together to achieve them.

Second economy

Long-term growth prospects are brighter today in South Africa than at any other time in its recent history. The macroeconomy is in good shape and is well managed; new state and civic institutions are growing in authority and competence; developmental strategies have been tested and modified, and are now making headway. The country is stable and the government has elicited new levels of trust and confidence. All this is good for the denizens of the first economy – but can we build bridges that connect to the marginalised poor, and can we roll back persistent pockets of poverty and unemployment?

The government's second economy strategy has four main themes, beyond the mechanisms of relief through social transfer payments: temporary work opportunities, human resource development, access to capital, and better information flows. This is in addition to existing programmes to improve the social and economic infrastructure – roads, telecommunications, sanitation and water, schools and clinics. We now have a better sense of what is happening, and what could work. Difficulties include prioritisation and co-ordination between national departments and agencies, and between the different spheres of government.

The Expanded Public Works Programme (EPWP) is broadening, especially in labour-intensive construction, conservation, and water and sanitation programmes. What has been much slower to implement are the social interventions – state-supported early childhood development (ECD – pre-school education), where there is the potential for improving quality and creating jobs in the private and non-governmental organisation (NGO) sectors, and the field of home- and community-based health care. The institutional modalities are complex – though some local governments and provinces have successful initiatives, national programmes have struggled to get off the ground.

Another element that has taken considerably longer than planned to roll out is the 'Apex fund' – a wholesale fund to support micro-loans to micro-businesses and poor households. While some delivery institutions for Apex, mostly financial NGOs, are up and running, and have accumulated valuable experience mostly supported by donor and development agency funds, the national fund also suffered from the lack of a common national vision and poor co-ordination at a national level. Reform of banking law and the elements of the outcome of the BEE charter for the financial services sector should have a huge positive impact when they extend deposit-taking and credit services into, as yet, inaccessible markets.

In terms of human resource development, the key focal areas have been the improvement of general education and the development and spreading of learnerships for the unemployed. One key second-economy intervention strategy that demands more attention and support is Adult Basic Education and Training (ABET) because of the effect it can have on the viability of sustainable livelihood strategies, and on the context for the nurturing of the next generation. Another potential point of intervention is the system of technical high schools (Further Education and Training), which needs revamping, and could be, where appropriate, more effectively tailored to the needs of the second economy.

The fourth element is the flow of information. The marginalised poor have limited access to that information which is critical for managing their lives and strategising for the future. Information sources are improving – radio and television penetration is very deep, and the government is improving access to government information and services through the establishment of multipurpose community centres, the establishment of an all-purpose government website (the Batho Pele Gateway) and a toll-free number linked to an all-purpose government call centre. But even these innovative strategies promise to improve access steadily rather than spectacularly.

On the converse side of the information problem, the policy and strategy institutions do not have sufficient information about the marginalised poor, especially on how they make strategic decisions. Social data is improving, but it is not yet at the qualitative level that we can answer with any certainty why very poor people live where they live, migrate as they do, send children to school or withdraw them from school, seek work or choose not to seek work. The government will need to implement strategies that provide better information about the poor.

Our inventory of strategies implemented, strategies in development and strategy gaps is long and daunting, but there are reassuring circumstances. Firstly, the list of successfully implemented strategies is growing longer. Secondly, there is a growing level of consensus amongst key social actors about what is working and what it needed. Institutions such as Nedlac, the Millennium Labour Council, the Presidential working groups for business and labour and the joint working group – these institutions of formal negotiation and informal discussion, of the state and of civil society – are converging on a common vision for South Africa. Thirdly, the credibility of the government has grown after three national democratic elections, and a string of well-conceived and well-executed budgets.

Perhaps most important though, is that government is gaining self-confidence, based on the growing experience and growing knowledge of its leaders and managers. Fear of mistakes, growing debt, and losing sovereignty to international finance capital has receded, as confidence in policies and the effectiveness of instruments has grown. The government is now more ready and better equipped than before to meet the combined challenges of rolling back poverty and inequality and increasing the rate of economic growth.

Note

1. The poverty line indicates an annual household income of R12 982.50 as the poverty line level. This was based on the 1995 household poverty line of R903 per month, drawn from May (1998) and updated using the core inflation figures for the period 1995 to 1999.

Asking new questions

How would the new South Africa balance the tasks of setting the economy on a path of economic growth, to lay the basis for prosperity and, simultaneously, redistribute income, wealth and other resources such as human capital to meet the objectives of social justice and long-term sustainability? This was the central question posed for economic policy when the democratic government was elected in 1994.

The Reconstruction and Development Programme (RDP), as indicated in the introduction to this book, addressed this conundrum by positing a virtuous circle: infrastructure development aimed largely at providing access for the poor, would also contribute to economic growth through opening up the domestic market and increasing the efficiency of the economy. In turn, this would allow further improvements in the lives of the voters. The RDP also contained an acceptance of the inevitability and necessity of globalisation, with tight macroeconomic parameters and a commitment to trade reform. Nevertheless, conservative and business circles felt that the RDP posed a danger to macroeconomic stability.

During the 1990s the state leaned towards caution. The predominant concern of the new government was to retain its sovereignty, not to risk mortgaging the country's future before the new regime was firmly in the saddle. This was particularly true once an ANC leader became Finance Minister. The ability of the country to implement the RDP was limited – the state apparatus was weak and not strengthened in the short term by intensive transformation.

Both the state and the public enterprises, perhaps with the exception of Eskom, had lost their ability to scale up infrastructure investments. So while the rollout of housing and related infrastructure for the poor was fairly successful during this period, the scale of public sector investment remained relatively low.

Trevor Manuel, the Finance Minister, later described the period after he assumed office as 'a period of fiscal consolidation' (Manuel 2004). It followed a period of fiscal indiscipline in the early 1990s and only a partial correction of this in the 1994–96 period, with an average budget deficit of 4.7%, and government debt approaching 50% of GDP (gross domestic product). The emphasis in the late 1990s was on fiscal planning, increasing transparency in public finances, tax reform, reform of revenue administration capacity, and ultimately co-ordination of fiscal and monetary policy through the deployment of inflation targeting in 2001. In retrospect, it was a period of taking control of the system, before which the results of a more expansionary programme would have been unpredictable.

The government hoped that private sector investment, particularly from abroad, would make a bigger contribution in this period – this expectation of the Growth, Employment and Redistribution (GEAR) strategy was much criticised when GEAR missed its growth projections. Slow private sector investment provided ammunition for the anti-globalisation lobby and other supporters of an inward-focused development path. Private investment remained lower than hoped, even though government cutbacks were intended to make room for private investors. The currency shocks of 1996 and 1998 and the South African Reserve Bank's (SARB's) heavy-handed response increased the cost of capital and the investment hurdle rate, rather than reducing them. Added to this, the first black government in South Africa had to fight far harder for credibility for its policies than its white predecessors, even though its policies were better and its political base very firm. GEAR did not predict the Asian crisis, or the central bank's response, nor did it take into account the extra effort required of a new black government to obtain credibility in financial markets.

Though the GEAR (or 'fiscal consolidation') phase disappointed in its growth performance, it delivered macroeconomic stability. On the basis of a very low budget deficit, declining public debt, and lower costs of borrowing, the government shifted its stance in the budget year 2001/02. There were three main elements of the shift. The first was a significant tax-cut, especially for the lower middle class and the working class. The second was a commitment to speeding up public infrastructure spending, and the third was a commitment to accelerate and broaden the roll-out of social security transfers – the state pension, the newly structured disability grant, the foster-care grant, and the recently introduced child support grant. With the state as yet not strong enough to roll out investment as rapidly as desired, the tax-cut and the social grants played bigger roles in the early 2000s. From an austere outward-looking state, the South African state slipped into Keynesian mode. The Expanded Public Works Programme (EPWP) announced in 2003 was another recognisably Keynesian element.

The strengthening of redistribution through tax-cuts and the social grants were meant to complement a strategy for competitiveness and exports beyond natural resources. But the fiscal expansionary phase coincided with a period of rapid and far-reaching strengthening of the currency. This resulted partly from tight monetary policy after the 2001 shock, partly from the weakness of the US dollar, and partly from the worldwide commodity boom driven by rising Chinese imports of industrial inputs. So, while platinum, steel, iron ore, coal and aluminium producers could export in spite of the strengthening rand, the agriculture, manufacturing and services sectors faced rising rand costs without the compensation of booming international prices.

It was as if the path had shifted from export competitiveness to inward industrialisation, except for the fact that the rand became so strong that domestic producers could not take full advantage of the consumption boom and were forced to compete with imports, especially in consumer durables such as Korean refrigerators and European cars. So it happened that South Africa experienced its first-ever boom based on a broad-based expansion of domestic consumption, alongside a reasonably healthy minerals and metals export sector.

One of the most striking and novel features of the boom of the mid-2000s was the role played by the emerging black middle strata. From white-collar workers through to professionals and managers of the very highest economic stratum, the progress of black people in the economy was one of the key drivers of domestic demand and growth. A merchant bank put it this way in a report for investors: 'On both an 18-month and five-year view, we expect the emerging black market to continue to support volume growth across the South African economy' (Moola and Moloto 2004: 3).

This broad-based rise in consumption is being driven by a significant shift in the position of the black middle strata. The Bureau for Market Research reported:

> In 2001 4.1 million out of 11.2 million households in South Africa lived on an income of R9 600 and less per year. This decreased to 3.6 million households in 2004, even after taking the negative effects of price increases on spending power into account. On the other hand, households receiving a real income of R153 601 and more per annum rose from 721 000 in 1998 to more than 1.2 million in 2004 (Bureau for Market Research 2005).

Trends for groups between R9 600 and R153 601 are similarly positive, indicating significant real improvements in all these levels between 1998 and 2004. At the lowest level, the expansion of the social grants has impacted on the poor, reducing levels of extreme poverty and significantly strengthening their purchasing power. The percentage of poor households as defined in the terms used by the Bureau for Market Research shrunk from 40.3% of households to 29.8% between 1998 and 2004. At the opposite end of the scale, of South Africa's 23 000 multimillionaires, 11 000 are white and 12 000 are 'black' (including Africans, coloureds and Indians) (*Sake Rapport* 30 January 2005).

In short, the impact of employment equity and economic empowerment pressures have been to create a new dynamic within the economy of a very broad set of households that is able to accumulate private real assets for the first time in history. Combined with the impact of the social grants and the tax-cuts of 2001, the expansion and strengthening of the broad black middle strata has added a significant new element to the growth story in South Africa. Perhaps this is best captured in the fact that a very large proportion of the foreign inflows into the Johannesburg Stock Exchange in 2003, 2004 and 2005 were directed at domestic market-oriented stocks, especially in financial and service sectors, rather than the traditional natural resource counters.

So there would seem to be a virtuous circle between redistribution and growth, perhaps even more than ANC leaders expected in the early 1990s. But exciting as this outcome is, serious challenges remain. Indeed, some are serious enough to pose significant threats to the future of the South African economy. Several of these were dealt with in the previous chapter: the challenge of raising investment levels; the challenge of improving human resource development standards and throughput; and the challenge of integrating the second economy into the modern industrial economy. Beyond these challenges, recent peculiarities in South Africa's economic performance remind us that macroeconomic policy remains less than optimal – perhaps the key challenge is in the co-ordination of fiscal and monetary policy.

In a recent and as yet unpublished Investment Climate Survey by the World Bank and the South African government, firms were asked what the main obstacles to growth were. While the shortage of skills, the threat of crime and labour regulations were prominent answers amongst manufacturers, one of the highest responses pointed to 'macroeconomic instability'. With steady low inflation rates and relatively low interest rates, the only logical conclusion is that these manufacturing firms were challenged by the volatile and unpredictable currency. A currency that veers regularly by 20% or more, most recently strengthening by 50% against the dollar over three years, makes effective integration into the world economy extremely difficult. This recent 'positive' currency shock was the fourth currency shock in the 10 years since 1994, following negative currency shocks of more than 20% in 1996, 1998 and 2001. Observation has suggested for several years, and the World Bank survey now confirms, that the volatility of the currency is the single greatest obstacle to higher rates of investment by the private sector.

In one sense this is a positive development – other obstacles to investment symptomatic of serious malfunctioning of the state, such as crime or health-related concerns, have now subsided, and more purely economic policy matters have come to the fore. This indicates that the new democratic state has convinced investors that it is effectively addressing public service management issues, even if challenges remain. But the volatility of the currency remains a frustrating obstacle to a really significant increase in the rate of growth.

To what extent could this volatility be countered? What are the options for a relatively small open economy? South Africa does not have huge scope to adjust its relationship to international markets, but there are some significant instruments, and they are not trivial. The central bank can build its reserves, which remain low by international standards; exchange controls could be further loosened; the interest rate remains a valid instrument to address over- or under-valuation of the currency; and what the SARB Governor calls 'open mouth operations' or talking the currency up or down could be an effective instrument.

What is absolutely necessary, though, is effective co-ordination of fiscal and monetary policy. For example, if the currency is seen to be over-valued because South Africa's real interest rate is considerably higher than in most significant economies, the SARB can reduce interest rates to reduce the interest rate differential. The risk is that this move might overheat the domestic economy, which could lead to a rise in inflation, putting the SARB's mandate of inflation targeting at risk. However, if fiscal policy worked in consonance with this monetary policy move, and was able to moderate domestic demand, the risk to the inflation target would be reduced, which would allow an appropriate monetary policy stance. Inflation targeting is the central tool used to co-ordinate fiscal and monetary policy, but without deepening that co-ordination, inflation targeting becomes too blunt an instrument, with potentially serious unintended consequences.

There is scope for further co-ordination of fiscal and monetary policy. If this were achieved, the potential for growth would be considerably greater. The economy would not veer as giddily between export competitiveness and domestic demand as drivers of alternate periods of growth when the rand is weak and strong respectively, and would move towards greater balance and stability. It might hit the 'sweet spot' that some investment analysts have recently written about, when South Africa can take advantage of both its strongly booming domestic demand and its export opportunities for commodities and manufactures and services.

How the key questions have shifted in the 11 years since the first democratic elections is a sign of South Africa's progress. In 1994 the question was: how can we combine growth and redistribution so that the economy prospers and poverty and inequality are significantly reduced? Today, in 2005, I think it is fair to say that we know the answers to this question. The challenge of redistributing assets remains great, but the success in redistributing income is gathering pace. The performance of the economy has been strong, with post-1998 being the longest continuous period of growth in South Africa's recorded national accounts history, also achieving a 46-year low in inflation and a 24-year low in interest rates. The question today is: how do we take the economy to a higher growth plane so that we can effectively sustain our programme of redistribution and the integration or elimination of the second economy? Many analysts inside and outside of government do not think it is too hard to answer the new question, as we discussed in the previous chapter.

Perhaps a fictitious analogy would help to explain where we seem to be. Eleven years ago, a young and enthusiastic team took over the management of a rally car. The car, though well built, was battered and old, and had failed to obtain a podium finish for decades. Of late, it had failed to complete most races. Often it ran short of fuel because of shortages of funds. Because the races never stop in this rally series, the new team was forced to learn to drive the vehicle and to begin to modify it simultaneously. First it cut back on costs, and then it began to invest in skills and equipment. After six or seven years, the vehicle was running reliably, finishing races and performing well on some courses. The rally team was sustainable, if not thriving. Further modifications over the next few years clearly improved the performance of the vehicle, but this was not enough to take it to the podium. Though teamwork was improving, it wasn't good enough. What is lacking is a higher level of co-ordination between the designers, the mechanics, the driver and the navigators, not to mention the financiers. Once this is overcome, success will be around the corner.

Current projections for the South African economy generally indicate growth in the vicinity of 4% for the next three to four years.[1] This suggests that South Africa has stepped up a level from average growth of around 2.9% in the first 10 years, to an average rate of growth around 1% higher. Government and businesses in South Africa have learned to manipulate the levers of growth, and redistributive policies are reinforcing the positive growth trajectory. Where the ceiling is no one really knows – the rate of investment is constrained by capital flows, the rate of savings and the availability of skills. It looks increasingly feasible that South Africa can attain growth in the vicinity of 5-6% consistently. South Africa last saw growth at those levels in the 1960s and 1970s but then the economy was built on an undemocratic society with deep inequalities of wealth and income, which both politically and economically limited the growth rate in the long term. This time the growth surge is built on and fed by a democratic state striving to reduce poverty and inequality.

Note

1. Several of the locally based bank research units in organisations such as Standard
   Bank, Deutsche Bank and others have made similar projections for the next
   three to four years as of early 2005.

Select bibliography

Abedian, I. 2004. Beyond Budget 2004: job creation and poverty alleviation in South Africa: what should we be doing? Institute for Justice and Reconciliation. Public symposium. Cape Town: Graduate School of Business, University of Cape Town.

African National Congress (ANC). 1949. Programme of Action. In S. Johns and R. Hunt Davis Jr. (eds.), 1991, *Mandela, Tambo, and the African National Congress: The Struggle against Apartheid 1949–1990: A Documentary Survey.* New York: Oxford University Press.

———. 1955. Freedom Charter. In S. Johns and R. Hunt Davis Jr. (eds.), 1991, *Mandela, Tambo, and the African National Congress: The Struggle against Apartheid 1949–1990: A Documentary Survey.* New York: Oxford University Press.

———. 1969. Strategy and Tactics. Abridged in T.G. Karis and G.M. Gerhart, 1997, *From Protest to Challenge, Volume 5: Nadir and Resurgence.* Bloomington: Indiana University Press.

———. 1979. Report of the Politico-Military Strategy Commission to the ANC National Executive Committee (the Green Book). Abridged in T.G. Karis and G.M. Gerhart, 1997, *From Protest to Challenge, Volume 5: Nadir and Resurgence.* Bloomington: Indiana University Press.

———. 1988. Constitutional guidelines for a democratic South Africa. In I. Liebenberg, c.1989, *Responses to the ANC Constitutional Guidelines.* Cape Town: IDASA.

———. 1989. Declaration of the OAU ad-hoc committee on southern Africa on the question of South Africa, 21 August, Harare. In K. Asmal et al., 2005, *Legacy of Freedom: The ANC's Human Rights Tradition.* Johannesburg: Jonathan Ball.

———. 1991a. *Draft Resolution on ANC Economic Policy for National Conference.* Cape Town: Centre for Development Studies, University of the Western Cape.

———. 1991b. *Workshop Package: Economic Policy.* Cape Town: University of the Western Cape.

——. c.1991c. Draft: some notes on the ANC's strategic approach to business. Undated memo.

——. 1991d. Department of Economic Policy briefing document: meetings with foreign investors. Unpublished memo. 8 April.

——. 1992. *Ready to Govern: ANC Policy Guidelines for a Democratic South Africa*. Johannesburg: ANC Policy Unit.

——. 1994a. *The Reconstruction and Development Programme: A Policy Framework*. Johannesburg: Umanyano Publications.

——. 1994b. ANC trade and industry policy guidelines. Unpublished.

——. 1997a. Challenges facing the South African economy. Background document prepared for the ANC National Conference, December.

——. 1997b. 50th National Conference Report. http://www.anc.org.za.

——. 1997c. Resolutions from the 50th National Conference, December. http://www.anc.org.za.

——. 2004. A people's contract to create jobs and fight poverty. http://www.anc.org.za/elections/2004/manifesto/manifesto.html.

African National Congress and COSATU. 1990. ANC and COSATU recommendations on post-apartheid economic policy. Mimeo. Discussed in a consultative conference 28 April–1 May, Harare.

African National Congress (Department of Economic Policy). 1990. Forward to a democratic economy. Workshop documents, 20–23 September, Harare.

Amsden, A.H. 1989. *Asia's Next Giant: Late Industrialisation in South Korea*. Oxford: Oxford University Press.

Archer, S. et al. 1990. Unemployment and labour market issues: a beginner's guide. In N. Nattrass and E. Ardington (eds.), *The Political Economy of South Africa*. Oxford: Oxford University Press.

Asmal, K., D. Chidester and C. Lubisi (eds.). 2005. *Legacy of Freedom: The ANC's Human Rights Tradition*. Johannesburg: Jonathan Ball.

Badroodien, A. 2003. Enterprise training. In A. Kraak and H. Perold (eds.), *Human Resources Development Review 2003: Education, Employment and Skills in South Africa*, Cape Town: HSRC Press.

Baker, P., A. Boraine and W. Krafchick (eds.). 1993. *South Africa and the World Economy in the 1990s*. Cape Town: David Philip and Washington, DC: Brookings Institution Press.

Baskin, J. 1991. *Striking Back: A History of COSATU*. Johannesburg: Ravan Press.

Bell, T. and N. Caettaneo. 1997. *Foreign Trade and Employment in the South African Manufacturing Industry*. Geneva: International Labour Office (ILO).

Bhorat, H. 2003. Employment and unemployment trends in post-apartheid South Africa. Unpublished paper prepared for The Presidency's Ten Year Cabinet Review.

Bird, A. 1991. Negotiation for change: the Cosatu view of changes needed in the provision of adult education and training in South Africa. Paper presented at a conference on Manpower Development for the New South Africa, Pretoria, October 1991.

Birdsall, N. and J. Londono. 1997. Asset inequality matters: an assessment of the World Bank's approach to poverty reduction. *American Economic Review* 87.

Black, A. 1991. Manufacturing development and the economic crisis: a reversion to primary production? In S. Gelb (ed.), *South Africa's Economic Crisis*. Cape Town: David Philip.

Black Economic Empowerment Commission (BEECom). 2001. *A National Integrated Black Economic Empowerment Strategy*. Johannesburg: Skotaville.

Blinder, A.S. 1998. *Central Banking in Theory and Practice*. Cambridge, MA: MIT Press.

Board of Trade and Industry. 1988. A policy and strategy for the development and structural adjustment of industry in the Republic of South Africa. Report No. 2614. Pretoria.

Bond, P. 1991. *Commanding Heights and Community Control: New Economics for a New South Africa*. Johannesburg: Ravan Press.

Bundy, C. 1979. *The Rise and Fall of the South African Peasantry*. London: Heinemann.

Bunting, B. 1969. *The Rise of the South African Reich*. London: Penguin and Berkeley: University of California Press.

Bureau for Market Research. 2005. *National Personal Income of South Africans by Population Group, Income Group, Life Stage and Life Plane 1960–2007*. Pretoria: UNISA.

BusinessMap Foundation. 2003. *Empowerment Guidelines for Investors 2003: Mapping State Requirements and Investor Experiences*. Johannesburg: BusinessMap Foundation.

Capie, F., C. Goodhart, S. Fischer and N. Schnadt. 1994. *The Future of Central Banking*. Cambridge: Cambridge University Press.

Cargill, J. (ed.). 1999. *Empowerment 1999: A Moving Experience*. Johannesburg: BusinessMap Foundation.

Cassim, R., D. Onyango and D.E. van Seventer. 2002. *The State of Trade Policy in South Africa*. Johannesburg: TIPS.

Cassim, R., D. Onyango, Z. Skosana and D.E. van Seventer. 2003. A review of the changing composition of the South African economy. Unpublished paper prepared for The Presidency's Ten Year Cabinet Review. http://www.sarpn.org.za.

Chabane, N., J. Machaka, N. Molaba, S. Roberts and M. Taka. 2003. 10 year review: industrial structure and competition policy. Unpublished paper. http://www.sarpn.org.za.

COSATU, NACTU and FEDSAL. 1996. Social equity and job creation: the key to a stable future. http://www.cosatu.org.za.

COSATU, NACTU and FEDUSA. 1998a. Creating jobs in South Africa: key issues and strategies. Labour's input to the Presidential Jobs Summit, April. Mimeo.

———. 1998b. Labour's input to the Presidential Jobs Summit, presented by John Gomomo, 30 October. http://www.polity.org.za.

CREFSA. 1996. Foreign portfolio investment flows to South Africa. *CREFSA Quarterly Review* (July). London: London School of Economics.

———. 1997. South Africa's external debt: maturity and liquidity issues. *CREFSA Quarterly Review* (January). London: London School of Economics.

Crush, J., A. Jeeves and D. Yudelman. 1991. *South Africa's Labor Empire: A History of Black Migrancy to the Gold Mines*. Boulder: Westview Press.

Cull, P. (ed.) 1992. *Economic Growth and Foreign Investment in South Africa*. Cape Town: IDASA.

Davies, R. 1979. *Capital, State and White Labour in South Africa, 1900–1960*. Brighton: Harvester Press.

———. 1987. Nationalisation, socialisation and the Freedom Charter. *South African Labour Bulletin* 12(2).

Davies, R. and D.E. van Seventer. 2004. A three-gap and macro-decomposition analysis for South Africa, 1993–2002. *Development Southern Africa* 21(1).

Department of Arts, Culture, Science and Technology (DACST). 2001a. A national biotechnology strategy for South Africa. http://www.dst.gov.za/programmes/biodiversity/ biotechstrategy.pdf.

———. 2001b. National research and development strategy. http://www.dst.gov.za.

Department of Finance. 1996. Growth Employment and Redistribution: a macro-economic strategy. http://www.treasury.gov.za.

Department of Labour. 2003a. Annual report: Commission for Employment Equity 2002–2003. http://www.labour.gov.za.

———. 2003b. Growth and Development Summit 2003: building a partnership for growth and development. Pretoria: Department of Labour.

Department of Science and Technology. 2005. National survey of research and experimental development (R & D) (2003/04 fiscal year): high level results. Pretoria: Department of Science and Technology.

Department of Trade and Industry (DTI). 1998a. Annual report, 1996–1997. RP57/98.

———. 1998b. South African foreign trade: selected statistics July 98. Unpublished.

———. 1998c. Incentive schemes.

———. 1999. Five year assessment of DTI policies. Unpublished draft. 2002. Integrated Manufacturing Strategy. http://www.nedlac.org.za.

———. 2003a. South Africa's economic transformation: a strategy for broad-based black economic empowerment. http://www.info.gov.za.

———. 2003b. Unlocking potential in an enterprising nation: the integrated small business development strategy in South Africa 2004–2014. Unpublished paper.

Department of Transport. 1998. Moving South Africa. http://www.transport. gov.za/projects.

Dornbusch, R. 1998. Cross-border payments, taxes and alternative capital account regimes. In G.K. Helleiner (ed.), *Capital Account Regimes and the Developing Countries*. London: Macmillan.

Du Plessis, P.G. 1979. An international comparison of economic concentration. *South African Journal of Economics* 4(1).

Edwards, L. 2001. Globalisation and the skills bias of occupational employment in South Africa. *South African Journal of Economics* 69(1).

Edwards, S. 1998. Capital flows, real exchange rates and capital controls: some Latin American experiences. NBER Working Paper No. 6800. Cambridge, MA: NBER.

Eijffinger, S.C.W. and J. de Haan. 1996. *The Political Economy of Central-Bank Independence*. Princeton: Princeton University.

Ellis, S. and T. Sechaba. 1992. *Comrades against Apartheid: The ANC and the Communist Party in Exile*. London: James Currey.

EmpowerDEX. 2003. From the starting block: a decade of black economic empowerment. Unpublished paper prepared for The Presidency's Ten Year Cabinet Review.

———. 2005. A snapshot of black economic empowerment on the JSE. Unpublished paper submitted by EmpowerDEX to The Presidency, 16 February.

Erwin, A. 1978. An essay on structural unemployment. *South African Labour Bulletin* 4(4).

———. 1989. Towards a planned economy. South African Labour Bulletin 14(1).

———. 1998. A report on the Presidential Jobs Summit by the government delivered by Minister Alec Erwin. 30 October. http://www.polity.org.za.

Fallon, P. 1993. The implications for South Africa of using World Bank facilities. In P. Baker et al. (eds.), South Africa and the World Economy in the 1990s. Cape Town: David Philip and Washington, DC: Brookings Institution Press.

Fallon, P. and L. Perreira da Silva. 1994. South Africa: economic performance and policies. Discussion Paper 7, April. Washington, DC: World Bank Southern Africa Department.

Fallon, P. and R. Lucas. 1998. South Africa Labour Markets: Adjustment and Inequalities. Washington, DC: World Bank Southern Africa Department.

Fields, G. 2000. Distribution and Development: A New Look at the Developing World. Cambridge, MA: MIT Press.

Fine, B. and Z. Rustomjee. 1996. The Political Economy of South Africa: From Minerals-Energy Complex to Industrialisation. Boulder: Westview.

Fischer, S. 1994. Modern central banking. In F. Capie et al., The Future of Central Banking. Cambridge: Cambridge University Press.

Forder, J. 1998. Central Bank independence: conceptual clarifications and interim assessment. Oxford Economic Papers 50(3).

Fourie, F.C.V.N. 1996. Industrial concentration levels and trends in South Africa: completing the picture. South African Journal of Economics 64(1).

Freund, B. 1991. South African gold mining in transformation. In S. Gelb (ed.), South Africa's Economic Crisis. Cape Town: David Philip.

Garelli, S. 1998. World Competitiveness Yearbook: World Competitiveness – New Frontiers in 1998. Switzerland: Institute of Management Development.

Gelb, S. 1991a. South Africa's economic crisis: an overview. In S. Gelb (ed.), South Africa's Economic Crisis. Cape Town: David Philip.

———. (ed.). 1991b. South Africa's Economic Crisis. Cape Town: David Philip.

———. 2001. Fixed investment in South Africa: overview report. Unpublished report for The Presidency.

Gerson J. and B. Kahn. 1988. Factors determining real exchange rate changes in South Africa. South African Journal of Economics 56(2).

Harber, A. and B. Ludman (eds.). 1995. A–Z of South African Politics: The Essential Handbook. London: Penguin.

Hart, G.P. 1972. Some Socio-Economic Aspects of African Entrepreneurship. Grahamstown: Institute of Social and Economic Research, Rhodes University.

Hayter, S. 1999. Assessing the social impact of globalization: trade liberalization and employment. *Trade and Industry Monitor* 9 (March).

Helleiner, G.K. 1998a. Capital account regimes and the developing countries: issues and approaches. In G.K. Helleiner (ed.), *Capital Account Regimes and the Developing Countries*. London: Macmillan.

———. 1998b. *Capital Account Regimes and the Developing Countries*. London: Macmillan.

Hindson, D. 1987. *Pass Controls and the Urban African Proletariat in South Africa*. Johannesburg: Ravan Press.

Hirsch, A. 1987. The industrialisation of Dimbaza: population relocation and industrial decentralisation in a Bantustan. In R. Tomlinson and M. Addelson (eds.), *Regional Restructuring under Apartheid: Urban and Regional Policies in Contemporary South Africa*. Johannesburg: Ravan Press.

———. 1989. Sanctions, loans and the South African economy. In M. Orkin (ed.), *Sanctions against Apartheid*. Cape Town: David Philip.

———. 1992a. Prospects and policy implications. In P. Cull (ed.), *Economic Growth and Foreign Investment in South Africa*. Cape Town: IDASA.

———. 1992b. The external environment and the South African trade policy debate. Economic Trends Research Group, Working Paper No.13. Cape Town: Development Policy Research Unit, University of Cape Town.

———. 1993. *Trading up: Trade Policy for Industrialisation*. Cape Town: Industrial Strategy Project, Development Policy Research Unit, University of Cape Town.

———. 1995. From the GATT to the WTO: the global trade regime and its implications for South Africa. In G. Mills, A. Begg and A. van Nieukerk (eds.), *South Africa in the Global Economy*. Johannesburg: South African Institute for International Affairs.

Holden, M. 1990. The growth of exports and manufacturing in South Africa from 1947 to 1987. *Development South Africa* 7(3).

Holden, M. and A. Gouws. 1997. Determinants of South African exports. Paper presented at the Trade and Industry Policy Secretariat Annual Forum, Muldersdrift.

Horwitz, R. 1967. *The Political Economy of South Africa*. London: Weidenfeld and Nicholson.

Human Sciences Research Council (HSRC). 2003. Measuring the impact of government programmes using administrative data. Unpublished paper commissioned by The Presidency.

Industrial Development Corporation (IDC). 1990. *Modification of the Application of Protection Policy*. June. Sandton.

————. 1998. *Core Economic Indicators*. July. Sandton.

Innes, D. 1984. *Anglo American and the Rise of Modern South Africa*. New York: Monthly Review Press and London: Heinemann.

International Monetary Fund (IMF). 2004. World economic outlook. http://www.imf.org/external/pubs/ft/weo/2004/02.

Joffe, A., D. Kaplan, R. Kaplinsky and D. Lewis. 1995. *Improving Manufacturing Performance in South Africa: The Report of the Industrial Strategy Project*. Cape Town: University of Cape Town Press.

Johns, S. and R. Hunt Davis Jr. (eds.). 1991. *Mandela, Tambo, and the African National Congress: The Struggle against Apartheid 1948–1990: A Documentary Survey*. New York: Oxford University Press.

Kahn, B. 1987. Import penetration and import demand in the South African economy. *South African Journal of Economics* 55(3).

————. 1991. The crisis in South Africa's balance of payments. In S. Gelb (ed.), *South Africa's Economic Crisis*. Cape Town: David Philip.

————. 1992. South Africa's exchange rate policy: lessons from the past. Economic Trends Working Paper No. 15. Cape Town: Development Policy Research Unit, University of Cape Town.

Kaplan, D. 1977. Class conflict, capital accumulation and the state: an historical analysis of the state in twentieth century South Africa. Unpublished Ph.D. thesis, University of Sussex.

Kaplan, D. and R. Kaplinsky. 1998. Trade and industrial policy on an uneven playing field: the case of the deciduous canning industry in South Africa. Mimeo.

Kaplinsky, R. and C. Manning. 1998. Concentration, competition policy and the role of small and medium-sized enterprises in South Africa's industrial development. *Journal of Development Studies* 31(1).

Karis, T.G. and G.M. Gerhart. 1997. *From Protest to Challenge. Volume 5: Nadir and Resurgence*. Bloomington: Indiana University Press.

Kasekende, L., D. Kitabire and M. Martin. 1998. Capital inflows and macroeconomic policy in sub-Saharan Africa. In G.K. Helleiner (ed.), *Capital Account Regimes and the Developing Countries*. London: Macmillan.

Khatri, Y., J. Leape and E. van der Merwe. 1997. Capital flows and macroeconomic policy in South Africa. *CREFSA Quarterly Review* (1).

Khosa, M. 1990. The black taxi revolution. In N. Natrrass and E. Ardington (eds.), *The Political Economy of South Africa*. Oxford: Oxford University Press.

Kraak, A. 2004a. Training policies under late apartheid: the historical imprint of a low skills regime. In S. McGrath et al. (eds.), *Shifting Understandings of Skills in South Africa: Overcoming the Historical Imprint of a Low Skills Regime*. Cape Town: HSRC Press.

———. 2004b. The National Skills Development Strategy: a new institutional regime for skills formation in post-apartheid South Africa. In S. McGrath et al. (eds.), *Shifting Understandings of Skills in South Africa: Overcoming the Historical Imprint of a Low Skills Regime*. Cape Town: HSRC Press.

Kraak, A. and H. Perold (eds.). 2003. *Human Resources Development Review 2003: Education, Employment and Skills in South Africa*. Cape Town: HSRC Press.

Krugman, P. 1999. The return of depression economics. *Foreign Affairs* 78(1).

Leftwich, A. (ed.). 1974. *South Africa: Economic Growth and Political Change*. London: Alison & Busby.

Legassick, M. 1974. Legislation, ideology and economy in post-war South Africa. *Journal of Southern African Studies* 1(4).

Levy, A. and Associates. 2003. *Andrew Levy Strike Report*. 30 June.

Levy, B. 1992. *How can South African Manufacturing Efficiently Create Employment? An Analysis of the Impact of Trade and Industrial Policy*. Washington, DC: World Bank Southern Africa Department.

Lewis, D. 1991. Unemployment and the current crisis. In S. Gelb (ed.), *South Africa's Economic Crisis*. Cape Town: David Philip.

———. 1995. Markets, ownership and manufacturing performance. In A. Joffe et al., *Improving Manufacturing Performance in South Africa: Report of the Industrial Strategy Project*. Cape Town: University of Cape Town Press.

Liebenberg, I. c.1989. *Responses to the ANC Constitutional Guidelines*. Cape Town: IDASA.

Lipton, M. 1986. *Capitalism and Apartheid: South Africa, 1910–1986*. Aldershot: Wildwood House and Cape Town: David Philip.

Louw, R. (ed.). 1989. *Four Days in Lusaka: Whites in a Changing Society*. Johannesburg: Five Freedoms Forum.

Macroeconomic Research Group (MERG). 1993. *Making Democracy Work: A Framework for Macroeconomic Policy in South Africa*. Cape Town: Centre for Development Studies, University of the Western Cape.

Mandela, N. 1955. People are destroyed. In S. Johns and R. Hunt Davis Jr. (eds.). 1991. *Mandela, Tambo, and the African National Congress: The Struggle against Apartheid 1948–1990: A Documentary Survey*. New York: Oxford University Press.

———. 1956. Freedom in our lifetime. In S. Johns and R. Hunt Davis Jr. (eds.). 1991. *Mandela, Tambo, and the African National Congress: The Struggle against Apartheid 1948–1990: A Documentary Survey*. New York: Oxford University Press.

———. 1959. Verwoerd's tribalism. In S. Johns and R. Hunt Davis Jr. (eds.). 1991. *Mandela, Tambo, and the African National Congress: The Struggle against Apartheid 1948–1990: A Documentary Survey.* New York: Oxford University Press.

———. 1965. *No Easy Walk to Freedom.* Edited by Ruth First. Oxford: Heinemann.

———. 1990. Speech to South African business executives hosted by the Consultative Business Movement. 23 May, Johannesburg. http://www.anc.org.za.

———. 1991. Address on the occasion of the signing of a statement of intent to set up a national capacity for economic research and policy formulation. 23 November. http://www.anc.org.za.

———. 1992a. Speech to the World Economic Forum in Davos on February 2, 1992. http://www.anc.org.za.

———. 1992b. Welcoming address to workshop on Anti-trust, Monopolies, and Mergers Policy. 4 December. http://www.anc.org.za.

Manuel, T. 1996. Address to the National Assembly by Minister of Finance: Finance Budget Vote (Vote 13). 14 June. Press release text.

———. 1999. Budget speech. 17 February. http://www.finance.gov.za.

———. 2004. Longer term fiscal policy issues in South Africa. Bureau for Economic Research 60th Anniversary Conference. November, Somerset West.

Marais, H. 1998. *South Africa: Limits to Change: The Political Economy of Transition.* London: Zed Books and Cape Town: University of Cape Town Press.

May, J. (ed.). 1998. *Poverty and Inequality in South Africa: Final Report.* Report prepared for the Executive Deputy President and the Inter-Ministerial Committee on Poverty and Inequality. Durban: Praxis.

Mbeki, G. 1984. *South Africa: The Peasants' Revolt.* London: International Defence and Aid Fund for Southern Africa.

Mbeki, T. 1996. Reconstruction, development and macro-economic policy. Speech at the National Assembly, 14 June. In T. Mbeki, *Africa, the Time has Come: Selected Speeches.* Cape Town: Tafelberg and Johannesburg: Mafube.

———. 1998a. *Africa, the Time has Come: Selected Speeches.* Cape Town and Johannesburg: Tafelberg and Mafube.

———. 1998b. Statement of the President of the African National Congress at the meeting of the Central Committee of COSATU. 22 June, Johannesburg. http://www.anc.org.za.

———. 1999. Speech at the annual national conference of the Black Management Forum. 20 November. http://www.anc.org.za.

———. 2003a. Letter from the President: bold steps to end the two nations divide. ANC *Today*. 26 August. www.anc.org.za/ancdocs/anctoday.

———. 2003b. Two parallel economies: challenges of socio-economic development in South Africa. Reflections of the July 2003 Cabinet Lekgotla. Unpublished.

———. 2004. Address of the President of South Africa to the first joint sitting of the third democratic parliament. 21 May, Cape Town.

McCarthy, C. 1988. Structural development of South African manufacturing. *South African Journal of Economics* 56(1).

———. 1991. *Stagnation in the South African Economy: Where did Things go Wrong?* Stellenbosch: Stellenbosch Economic Project.

McClennan, B. 1990. *Apartheid: The Lighter Side.* Cape Town: Chameleon.

McGrath, S., A. Badroodien, A. Kraak and L. Unwin (eds.). 2004. *Shifting Understandings of Skills in South Africa: Overcoming the Historical Imprint of a Low Skills Regime.* Cape Town: HSRC Press.

Mji, D. 1976. Speech by President to General Students Council of SASO, Hammanskraal, July. Abridged in T. Karis and G. Gerhart, 1997, *From Protest to Challenge. Volume 5: Nadir and Resurgence.* Bloomington: Indiana University Press.

Moll, T. 1990. From booster to brake: apartheid and economic growth in comparative perspective. In N. Nattrass and E. Ardington (eds.), *The Political Economy of South Africa.* Oxford: Oxford University Press.

Moola, N. and R. Moloto. 2004. The emerging black middle class 'rocketing'. Merrill Lynch, 18 October.

Morris, M. 1976. The development of capitalism in South African agriculture: class struggle in the countryside. *Economy and Society* 5.

Moss, G. and I. Obery (eds.) 1987. *South African Review 4.* Johannesburg: Ravan Press.

National Advisory Council on Innovation. 2003. *An Advanced Manufacturing Strategy for South Africa.* Pretoria: Department of Science and Technology.

———. 2004. *South African Innovation Key Facts and Figures 2004.* Pretoria: Department of Science and Technology.

National Treasury. *Estimates of National Expenditure.* Various.

Nattrass, N. 1990a. Economic power and profits in post-war manufacturing. In N. Nattrass and E. Ardington (eds.), *The Political Economy of South Africa.* Oxford: Oxford University Press.

———. 1990b. The small black enterprise sector: a brief note of caution. In N. Nattrass and E. Ardington (eds.), *The Political Economy of South Africa*. Oxford: Oxford University Press.

———. 1998. Globalization and the South African labour market. Paper for the Conference on Restructuring the South African Economy, Midrand.

Nattrass, N. and E. Ardington (eds.). 1990. *The Political Economy of South Africa*. Oxford: Oxford University Press.

Nedlac. 1998a. Summary of Jobs Summit declaration. 30 October. http://www.polity.org.za/govdocs/summit/summit.html.

———. 1998b. Report on competition policy. http://www.nedlac.org.za.

Nelson, J.M. (ed.). 1994. *Intricate Links: Democratization and Market Reforms in Latin America and Eastern Europe*. New Jersey: Transaction Publishers.

Nolutshungu, S.C. 1983. *Changing South Africa: Political Considerations*. Cape Town: David Philip.

O'Dowd, M. 1964. South Africa in the light of the stages of economic growth. Mimeo. Later published in A. Leftwich (ed.), 1974. *South Africa: Economic Growth and Political Change*. London: Alison & Busby.

O'Meara, D. 1983. *Volkskapitalisme: Class, Capital and Ideology in the Development of Afrikaner Nationalism, 1934–1948*. Johannesburg: Ravan Press.

Orkin, M. (ed.). 1989. *Sanctions against Apartheid*. Cape Town: David Philip.

Ovenden, K. and T. Cole. 1989. *Apartheid and International Finance: A Programme for Change*. Australia: Penguin Books.

Padayachee, V. 1998. Progressive academic economists and the challenge of development in South Africa's decade of liberation. *Review of African Political Economy* 25(77).

Paton, A. 1948. *Cry the Beloved Country*. London: Jonathan Cape.

Policy Co-ordination and Advisory Services, The Presidency. 2003. *Towards a Ten Year Review: Synthesis Report of the Implementation of Government Programmes*. Pretoria: The Presidency.

Porter, M.E. 1990. *The Competitive Advantage of Nations*. London: Macmillan.

Posel, D. and D. Casale. 2003. Exploring labour force participation in South Africa, 1995–2001. Unpublished paper for the Human Sciences Research Council.

Ramphele, M. and C. McDowell (eds.). 1991. *Restoring the Land: Environment and Change in Post-Apartheid South Africa*. London: Panos.

Roberts, S. 1998. *A Preliminary Analysis of the Impact of Trade Liberalization on Manufacturing in South Africa*. Muldersdrift: TIPS Annual Forum.

Rogerson, C. 1987. The state and the informal sector: a case of separate development. In G. Moss and I. Obery (eds.), *South African Review 4*, Johannesburg: Ravan Press.

Rustomjee, Z. 1991. Capital flight from South Africa, 1970–1988. *Transformation* 15.

SALDRU. 1993. South African Living Standards and Development Survey. University of Cape Town.

Sassoon, D. 1996. *One Hundred Years of Socialism: The West European Left in the Twentieth Century.* New York: The New Press.

Saul, J. and S. Gelb. 1981. *The Crisis in South Africa: Class Defence, Class Revolution.* New York: Monthly Review Press.

Simkins, C. 1982. Structural unemployment revisited: a revision and update of earlier estimates incorporating new data from the current population survey and the 1980 census. Southern African Labour and Development Research Unit Working Paper, University of Cape Town.

Simons, H.J. and R. Simons. 1969. *Class and Colour in South Africa, 1850–1950.* London: Penguin.

Slovo, J. 1990. Has socialism failed? *South African Labour Bulletin* 14(6).

Smal, M.M. 1996. Exchange rate adjustments as an element of a development strategy for South Africa. *South African Reserve Bank Quarterly Bulletin* (June).

South Africa Foundation. 1996. *Growth for All: An Economic Strategy for South Africa.* Johannesburg.

South African Chamber of Business (SACOB). c.1993. *Defining the Role of the South African Reserve Bank in the Formulation and Implementation of Monetary Policy.*

South African Communist Party. 1989. The path to power: programme of the South African Communist Party as adopted at the seventh congress.

South African Reserve Bank (SARB). 1994a. *Quarterly Bulletin* (June).

———. 1994b. *Quarterly Bulletin* (September).

———. 1995. *Quarterly Bulletin* (March).

———. 1996a. *Quarterly Bulletin* (March).

———. 1996b. *Quarterly Bulletin* (June).

———. 1997. *Quarterly Bulletin* (March).

———. 1998a. *Quarterly Bulletin* (March).

———. 1998b. *Quarterly Bulletin* (September).

———. 1998c. *Quarterly Bulletin* (December).

———. 2004. *Quarterly Bulletin.* (December).

———. 2005. *Quarterly Bulletin.* (March).

Stals, C.L. 1994a. Money supply guidelines for 1994. South African Reserve Bank *Quarterly Bulletin* (June).

———. 1994b. The role of monetary policy in support of economic development. South African Reserve Bank *Quarterly Bulletin* (September).

————. 1995. Monetary policy in 1995. South African Reserve Bank *Quarterly Bulletin* (March).

————. 1997. Monetary policy: options and strategies. South African Reserve Bank *Quarterly Bulletin* (March).

————. 1998. Monetary policy and Reserve Bank accommodation procedures. South African Reserve Bank *Quarterly Bulletin* (March).

Standard Bank. 1991. An industrial policy for South Africa. *Standard Bank Economic Review* (June).

Standing, G., J. Sender and J. Weeks. 1996. *Restructuring the Labour Market: The South African Challenge.* Geneva: International Labour Organisation.

Stassen, A. and T. Kirsch. 1999. The refinancing challenges. In J. Cargill (ed.), *Empowerment 1999: A Moving Experience.* Johannesburg: Business-Map Foundation.

Statistics South Africa. 1998. Unemployment and employment in South Africa. Executive summary, Pretoria. http://www.statssa.gov.sa.

————. 2003. Census 2001: census in brief. http://www.statssa.gov.sa.

————. 2005. Labour Force Survey September 2004. http://www.statssa.gov.za.

Texeira C. and R. Masih. 2003. South Africa growth and unemployment: a ten-year outlook. Global Economics Paper No. 93. March, Goldman Sachs.

Tomlinson, R. and M. Addelson (eds.). 1987. *Regional Restructuring under Apartheid: Urban and Regional Policies in Contemporary South Africa.* Johannesburg: Ravan Press.

Tsikata,Y. 1998. Liberalization and trade performance in South Africa. World Bank Southern Africa Department: informal discussion papers on aspects of the economy in South Africa.

Van Onselen, C. 1996. *The Seed is Mine: The Life of Kas Maine, a South African Sharecropper, 1894–1985.* New York: Hill & Wang.

Wade, R. 1990. *Governing the Market: Economic Theory and the Role of Government in East Asian Industrialization.* Princeton: Princeton University Press.

Waldmeir, P. 1997. *Anatomy of a Miracle: The End of Apartheid and the Birth of the New South Africa.* London: Viking.

Westphal, L. 1990. Industrial policy in an export-propelled economy: lessons from South Korea's experience. *Journal of Economic Perspectives* 4(3).

Wilson, F. 1992. *Migrant Labour in South Africa.* Johannesburg: South African Council of Churches/SPRO-CAS.

Wilson, F. and M. Ramphele. 1989. *Uprooting Poverty: The South African Challenge.* Cape Town: David Philip.

Wolpe, H. 1972. Capitalism and cheap labour power in South Africa: from
    segregation to apartheid. *Economy and Society* 1(1).
Wood, A. 2002. Could Africa be like America? http://ssrn.com/abstract=
    315240.
Wood, A. and J. Mayer. 2000. Africa's export structure in a comparative
    perspective. *Cambridge Journal of Economics* 25(3).
Woolard, I. and H. Bhorat. 2004. Key empirical parameters of the South
    African labour market: input to Business Trust. Employment Challenge
    document.
World Bank. 2000. *World Development Report 1999/2000*. Washington, DC:
    World Bank.
World Travel and Tourism Council. 1998. *South Africa's Travel and Tourism:
    Economic Driver for the 21st Century*. London.
Yudelman, D. 1983. *The Emergence of Modern South Africa: State, Capital and
    the Incorporation of Organized Labor on the South African Gold Fields 1902–
    1939*. Westport: Greenwood Press.

Index

Abedian, Iraj   186
Adult Basic Education and Training
   (ABET)   253
affirmative action   52, 210, 229, 242
African Merchant Bank   217
African National Congress (ANC)
   1-6, 10
   achievement in 10 years   235-237
   BEE strategy   210-214, 221-230
   Congress Alliance   32-35, 39
   economic policy   29-62, 65-70,
      84, 91, 93-108, 110, 118, 122-
      123, 125-130, 141-148, 155-
      156, 164-167, 188-189, 196,
      199-201, 210-211, 233-255,
      257-264
   Economic Policy, Department of
      (DEP)   48-51, 56
   election campaign, 2004   191
   industrial policy   124-125, 143
   infrastructure programme   190
   macroeconomic policy   6-7, 97,
      100-101, 163, 166, 181, 243,
      248-249, 252
   monetary policy   95, 97, 98-99,
      101, 106-107
   skills development strategy   186-
      187 see also skills
   small business development   201-
      204
   support strategy   153-154, 159
   trade reform   53, 94, 109-111,
      118-119, 122, 126-135, 166,
      181, 210, 236
   trade relations   136-137
   tripartite alliance   96, 111, 163,
      166-167, 176, 196, 210
   Western Cape   111

Afrikaner *Sakekamer*   206
Afrikaners   216, 222
agriculture   113-114, 125
   African   205
   labour   12
   market access   136
   products   114-115, 128-130,
      250, 259
   subsistence   183
AIDS   191, 235, 242
aluminium industry   250, 259
Amsden, Alice   38
Anglo American Corporation   43,
   113, 131, 157, 195-196, 198,
   215-216
Anglovaal   195
Angola   138
apartheid   1, 9-28, 32, 37-41, 43,
   69, 139, 171, 179, 182, 188,
   193, 200, 206-208, 222, 224,
   241, 245
Apex fund   253
apprenticeship   185, 187 see also
   learnerships
Armscor   131
Asia   4, 35, 38, 57, 106, 117, 121,
   238, 250, 258
   East   38, 57, 117-119
   South-East   38, 117
Asmal, Kader   125-126
Australia   22, 112, 240
Azanian People's Organisation
   (AZAPO)   10

balance of payments   24-25, 80, 97,
   131
bank rate   81-82, 87, 100, 102-104

banking law   253
Bantu Education Act, 1953   17
Bantustans   140, 175-176
    traders   207
Basic Conditions of Employment Act,
    1997   183
Batho Pele Gateway   254
Bell, Trevor   121
BHP Billiton   198, 216
Biotechnology Regional Innovation
    Centres   151
Bird, Adrienne   186
Black Economic Empowerment (BEE)
    7-8, 143, 158-159, 193-199,
    202-203, 210-214, 217-218,
    236, 251, 253
    effectiveness   228-230
    financing   218-221, 227, 229
    political significance   210
Black Economic Empowerment Act,
    No. 53 of 2003   220-223, 228
Black Economic Empowerment
    Advisory Council   222-223
Black Economic Empowerment
    Commission (BEECom)   221-
    222
Black Management Forum (BMF)
    220-221
blacks in business   194, 204-210
blacks, employment   193
Blinder, Alan   79
Board of Trade and Industry (BTI)
    118, 131
Bond, Patrick   121
Botha, P.W.   24, 65-66, 131
Botswana   137
bourgeoisie, black   34, 221
BRAIN (Business Referral and
    Information Network)   203
Brazil   106, 139
Bretton Woods agreement   20-21,
    80, 174
budget   165
    deficit   70, 77, 95, 102, 106, 166,
    224, 258-259
Business South Africa   200
Business Unity South Africa (BUSA)
    210-211

Camdessus, Michel   91
Canada   22, 39, 54, 112, 136
Cancun   115
capital flow   83, 89-93, 97, 101, 103
capitalisation   195
capitalism   12-14, 36-38, 156-157,
    177-178, 188, 193, 210
    Afrikaner   216
    black   216
casualisation   234
Centre for Small Business Promotion
    201
Chabane, N.   197
Chile   91, 136, 139
China   238
    imports from   259
class
    middle, black   87, 140, 178, 210,
    260-261
    working, black   87, 164
Clinton, Bill   110-111, 129
clothing industry   110-111, 198, 250
colonialism   35, 193, 245
Common Monetary Area (CMA)   86
communications   16, 27, 153, 236
    technology   149
competition   157-159, 196, 199-201
Competition Act, No. 89 of 1998
    159, 197, 199-201
Competition Commission   159
Competition Tribunal   197
Competitiveness Fund   155
conglomerates   194-196, 201, 214
'Congress of the People', Kliptown   32
Congress of South African Trade
    Unions (COSATU)   44-45,
    59-62, 96, 101, 109-111, 118,
    122, 126, 127, 130, 163-167,
    186
conservation programmes   191
Constitution, South Africa   77-78,
    215
Constitutional Guidelines   40, 43
construction, labour-intensive   190
Consultative Business Movement
    (CBM)   67
consumer price index (CPI)   80-81
corruption   235

COSATU *see* Congress of South African Trade Unions
cost of living 176, 182-184
Council for Industrial and Scientific Research (CSIR) 149-151
credit 105, 235
  services 253
Credit Guarantee Insurance Corporation 134
crime 235, 240, 242, 261-262
Critical Infrastructure Programme 145
Cronin, Jeremy 96
Cuba 39, 65
currency 6, 21, 25, 77, 78-80, 82-83, 104
  foreign 86, 88
  stabilisation 88, 248, 258-259
  volatility 21, 242, 261-262
  see also rand value
Cypionka, Nico 3

Davies, Rob 62, 242
De Klerk, F.W. 29, 66, 110-111, 126
debt, government 98, 106, 112, 164, 225, 235, 241, 243, 248, 255, 258-259
decentralisation, industrial 140
defence cuts 73
deficit, fiscal 112
Democratic Alliance (DA) 222
Democratic Party 3
depreciation 88
devaluation 89
'developing' countries 109-110
Dhlamini, Chris 62
Dornbusch, Rudiger 91
Du Plessis, Barend 66

Economic Planning, Department of (DEP) 123
Economic Research on South Africa (EROSA) 44, 46-47, 55
Economic Trends group (ET) 45-47, 57
economies, two 188 *see also* second economy
economy, mixed 31, 245

education 17-19, 27, 106-107, 119, 150-151, 174, 178, 182, 185, 187, 191, 243, 252-253
  Bantu 9, 17-19, 208
  black 178
  expenditure 73, 107, 246, 248
  see also training
Edwards, Sebastian 90-91
Egypt 35
election, 1994 1, 91, 125
election, 1999 212
election, 2004 234
electricity 107, 236-237, 248
employment 23, 129, 171-173, 191, 198, 249
  conditions 183
  equity 229-230
  figures 245
Employment Conditions Commission 180
Employment Equity Act, 1998 183, 229
empowerment, blacks 203, 210-211, 213, 218, 220-224, 226, 229, 242, 252, 261
entrepreneurs
  African 205-207
  coloured 206, 209
  Indian 206, 209
equality, racial 194, 261
EROSA *see* Economic Research on South Africa
Erwin, Alec 45, 62, 72, 93, 123, 127, 147, 158, 177, 181, 199, 227
Eskom 22, 250, 258
European Union (EU) 114, 136, 138-139
European Union-South Africa free trade agreement 114
exchange control 21, 69, 84-87, 90-91, 94, 99-100, 139, 195, 248, 262
exchange rates 80-81, 89-91, 100, 103-104, 131, 236
Expanded Public Works Programme (EPWP) 189-191, 253, 259
expenditure, government 71-72
Export Finance Scheme for Capital Projects 134

Export Marketing and Investment
    Assistance Programme   135
exports   24–25, 27, 58, 85, 95, 100,
    103, 105, 113–115, 118–119,
    121, 127, 130–139, 180–181,
    203, 236, 250, 259, 260, 263

Fallon, Peter   175
Fanaroff, Bernie   60
farms, black   13
Federale Mynbou/General Mining   216
financial rand   84–85
Financial Sector Charter   223–224,
    228
financial services, empowerment   185
Fine, Ben   120
fiscal deficit   105, 235 *see also* debt,
    government
fiscal policy   106–107, 241, 249,
    261–263
Fischer, Stanley   78
food prices   251
foreign exchange   78, 88
foreign reserves   88
free market economies   209
free trade   137–138
Freedom Charter   32–34, 40–41, 44
Frelimo   113
fruit exports   114, 136
Fund for Research into Growth,
    Development and Equity
    (FRIDGE)   134
furniture industry   198
Further Education and Training   253
futures exchange   86, 88

GATT   *see* General Agreement on
    Tariffs and Trade
GEAR   *see* Growth, Employment
    and Redistribution
Gelb, Stephen   45, 121
Gencor   143, 216
gender equity   230
General Agreement on Tariffs and
    Trade (GATT)   6–7, 53, 109–
    110, 125–128, 130, 132, 180
Generalised Export Incentive Scheme
    (GEIS)   127, 130–132, 135

Ghana   35
Ginwala, Frene   123
globalisation   6, 188, 245, 257
gold   20
    price   21–22, 25–26, 66, 113, 131
    production   112–113
Gorbachev   38–39
Gordhan, Ketso   49
Gordhan, Pravin   106
Gouws, Rudolf   72
government of national unity (GNU)
    66, 68, 126, 141, 211
grants, social   107, 246, 260–261 *see
    also* social welfare
gross domestic fixed investment
    (GDFI)   139–140
gross domestic product (GDP)   24,
    57, 70, 72, 77, 80–81, 95, 98,
    102, 105–106, 112, 114–115,
    137, 139–140, 149, 236, 239–
    241, 243–244, 246–248, 258
gross fixed capital formation (GFCF)
    239–241
Group Areas Act, 1950   16, 206
'group of 22'   139
growth, economic   237–244, 260–
    264
Growth and Development Summit,
    2003   169, 187–191
Growth for All   94–96, 176
Growth, Employment and
    Redistribution (GEAR)   4, 6,
    57, 98–108, 145, 163–167, 179,
    241–243, 258–259
Gulf War, 1992   22

Hanekom, Derek   50, 62
Harare Declaration, 1989   40, 43
health   182, 191, 235, 243, 252–253
    expenditure   73, 106, 248
Helleiner, Gerry   54
Hirsch, Alan   127
Holden, Merle   118
homelands   12, 76
Hong Kong   117, 119
Household Survey   *see* October
    Household Survey
housing   59, 236–237, 258
    expenditure   73, 228

human resources   253, 261
human rights   182

immigration, illegal   183
imports   80, 85, 100, 105, 130, 159,
   181, 236, 259
income
   household   183, 192 n.2, 245,
      255 n.1, 260-261
   per capita   238
   personal   2, 112, 194, 244
Income Tax Act   179
Independent Communications
   Authority of South Africa
   (ICASA)   218
India   139, 238
Industrial Development Corporation
   (IDC)   47, 118-119, 128, 133,
   135, 142-144, 154, 179, 203,
   213-214, 224, 226, 250
industrial relations 208
Industrial Strategy Project (ISP)   51,
   55, 57-59, 153-154, 198-199
industrialisation   121-125, 259
industry   116-125, 197 *see also*
   manufacturing
inequality   1, 170, 179, 234, 237,
   245, 247-248, 255, 263-264
inflation   3, 20-21, 27, 36, 78-82,
   87, 90, 98-100, 103-105, 235-
   236, 241-242, 248-249, 258,
   261-263
influx control   10, 66, 171
informal sector   209, 245
information technology   223, 254
infrastructure   23, 27-28, 73, 107,
   139, 141, 145-148, 190, 207,
   225, 227, 236, 243-244, 248,
   251-252, 257-259
Inkatha Freedom Party   66
Innovation Fund   151
Integrated Manufacturing Strategy
   159
Interest rates   72, 78, 80-83, 87-93,
   98, 101-103, 164, 166, 178-
   179, 235, 240-242, 248-249,
   259, 261-263
International Development Research
   Centre (IDRC)   54

International Monetary Fund (IMF)
   5, 22, 52, 69, 75, 78, 91-92,
   112, 117, 176, 211
investment   3, 25, 38, 74, 82, 84, 89,
   100, 105-108, 120, 121, 139-
   148, 160, 169, 178-179, 181,
   189, 196, 226-227, 238-244,
   248, 252, 258-259, 261-264
   foreign   22, 30-32, 53, 82-83,
      85, 90, 92, 101, 103-104, 137,
      139-140, 142, 157, 165, 210,
      242, 258, 261
   offshore   86-87
Iscor   22, 47, 131, 239
Isibaya Fund   227
Israel   5, 136, 140

Japan   38, 58, 110, 114-119, 139
Japanese Grant Fund   132-134,
   141-142, 154-155
job
   creation   20, 31, 94, 96, 105,
      120-122, 124, 141, 144-146,
      163, 173-174, 181, 185, 189,
      194, 209, 234, 253
   losses   111, 179-181, 185, 234
   reservation   17, 207-209
Jobs Summit, 1998   163-164, 166-
   168, 176, 180-181, 188-190
Johannesburg Stock Exchange (JSE)
   92, 195-196, 214-215, 227-
   229, 261
Johnnic   215, 217, 219
Jones, J.G.F.   216
Jourdan, Paul   50, 119, 146

Kantor, Brian   75
Kaplinsky, Raphael   198
Kaunda, Kenneth   35
Keynes, John Maynard   34, 60, 91, 259
Keys, Derek   65-67, 70, 92, 125-
   127, 131, 196
Khosa, Ruel   220
Khula Enterprise Finance Ltd   201-
   203
Korea   38, 58, 117-119, 132, 240,
   259
Kotze, Philip   133

Krugman, Paul   80

labour
    costs   7, 182–187, 205
    laws   174, 183, 200, 261
    markets   94–96, 100, 102, 166,
        174–177, 179, 181–182, 190,
        209, 242
    migrant   9–12, 26, 112, 173, 205,
        208
    mine   13, 112, 205, 207
    skills   7, 27, 185–186
Labour, Department of   102
Labour Force Survey (LFS)   170–172
Labour Party, UK   34
Labour Relations Act, 1995/96   95,
    183
labour-intensive projects   190–191,
    250, 253
land
    reform   35, 58, 114
    tenure   2, 13, 15–16, 27
Land Act, 1913   205
Land Bank   203
Leape, Jonathan   88, 104
'learnerships'   187, 189, 191, 253
Lebombo initiative   147
Lesotho   137
Levy, Brian   120, 161 n.2,3, 192 n.1
Lewis, David   177, 195–196, 199
Liberal Party, UK   34
Liberty Group   195–196
Liebenberg, Chris   67, 76, 85, 93, 98
Lipton, Merle   178
Liquid Fuels Industry Charter   223
living standards   176, 183
Local Business Service Centres   202
local government restructuring   243
Lomé Convention   136, 138
Lucas, Robert   175

M3   81–82, 87, 90
macroeconomic policy   105, 248–
    249, 261 *see also* African
    National Congress, macroeco-
    nomic policy
Macroeconomic Research Group
    (MERG)   54–57, 59, 95

malaria   191, 235
Malawi   138
management   194, 260
    equity   230
Mandela, Nelson   4–5, 9, 16, 29–31,
    41, 49, 52, 55, 67–68, 93, 110,
    126, 164, 167, 215
Manning, Claudia   198
Mantashe, Gwede   96
Manuel, Trevor   4, 30, 49–50, 62,
    68, 85–86, 93–94, 97–98,
    101–102, 106, 109–111, 123,
    133, 145, 156–158, 164–165,
    196, 258
manufacturing   20, 22–23, 113,
    115–118, 122, 124, 131, 148–
    150, 180, 185, 251, 259
    protection   129
Manufacturing Advisory Centres   202
Maputo   146–147
Maree, Sydney   226–227
marginalisation   245, 252, 254
markets
    blacks   260
    concentration   197
    control   194
    domestic   257
    efficiency   200
    power   199
    structure   156
Marrakech Agreement   125–126
Marxism   36, 116, 165
Mauritius   138, 155
Mbeki, Thabo   68, 93, 101, 166,
    168–169, 184, 188, 191, 212,
    215, 221, 233–234, 237, 244,
    246, 250
Mboweni, Tito   29–30, 42, 46, 49,
    62, 95, 123, 127
McMenamin, Vivienne   49
Metal and Allied Workers' Union
    (MAWU)   186
metal industry   113, 117, 143, 176
    protection   129
Metlife   214, 216, 224
Mexico   136, 139
microeconomics   249–252
Millennium Labour Council   254

mining 120, 205, 223, 250
  houses, diversification 195
  production 115
Mining Charter 223
Mji, Diliza 37
monetary policy 105, 108, 235, 241, 249, 261–263
Monitor Group 153
Moseneke, Dikgang 215, 217
Motlana, Nthatho 214–215, 217
Motor Industries Development Programme 159, 250
motor industry 236, 250
  protection 129, 135
Mozambique 12, 44, 112–113, 138, 141, 146, 183
Mpumalanga 141, 146
Mufamadi, Sydney 10, 37
Municipal Infrastructure Grant (MIG) 190, 244

Naidoo, Jay 38, 60, 123, 127
Namibia 137
Nasser, Abdel Gamal 35
National Economic Development and Labour Council (Nedlac) 133, 135, 142, 144,154–155, 168, 174, 189, 200–201, 254
National Economic Forum (NEF) 66, 127–128, 133
National Empowerment Consortium 215
National Empowerment Fund (NEF) 224, 226–227
National Empowerment Fund Act, No. 105 of 1998 226
National Institute for Economic Policy (NIEP) 95
National Manufacturing Advisory Centre (NAMAC) 203
National Party (NP) 12, 41, 68, 111, 140, 206, 209, 216, 222
National Small Business Council 202
National Treasury's Preferential Procurement Policy Framework Act, 2000 212–213
National Union of Metalworkers of South Africa (NUMSA) 45, 96, 116

National Union of Mineworkers (NUM) 215
nationalisation 33–35, 41–42, 44, 47, 51–52, 55, 196, 211
Native (Urban Areas) Act, 1923 9, 205
Naudé, Stef 109
Ndulu, Benno 54
Nedlac *see* National Economic Development and Labour Council
Nelson, Joan 70
neo-liberalism 5
New African Investments Limited (NAIL) 214–220
Nkrumah, Kwame 5, 35
non-governmental organisations (NGOs) 253
Normative Economic Model (NEM) 97
North American Free Trade Agreement (NAFTA) 137
Nqakula, Charles 167
Nqula, Khaya 144
Ntsika Enterprise Promotion Agency 201–203
Nyerere, Julius 35

October Household Survey (OHS) 170–171
oil price 21, 66
Oppenheimer, Harry 216
O'Reilly, Tony 75
Organisation of African Unity (OAU) 40
ownership 194–197, 223
  black 212–213, 218–220, 224, 227–229

Pan-Africanist Congress (PAC) 215
pass laws 9–10, 12
Patel, Ebrahim 61
Paton, Alan 15
petroleum industry 228
Pillay, Vella 44, 95
platinum 236, 250, 259
population 173
Porter, Michael 153–154

poverty   12, 112, 169–170, 179, 191,
    234–236, 244–248, 252
  relief   95, 238, 247, 260, 263–264
poverty line   2, 188, 245, 255
power   149
  economic   194
  economic/political   222
Presidential Conference on Small
    Business, 1995   201
privatisation   47, 74, 95, 99–100,
    102, 140, 163–164, 209, 213,
    224–225, 249
  share distribution   226
procurement   212–213, 223
productivity   53–54, 100, 113–114,
    155, 239
Proudly South African campaign   168
Provincial Infrastructure Grant (PIG)
    190, 244
Public Investment Corporation (PIC)
    227, 229
public sector investment   239, 242,
    244, 249, 258
public service   76, 98–100, 164, 191,
    229–230, 262
public spending   243
public works   189
Public Works, Department of   190
pulp and paper industry   113, 117, 197
  protection   129

racism   178, 185, 193, 209
railways   251
Ramaphosa, Cyril   38, 215, 217, 221
Ramos, Maria   103
Rand Merchant Bank   197
rand value   25, 78–79, 82, 84, 88,
    93–94, 96, 100, 102–104, 106,
    250, 258–259, 262–263 *see
    also* currency
Reconstruction and Development
    Programme (RDP)   2, 6, 59–
    61, 69, 73–74, 93–94, 97, 122,
    124, 200, 210–213, 234, 243,
    257
Regional Industrial Development
    Programme (RIDP)   141, 144
Relly, Gavin   43, 157

Rembrandt Group   195–197
research and development   149
reserves, financial   235–236
revenue collection   99, 106, 243,
    248, 258
Rhodes, Cecil   13, 204
roads   252 *see also* infrastructure
Roberts, Simon   180, 182
Ruiters, Alistair   111
Russia   22, 39, 103–104, 106
Rustomjee, Zavareh   50, 119–120,
    123–124, 132, 143

SA Mutual   195–196
SAB Miller   198
Sachs, Goldman   65
Sandler, Jonty   215, 217
Sanlam   113, 143, 195–196, 198,
    213–214, 216
Sasol   22, 47, 49, 239
savings   27, 87, 226, 242–243, 264
  dissavings   243
science and technology   151–152
second economy   188, 191, 233–
    255, 261, 263
Sector Education and Training
    Authorities (SETAs)   187, 189
Sectoral Partnership Fund (SPF)
    154–155
service sector   185, 259
services   2, 16, 102, 115, 180, 182,
    189, 225, 235
share prices   91–92, 223
shares
  BEE   219
  distribution after privatisation   226
Shilowa, Mbazima   101
Sibiya, Bheki   210
Simkins, Charles   176–177
Sisulu, Max   30, 48–49, 62
Sisulu, Walter   49, 215
Sisulu, Zwelakhe   215, 217
skills   95, 102, 117, 134, 152, 175,
    178–179, 181, 184–187, 189–
    191, 194, 207–209, 211, 233–
    235, 245, 252, 261, 264
Skills Development Act, 1998   183,
    186

Skills Development Levies Act, 1999 183

Slovo, Joe 39, 40

Small and Medium Enterprise Development Programme 144, 203

small and medium enterprises (SMEs) 198-199, 202

Small and Medium Manufacturing Development Programme (SMMDP) 144, 203

small business 194, 249, 252
   development 193-194, 201-204, 209, 211

Small Business Act 158

Small Business Development Corporation (SBDC) 202, 209

Small Enterprise Development Agency (SEDA) 203

social security 4, 73, 182, 246-247, 259

social services 73, 106, 191, 236

social welfare 107, 246-247

socialism 5, 30, 35-42
   African 35, 193

South African Broadcasting Corporation (SABC) 215

South African Chamber of Business (SACOB) 79, 94

South African Clothing and Textile Workers' Union (SACTWU) 110-111, 116

South African Communist Party (SACP) 10, 35, 39, 42, 59, 96, 101, 111, 122, 163, 165-167

South Africa Foundation 94-95

South African Municipal Workers' Union (SAMWU) 164

South African National Civics Organisation (SANCO) 59

South African Qualifications Authority 187

South African Reserve Bank (SARB) 4, 25-26, 57, 65-66, 76, 77-84, 87-90, 92, 100-105, 164, 235, 258, 262

South African Revenue Services (SARS) 106 *see also* revenue collection

South African Students' Organisation (SASO) 37

Southern African Customs Union (SACU) 136-139

Southern African Development Community (SADC) 86, 136-138

Soweto revolt, 1976 214

Spacial Development Initiatives 146-148, 203

Spacial Development Programme 146

'special purpose vehicle' (SPV) 219-220, 224

Spicer, Michael 157-158

stability, monetary 79-80

Stals, Chris 25, 65-67, 79-85, 87, 90, 97, 103-104

Standard Bank Liberty 198

steel industry 135, 250, 259

Strategic Investment Programme 145

strikes 184

subsidies 73, 114, 140, 152-153, 178, 182
   export 130-135, 140

Support Programme for Industrial Innovation (SPII) 150

sustainability 79, 246, 253, 257

Swaziland 137, 147

Taiwan 38, 117, 119, 140

Tambo, Oliver 43

Tanzania 35, 36, 138, 176, 183

tariff rates 105, 110-111, 114, 118, 122, 128-130, 135, 137-138, 180-181, 236, 249

taxation 55, 60, 72, 74, 91, 99, 106, 145, 166, 241, 243, 258-259, 261
   VAT 74, 95

taxi industry 209

TB (tuberculosis) 191, 235

Technology and Human Resources for Industry Programme (THRIP) 150

telecommunications 214, 248, 251-252

Telkom 150, 222, 225

textile industry 110, 135, 176, 250
   protection 129

Thatcherism 209
'third world economy' 233
Tobin, James 91
tourism 115, 147–148, 159–160,
236, 250
Trade and Industry, Department of
(DTI) 102, 132–135, 142,
145–147, 150, 153–155, 201–
203
trade liberalisation 180–183, 236,
248 *see also* African National
Congress, trade reform
Trade Policy Monitoring Project 55
trade reform 125–139, 257 *see also*
trade liberalisation
trade surplus 137
trade unions 10–11, 37, 42, 94,
102, 116, 174–175, 179–180,
182–183, 208, 222
black 177, 209
traders, African 205–207
training 152–155, 178, 184–187,
190, 211
health care 191
industrial 100, 185–186
levy 183, 186–187
Transkei 141, 147
Transnet 251
transport 27, 182
Turok, Ben 62, 69

Umkhonto we Sizwe 39
unbundling 196–198, 213–214, 218
unemployment 15, 36, 78, 94, 112,
141, 163, 167–182, 187–191,
209, 233–236, 238, 245, 247,
252–253
white 234
Union Bank of Switzerland (UBS)
92–93
United Democratic Front (UDF) 49
United States 37, 79, 109, 114–115,
136, 139, 146
dollar 86, 88, 104, 259, 261
gold production 112
urbanisation 208–209
Uruguay Round 110, 125, 130
Usury Act, 1992 87

Van Driel, Maria 164
Van Seventer, D.E. 242
Vavi, Zwelinzima 163, 165
Verwoerd, H.F. 17

Wade, Robert 38
wages 4, 7, 9, 11–12, 88, 99–100,
102, 112–113, 163, 174–177,
179–184
water 107, 236, 252
wealth creation 209
wealth redistribution 1, 47–48, 51,
58, 60, 104, 121, 200–201,
225–226, 240, 257, 259, 263–
264
welfare 47 *see also* grants, social
welfare state 34
Wiese, Christo 197
wine industry 197, 236, 250
women, status 10, 173–174, 229, 235
Wood, Adrian 250
wood products 129, 131
working class *see* class
Working Groups 169
Workplace Challenge 155
World Bank 1–2, 52, 57, 69, 74–75,
97, 112, 117, 120, 132–133, 155,
175, 179, 211, 261–262
World Economic Forum, 1991 29–
31
World Player Scheme 135
World Trade Organisation (WTO)
115, 136, 138–139

Young Communist League 39

Zambia 35, 45, 138
Zimbabwe 138, 211, 242